The Authority of the Consumer

The aim of this collection is to explore the implications of 'consumer society' charting out its specific meanings in particular contexts and debating the potential merits or otherwise of this way of understanding and constructing relations between 'providers' and 'recipients'.

In particular, this development has been seen as involving a radical shift of authority – away from the provider/producer, towards the recipient/consumer – in judging the value and meaning of the activities concerned, or in the character of the social relations involved in them. But there have been differing responses to this shift; some welcoming it in terms of democratization, anti-elitism or empowerment; others decrying it as commercialization, populism, loss of integrity, and the like. Some have been more sceptical that any such shift is really taking place.

These are the issues explored in this important and wide-ranging book. The authors have drawn from several disciplines in the social sciences and humanities and include several non-academics.

Russell Keat is Reader in Philosophy, **Nigel Whiteley** is Senior Lecturer and Head of the Department of Visual Arts and **Nicholas Abercrombie** is Professor of Sociology – all at the University of Lancaster.

The Authority of the Consumer

Edited by Russell Keat, Nigel Whiteley and Nicholas Abercrombie

Lancaster University Centre for the Study of Cultural Values

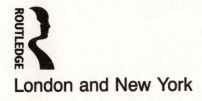

London and New York

First published 1994
by Routledge
11 New Fetter Lane, London EC4P 4EE

Simultaneously published in the USA and Canada
by Routledge
29 West 35th Street, New York, NY 10001

Phototypeset in Times by Intype, London

Printed and bound in Great Britain by Mackays of Chatham PLC, Chatham, Kent

British Library Cataloging in Publication Data

A catalogue record for this book is available from the British Library

Library of Congress Cataloging in Publication Data
The Authority of the consumer / edited by Russell Keat, Nicholas Abercrombie
and Nigel Whiteley.
    p. cm.
    'The papers presented in this volume derive from conferences and
workshops organized by the Center for the Study of Cultural Values at the
University of Lancaster'—CIP galley
    Includes bibliographical references and index.
    ISBN 0–415–08918–2 : $50.00.—ISBN 0–415–08919–0 : $17.95
    1. Consumer behavior—Congresses. 2. Consumption (Economics)—Social
aspects—Congresses. 3. Authority—Social aspects—Congresses.
4. Consumer education—Congresses. I. Keat, Russell. II. Abercrombie,
Nicholas. III. Whiteley, Nigel.
HF5415.32.A93   1993
658.8'342—dc20   93–24576
                                                                          CIP

ISBN 0–415–08918–2   ISBN 0–415–08919–0 (pbk)

Contents

Part Two   Consuming culture

Part Three   Consuming public services

Illustrations

Notes on contributors

Unless otherwise stated, the contributors are based at Lancaster University and are members of the Centre for the Study of Cultural Values (CSCV).

Nicholas Abercrombie, Professor of Sociology, has taught at Lancaster University since 1970. His current research interests are mainly in social theory, the sociology of popular culture, and the culture industries, particularly book publishing. Publications in those areas include: *Class, Structure and Knowledge* (Blackwell, 1980), *The Dominant Ideology Thesis* (1980), and *Sovereign Individuals of Capitalism* (1986) (both with S. Hill and B. Turner, for Allen & Unwin), and *Enterprise Culture* (edited with R. Keat, Routledge, 1991).

Norman Fairclough, Reader in the Linguistics department. His publications include *Language and Power* (Longman 1989), *Discourse and Social Change* (Polity Press, 1992), and he is the editor of *Critical Language Awareness* (Longman, 1992). He is currently writing a book about language in the media. His main research interests are in discourse analysis, and relationships between social/cultural change and linguistic change.

Oliver Fulton, Professor of Higher Education in the Centre for the Study of Education and Training. His current interests include policy-making and policy implementation in higher education, and the sociology of the academic profession. He recently edited *Access and Institutional Change* (Open University Press, 1989).

Paul Heelas, Senior Lecturer in the Sociology/Anthropology of Religion in the department of Religious Studies, and the current Director of CSCV. With Paul Morris he edited *The Values of Enterprise Culture: the Moral Debate* (Routledge, 1992). His current research interests include the de-traditionalization of religion in the contemporary west, with particular reference to the value ascribed to the self, and to the question of 'consumer culture'.

Tony Heward, Lecturer in Graphic Design in the department of Visual Arts. He combines the practice of the subject with studies of its theory and history. In addition, he works as a printmaker and graphic artist and has exhibited work in Brazil, Canada, France, Poland, Spain and the USA, as well as in Britain. Current research includes an investigation of 'retro' styles in graphic design.

Richard Hugman, Lecturer in social work and applied social science. He has a particular interest in old age and community care. He has undertaken research and published in the fields of professionalism and organization of health and welfare, social responses to old age, and mental health. He is co-editor of *The British Journal of Social Work*.

Russell Keat, Reader in Social Philosophy, and the former Director of CSCV, he is soon to take up the post of Professor of Political Theory at Edinburgh University. He has published extensively on twentieth-century continental philosophy and the philosophy of social science including *The Politics of Social Theory* (Blackwell, 1981) and, with J. Urry, *Social Theory as Science* (second edition, Routledge, 1982). He is currently researching the ethical and cultural implications of market economies. With Nicholas Abercrombie he co-edited *Enterprise Culture* (Routledge, 1991).

Baz Kershaw, Lecturer in Theatre Studies, and former Chair of the School of Creative Arts. He has worked extensively in alternative theatre as a director and writer. He co-authored *Engineers of the Imagination* (Methuen, 1990), and is the author of *The Politics of Performance* (Routledge, 1992).

Adam Lury is a founding partner of Howell Henry Chaldecott Lury. The agency was nominated *Campaign* Agency of the Year in 1989. Its current clients include Britvic Soft Drinks (Tango and R. Whites Lemonade), Mercury Communications, BHS, Lego and MTV.

Celia Lury lectures in Women's Studies and cultural studies in the Sociology department at Lancaster University. Her current research interests are identity, performance and cultural change. Publications include *Off-Centre: Feminism and Cultural Studies* (with S. Franklin and J. Stacey, Harper Collins, 1991), and *Cultural Rights* (Routledge, 1993).

Helen Rees, Head of Public Affairs, National Art Collections Fund, formerly, Director, Design Museum, London. Member of the Arts Council Art Panel, Governor of Design Dimension Educational Trust, Member of the Design Advisory Committee, Royal Society of Arts. Lecturer and contributor to numerous magazines on design and cultural policy.

Kieron Walsh, Professor of Public Sector Management in the Institute of Local Government Studies at the University of Birmingham. Author of a number of books and articles on aspects of public sector management, most recently *Competitive Tendering for Local Authority Services* (HMSO, 1991). He is currently conducting research on managing through contracts, the nature of networks and the nature of citizenship.

Alan Warde, Senior Lecturer in Sociology. He has written books about the Labour Party, urban and regional change, and the structure of British society. He is currently studying theories of consumption and researching aspects of changing food habits in the UK.

Nigel Whiteley, Senior Lecturer in the department of Visual Arts, has been its head since 1982. He is interested in the history, theory and values of design in recent and contemporary society. *Pop Design: Modernism to Mod* (Design Council, 1987) analysed design in Britain between 1952 and 1972, and *Design For Society* (Reaktion, 1993), is a critique of consumerist design and the 'design boom' of the 1980s. He is currently Chair of CSCV.

John Winward, Director of Research at the Consumers' Association in London. He has worked for a number of other consumer organizations in the UK, including the National Consumer Council, and is Senior Visiting Fellow in CSCV at Lancaster University.

Preface

The papers presented in this volume derive from conferences and workshops organized by the Centre for the Study of Cultural Values at the University of Lancaster. In the period 1988–90 the Centre took as its research theme 'The values of the enterprise culture' which resuited in two publications, *Enterprise Culture* (edited by R. Keat and N. Abercrombie, 1991) and *The Values of the Enterprise Culture* (edited by P. Heelas and P. Morris, 1992), both published by Routledge. In the following year, 1991, the Centre's work focused on contemporary forms of consumption and debates about the nature of consumer society which were replaced in a series of weekly workshops and four small conferences entitled: The New Consumer, Consuming Culture, Consuming Public Services, and Green Consumerism. These conferences were funded by the Nuffield Foundation to whom we give grateful thanks. Reflecting the Centre's commitment to interdisciplinary work across the social sciences and humanities, the contributors to these meetings were drawn from a wide range of academic disciplines represented within the Centre, and also included some with first-hand experience, as practitioners, of the areas they examined.

We would like to thank the following participants who presented papers to these meetings but who have not written for this volume: Richard Adams, Luciano Cheles, Susan Condor, Debra Davies, Mary Douglas, Lisa Gee, Robin Grove-White, Gerry Harris, Bob Hamilton, Paul Hatton, Christine King, Scott Lash, Richard Macrory, Mica Nava, Chris Rose, Jackie Stacey, Tessa Tennant, Steve Trivett, and John Urry. We also owe a special vote of thanks to Eileen Martin, who organized the workshops and conferences.

Introduction

*Russell Keat, Nigel Whiteley and
Nicholas Abercrombie*

A striking recent development is the tendency to refer to people as
consumers in a wide range of contexts where they had previously been
known by other and more varied names. Museum visitors, theatre audiences, sports spectators and TV viewers; university students, hospital
patients, social workers' clients, and even taxpayers and the public served
by the police – all are now deemed to be consumers, and those who are
involved as 'producers' in cultural and educational institutions and public
service organizations are constantly urged by their political mentors to
treat them accordingly.[1]

The aim of this volume is to examine what is meant by this current
extension of the status of consumer, to explore what, if anything, is going
on beneath the surface of the changing rhetoric, and to contribute to a
critical debate about the desirability or otherwise of such actual or possible changes from various cultural, political and ethical standpoints.

The papers in Parts Two and Three address these issues as they arise,
respectively, in the realm of cultural institutions and the organization of
public services. In Part One, attention is directed mainly at broader
processes of social change which concern the nature and significance of
consumption in contemporary society. The main themes and arguments
developed in these papers are outlined in later sections of this Introduction. But first we make some more general remarks about the central
concepts and questions that are involved here, and the bearing upon them
of this volume's title.

THE AUTHORITY OF THE CONSUMER

What might it mean to talk of cultural audiences and public service users
as 'consumers'? Perhaps the simplest, and nowadays the most literal,
sense of the term is that in which it is applied to the purchasers of goods
and services produced for exchange – that is, of 'commodities' – in a free
market economy. Yet this sense does not adequately express the complex
function of the concept of consumer in the kinds of developments with

which this volume is concerned. For on the one hand, whatever changes are taking place do not, for the most part, involve the direct relocation of previously publicly funded organizations in the private sector – that is, straightforward privatization. And on the other hand, this definition tells one little about what exactly is involved in being such a purchaser, or about the character of the relations between consumers and producers – and it is these kinds of questions that are of central importance here.

A somewhat different and more 'open-ended' starting-point, then, might be to distinguish at least two primary things that seem to be meant by those who advocate the conferral of this status of consumer, whilst recognizing that there are many more specific versions or interpretations of each of these. They are:

1 That the 'production' of such goods and services should be organized in ways that significantly mirror or parallel those involved in a free market economy, for example through the use of mechanisms enabling competition between rival producers, of contractually specified forms of exchange, and so on; and

2 That the 'consumers' of these goods and services should enjoy the kind of relationship with their 'producers' that may be thought to obtain between actual consumers and producers in a free market economy, and hence, for example, that these goods and services should satisfy their consumers' preferences, be responsive to their demands, and so on – depending on how that relationship is understood.

Thus the basic distinction is between the way in which the production of goods and services is to be organized, and the character of the relationship between their producers and consumers.[2] Of course, many of those who advocate (some specific version of) (1) do so in the belief that this will thereby ensure (some specific version of) (2). But others, who doubt whether this belief is correct, may none the less be sympathetic to the aim expressed in (2), that of 'consumer empowerment', and try to achieve it in other ways. As we shall see in Part Three, the different possible connections between (1) and (2) are a major source of debate in the reorganization of public services such as health-care, education and welfare.

By contrast, the papers in Part Two focus more on questions raised by the nature of the relationships between cultural producers and their audiences that may be implied by (2). In doing so, they also implicitly address issues that are more directly explored in Part One, where the main focus is on the question of what kinds of relationships between producers and consumers do in fact obtain in contemporary society, and what sorts of changes may be taking place in this respect.

It is at this point, we suggest, that the concept of consumer *authority* may usefully be brought into play, as a way of characterizing at least one kind of relationship that might obtain between consumers and producers – and more generally between consumers and other social groups – and of highlighting what may often be at issue in representing audiences and users as consumers.

Yet at first sight there may seem to be something very odd or paradoxical about attributing authority to consumers, for at least two reasons. First, more familiar uses of the concept of authority typically involve its attribution to specific individuals or social groups with a limited and fairly clearly defined membership. Second, and relatedly, its attribution to such individuals or groups is typically based on their claims to have some special abilities, qualifications, expertise, etc., which entitles them to exercise such authority in making – and enforcing – various kinds of judgements and decisions.

Consumers, by contrast, appear to lack these standard requirements for authority attributions. For they are, in effect, pretty much anyone and everyone – in principle no one is barred from membership of this 'group', even though many people's material circumstances may render their membership largely ineffective; and in making their judgements and decisions consumers neither necessarily possess, nor have to demonstrate their possession of, any special qualifications.

But, in a way, these paradoxical features of the concept of consumer authority bring out just what may be at issue here. For to attribute authority to consumers is typically to deny that any standard, more familiar forms of authority are operative in the particular context concerned. No one else has the right to make decisions in their place; no specially privileged social group may challenge their judgements. And if this is so, then it is at least arguable that the spread of market or quasi-market forms of organization brings with it a decline in other, more 'traditional' forms of authority – provided, of course, that the 'right kinds' of consumers are at work, and not consumers who deferentially and passively continue to accept the better judgement of their producer-superiors.

That there may indeed be different kinds of consumers, with different kinds of relationships to producers, is a possibility that tends to be concealed by the concepts of neo-classical economic theory, with its blanket attribution of 'sovereignty' to consumers and their 'preferences'. But at least some contributors to this volume would maintain, in effect, that this abstract conception of the consumer is only now beginning to be realized in the specific context of contemporary 'consumer' societies.

Others disagree, and instead emphasize the continuing ability of producers to exercise power over consumers, whether through the latter's acceptance of their authority or by other, more straightforwardly coercive or instrumental means. Relatedly, some contributors are inclined to regard apparent extensions of the status of consumer to cultural audiences or public service users as little more than misleading rhetoric – misleading because, if anything is going on here, it is more a matter of producers adopting and developing the discursive repertoires of advertising and marketing as a way of retaining their control over consumers; or indeed, more simply, of finding acceptable-sounding reasons for reducing public expenditure.

But there are also disagreements about whether, if consumers were to possess or be granted such authority, this would necessarily be desirable. For some contributors this would in principle be a welcome development, one that would challenge discredited forms of cultural elitism and professional authority, and would thus involve a movement towards genuine democratization. Others, however, are more doubtful about the benefits of empowerment conceived in this way, and regard the erosion of certain non-consumerist forms of authority as undermining the necessary bases for valuable and life-enhancing modes of experience, for instance in the aesthetic realm.

The latter kind of response might normally be understood as the expression of typically 'conservative' fears, of a kind that would belong, in political terms, to the so-called 'Old' Right, as distinct from the 'New' Right which largely displaced the former's political influence in the late 1970s and 1980s – the Thatcherite years. Yet those contributors who express such concerns would probably identify themselves as belonging to the Left – but to what might be called the 'Old' Left, whose conception of democracy and empowerment has been couched primarily in terms of the equalization of access to valued or valuable social goods.

By contrast one might say that for the New Left, democratic empowerment involves a direct 'democratization' of the criteria by which the value, and indeed meaning, of such social goods should be determined. Thus elitism, and inequality, are not so much a matter of restricted access to consensually agreed goods, but of the privileging of certain forms of experience or judgement at the expense of others, in ways that reflect relationships of power or domination 'unnoticed' by their predecessors. And hence, amongst other things, there is often an acute distrust of professional power and claims to expertise, and of traditional relations between professionals and their 'clients'.

But at this point there might seem to be certain resonances between the New Left and the New Right, which has likewise been strongly critical of professionals' power, and has often presented its radical programmes of reform as aiming to make them properly accountable. Its favoured device has been that of the market, with its supposed guarantee of consumer sovereignty. The New Left, of course, wishes to distance itself from this position, at least partly because of its markedly individualistic character, and also because its adherents continue, as socialists, to be hostile to the process of commodification. None the less, both amongst the contributors to this volume and more generally, it is hard to avoid the impression that the Old Left sometimes has more in common with the Old Right than with the New Left.

There is one further concept that needs to be noted here, one which brings with it an additional level of complexity to the (admittedly rather crude) political mapping that we have been suggesting. That is the concept of *citizenship* – or rather, a whole gamut of ways in which this term has recently been deployed in the kinds of debates that we have so far presented in terms of 'the consumer'. But we shall defer discussion of this concept until later in this Introduction, when we comment on the papers in Parts Two and Three.

SOCIAL CHANGE AND CONSUMPTION (PART ONE)

The papers in this part are concerned with a number of central questions about the nature and implications of consumption in contemporary society, and its relations to broader processes of social change. In particular: are important changes taking place in the character and significance of consumption in society, and if so, what are they? Can these be seen as connected with changes in authority, and if so, what are they? Can these be seen as connected with changes in authority, and if so, in what ways? Do they give individuals greater power to control their lives? And might they undermine aspects of human life which should have nothing to do with consumption, being valued instead for other, intrinsic reasons? → *civil rights — culture* *tradi*

In much recent work in the social sciences and humanities it has been argued or assumed that important social changes have been occurring that are associated in some way with the appearance or dominance of what is often called consumer society.[3] Writers may differ as to the precise dating of these changes, but there is rough agreement that they have taken place since the second world war.

According to this view, consuming things is an increasingly central life interest, and societies are increasingly organized around providing for that interest. The propensity to consume is being extended to an ever wider range of human activities, and people see themselves as consumers in more and more areas of their lives. Indeed, consumption seems now to embrace even certain forms of religion, as Paul Heelas suggests here in his discussion of New Age and self-religions.

An influential contributor to this body of work on the development of consumer society is Zygmunt Bauman, whose views are critically explored in Alan Warde's paper. Bauman puts the role of consumption at the very centre of the operation of the social world today. A new epoch of western society is being established in which the search for self-identity through acts of consumption is a key feature.

But these acts of consumption can no longer be understood as the acquisition of material objects for their instrumental utility. Instead, claims

Bauman, 'What is being sold is not just the direct use value of the product itself, but its symbolic significance as a building block of a particular cohesive life-style.' On this view, then, it is not just that the range of objects to be consumed is increasing, but that the *function* or cultural meaning of consumption itself is changing.

Similar claims have been made by cultural theorists such as Baudrillard – the replacement of use-value and even exchange-value by sign-value – and Bourdieu, for whom the consumption of goods and services in modern societies is no longer primarily orientated to the satisfaction of material wants or needs, but instead functions as a sign of a person's taste or position in a social group. These claims are contested here by John Winward, who argues that although some goods, especially those with a high 'cultural' content, are consumed primarily for their sign-value, a great deal of current consumption is still based on a rational weighing up of the advantages and disadvantages of particular goods and services for specific uses (and Warde has similar doubts about the centrality of life-style consumption).

Winward supports this view by describing the role of organizations such as the Consumers' Association, which both aid consumers in making rational choices and play a political role in uniting and representing them against producer interests. For him this indicates the active and potentially organized nature of consumers – though he accepts that the rationale for such forms of organization may be weakened by the decline of Fordist techniques of mass production and consumption (see Bagguley 1991).

This theme of the active consumer is also central to Adam Lury's paper. Drawing on his experience in the advertising industry, he sketches a two-stage development here. First, in the 1960s, the concept and techniques of marketing were introduced into the production–consumption cycle. What this effectively did was to induce the suppliers of goods and services of all kinds to orientate their output to the already discovered wishes and aspirations of the consumer: the system thus became increasingly consumer-led instead of producer-led.

None the less, he suggests, the consumer remained relatively passive in this process, or at least was assumed to be so by advertisers, who operated with relatively fixed and stereotypical conceptions of their audiences. More recently, however, as consumers have become more experienced, media-literate and critical, the old assumptions of advertisers are no longer tenable or effective, and a more equal relationship between them and their audiences becomes both possible and desirable.

If, in consumer society, attention increasingly shifts towards the satisfaction of consumer preferences, then it may also be argued that there are corresponding shifts in relations of authority. This is the central claim in Nicholas Abercrombie's paper. He maintains that despite the tendency of sociological theorists to ignore this, the relationship between producers and consumers can and should be understood in terms of this concept, and hence also involves issues about legitimacy.

The authority of producers, he suggests, is sustained by a variety of mechanisms, many of which are at present breaking down. Claims to expertise and knowledge, for example, have traditionally been made by producers, and accepted by consumers, particularly where professional services are concerned. The most important such mechanism in modern society, however, is the control of meaning. The authority of the producer is sustained by the capacity to define the meaning of the objects and transactions involved, and is correspondingly lost as consumers acquire that capacity. Such an outcome is especially likely in a society in which consumption is organized around images and life-styles, and where active consumers perpetually re-work the meanings of what they consume.

Russell Keat, in discussing the implications of consumer sovereignty for the conduct of cultural and educational practices, likewise suggests that the authority of producers lies in their right to define and judge the meaning and value of their products in terms of their own, or at least their practices', aims and standards, rather than those of the consumer. Such authority, however, itself depends on the legitimacy of cultural practitioners' claims to possess various kinds of knowledge, or the ability to make certain sorts of judgement. It is therefore vulnerable to the kinds of epistemological scepticism which seem to be an increasingly significant feature of contemporary society, and which make appeals to the idea of consumer sovereignty increasingly difficult to resist.

Related issues about the antitheses between consumer sovereignty and other forms or sources of authority are explored by Heelas in his discussion of the newly emerging self-religions. In these, he suggests, religion itself is often treated as an object of consumption, thereby undermining traditional patterns of religious authority. Religious authority lies with the believer, not with some external entity, whether divine or institutional: 'the locus of authority, or sovereignty, shifts from without to within'. In this respect, Heelas argues, the rise of New Age religions reflects a more general process of 'de-traditionalization, and the closely related development of a post-modern form of consumer culture'.

If consumer society involves a shift in authority towards the consumer, one might expect the consumer to be correspondingly empowered. Social theories based on neo-classical economic models provide a simple version of this proposition. The more that actual relationships between producers and consumers approach those depicted by such models of the competitive market, the more power and freedom consumers will have to make choices about what to purchase and from whom. Bauman, as discussed by Warde, offers a version of this hypothesis: 'The consumer market is therefore a place where freedom and certainty are offered and obtained together: freedom comes free of pain, while certainty can be enjoyed without detracting from the conviction of subjective autonomy' (Bauman 1988: 66).

Yet as Bauman himself emphasizes, things are not quite so straight-forward. For not only are many people excluded from this consumer paradise, but the organization of society around consumption depoliticizes society as a whole. But Warde is less impressed by the initial hypothesis, which depends, he suggests, on a particular, and unexamined, model of the consumer. Bauman, he claims, unites a model of the consumer drawn from neo-classical economics with a belief that consumers are motivated by a desire to construct their identities as members of a social group by acquiring consumer goods. Warde argues that this involves an unrealist-ically individualized, and undersocialized, account of the consumer, while at the same time exaggerating the capacity of consumption to provide satisfying forms of social membership or identity.

More generally, it is possible to argue that the apparent shift to a consumer society is a superficial or trivial change, or one that conceals the essential continuity of, for instance, class-based relationships of power. And, as will be seen in the discussion of the public services, in Part Three of this book, the claim that market mechanisms and 'discourses of the consumer' genuinely empower their users is problematic. But as Aber-crombie suggests here, there is a further level of complexity that needs to be considered in such debates.

Arguments that relate the growth of consumer authority to the empowerment of individuals often assume, he claims, that this is a long-term, secular, once-and-for-all change. But whilst agreeing that there has indeed been a recent shift of authority to consumers, Abercrombie argues that this is a *cyclical* change. Further, he proposes that the critical social relationship is *between* rival groups of producers who struggle for ascend-ancy. One weapon used by such groups is a process of commodification, which undermines the authority of hitherto dominant producers, transfer-ring it, if temporarily, to consumers. But once this dominant group has been deposed, other producers take their place and can assert their hegemony, drawing authority away from consumers by a process of de-commodification. Thus the authority of consumers may well be a short-lived phenomenon.

But even when there is a genuine shift towards consumer authority, and towards certain kinds of freedom or empowerment, it remains possible to argue that other, and less desirable consequences may flow from these changes. Heelas argues that the whole idea of consuming religion is essentially a contradiction in terms, because it undermines the concept of the sacred, the defining quality of religion. And when religion is seen in terms of what it can do to satisfy the consumer preferences of the believer, and not for any transcendental value, it can no longer perform such important functions as giving firm moral guidelines or alleviating existential anxieties.

In a somewhat similar vein, Keat argues that there are many social practices whose existence is dependent on a form of producer authority and would be undermined by any absolute consumer sovereignty. He does not deny that, for the provision of many goods and services, the market which serves expressed consumer preferences is the appropriate mechanism. But for other social activities, especially of a broadly cultural character, audiences (consumers) have to recognize or respect the authority of practitioners, which concerns 'their special relationship to the concepts, criteria and skills involved in the practice, and their acquired ability to evaluate particular attempts to realize these'. Keat's claim is that such recognition is necessary for the audience's own well-being, since without it they will be unable to understand, and hence judge for themselves, the value of the practice for their own lives. As we shall see, this argument is closely related to the themes explored in Part Two of this book.

CONSUMING CULTURE (PART TWO)

No doubt ever since the British Parliament first voted monies for subsidizing culture, arts bodies and organizations have complained about the inadequacy of the state's funding. But in the 1980s the complaints – from prestigious national companies and institutions such as the Royal Shakespeare Company and Tate Gallery, to local community arts groups – reached a new pitch of intensity. They were not, however, answered by increased funding in real terms but, as Celia Lury and Baz Kershaw describe in some detail in their papers, by a series of major revisions in state funding policy, including the 'encouragement' of artistic organizations to obtain sponsorship from the private sector to make up for the increasing shortfall in state-provided funds.

One outcome of this shift to private funding has arguably been a tendency to stage productions or exhibitions which are culturally 'safe' and uncontroversial, so that the commercial sponsor can be associated with established cultural capital, avoiding politically engaged or challenging work which might embarrass or enrage shareholders, or bring bad publicity to the corporate venture. And this effect, whether intended or not, would be welcome to a government that distrusted the previous 'arm's length' approach of bodies such as the Arts Council (and likewise, the universities and the BBC) which had permitted cultural institutions to promote anti-Conservative and even anti-enterprise values (see Keat and Abercrombie (eds) 1991, and Heelas and Morris (eds) 1992).

At another level, however, these changes of cultural policy can also be seen as intended to construct a new relationship between cultural producers and their audiences, one which involved, in line with the free

market ideology of the New Right, a shift towards consumer empowerment. When cultural organizations had been insulated from market pressures, they had been able to set an agenda and adopt standards which
mattered principally to the elite of producers and their peers, and to
pursue values which were as much at odds with those of the 'ordinary
man and woman' as the values of modernist architects were with those
of the Prince of Wales.

But now, producers would have to respond to consumer needs and
desires and, in so doing, would offer productions and exhibitions which
were popular and, consequently, financially successful. If an arts organization had to seek sponsorship, or was required to think of its audience as
consumers (whether directly, for example by the introduction of admission
charges for national museums and galleries, or indirectly, by the use of
commercially inspired marketing techniques and strategies), then it would
have to make its 'product' attractive to those consumers, and be responsive to their tastes and values. It is this kind of recasting of the relationship
between cultural producers and their audiences, as consumers, that is the
main focus of the papers in this section.

Taken to its extreme, the New Right espousal of consumer sovereignty
would seem to undermine the rationale for any form of state-enacted
cultural policy, and more generally for maintaining any distinction or
separation between the realms of culture and consumption. In these
respects it would be equally threatening to the Old Right, with its desire
to protect high cultural forms from the philistinism of commercialized
mass culture, and to the Old Left, whose view of cultural democracy
placed great emphasis on the widening of access to these non-commercial-
ized cultural forms.

Yet in fact, as Lury notes, the government continued to regard the arts
as a matter for cultural policy, albeit one which increasingly emphasized
their potential economic significance as parts of the 'culture industry',
especially at a regional level. Furthermore, she implies, recent changes in
Arts Council policies have done little to challenge its earlier model, which
assumed the state's (or other patrons') role to be that of enabling cultural
producers to provide a special form of experience that was deemed – in
effect by them – to be intrinsically worthwhile. The consumer (audience)
benefited by being able to have material access to the particular cultural
form, whether it was a symphony, a theatrical 'classic', or a sculpture.
The form was itself produced without direct reference to the consumer:
it was, to all intents and purposes, producer- rather than consumer-led.

Further, she argues, in continuing to see its aim as broadening the base
of the arts audience, the Arts Council has failed to acknowledge the
impact of popular culture and the mass media on the established hierarchy
of art forms and, more importantly, changes in the audience which has
become more visually aware and conceptually sophisticated. An audience

that is increasingly able to understand, for example, televisual conventions, and play with and manipulate meanings, is very different from the largely passive and deferential audience that was assumed by earlier stages of 'enlightened' cultural policy.

All of the contributors here would agree that the authority of high culture has been significantly eroded – partly for reasons associated with the more general decline in producer authority explored in Part One. The long-term socio-cultural changes from the late 1950s have produced a more educated and discriminating population which, allied to the economic affluence from which many people have benefited, have conspired to reduce considerably the power and authority of producers. The social conditions of the expansionist years of the 1980s gave the consumer confidence as well as perceived power, both reflected in and further fuelled by the political rhetoric of consumer sovereignty.

Furthermore, within the cultural realm itself the ordered hierarchies and supposed universal values of modernism have been rejected in favour of the mix-and-match options of post-modernism – a development which Nigel Whiteley traces through the Pop Art phenomenon of the 1960s. We now have 'Pavarotti in the Park', functional, everyday objects placed on the pedestals previously reserved for precious artefacts in international museums, and actors who can span Stratford (Shakespeare), Stratford (East) and Eastenders while retaining their credibility for television coffee commercials. Boundaries have been blurred or broken through. Meanings are no longer certain or authorial.

But the contributors differ markedly in their responses to these changes, displaying very different attitudes towards the status of high culture and producer authority in consumer society. Helen Rees, drawing on her experience as Director of the Design Museum, welcomes the opportunities brought about by an expanded field of culture which 'acknowledges meaning and value in contemporary commercial goods, as well as in art objects and historical artefacts'. The new conditions, she suggests, facilitate a new type of cultural institution which avoids the didactic paternalism or aesthetic formalism that dominated previous museums, and offer the possibility for an accessible, post-modern museum which can provide a 'critical commentary on the High Street'. That this was not fully achieved at the Design Museum, Rees concludes, was more a matter of inadequate financing than ideological conflict.

By contrast, Whiteley takes issue with those who have welcomed the blurring of boundaries between commerce and culture. He argues that the commercialization of culture, and the so-called 'aestheticization of daily life' resulting from the increasing cultural content of consumer goods, has in no way liberated or democratized the cultural realm. Instead it has homogenized cultural experience, reducing it to a level merely of 'liking things' which consumers may then choose to incorporate in one way or another into their life-styles.

Thus whilst Rees seems to accept Bourdieu's view of high culture as conferring status on privileged social groups, and Lury to associate it with forms of cultural elitism, Whiteley sees it as retaining a potential for 'otherness' from consumer society, whether through the realm of the aesthetic, or as a vehicle for generalizable critical reflection (cf. Keat in Part One).

But there are also disagreements here about the actual or potential character of an audience's typical mode of engagement with various cultural forms. For instance, whereas both Lury and Rees regard high culture as tending to involve passivity or deference on the part of audiences, and an uncritical acceptance of authoritative producer meanings and standards, Whiteley's argument implies that this is by no means necessarily so.

This question of the nature of audience experiences is of central concern to Kershaw. Focusing mainly on theatre, he argues that despite the hierarchical, class-based social meanings embedded in the physical design of most theatres, there are certain features of the experience of theatrical performance which potentially defy, and provide some basis for oppositional resistance to, the increasing commodification of cultural life in post-industrial, service-based economies – expressed, for example, in the accompaniment of exhibitions and theatrical productions by an ever-expanding range of souvenirs, T-shirts, and other merchandise that can be purchased and displayed by the consumer–audience. And he suggests that live performance can be an arena for a radically democratized empowerment of 'consumers', one that can transform audiences into what he calls 'collective co-producers'.

Whilst Lury is more sceptical about the radical potential of traditional cultural forms, she too is concerned with the democratization of culture, and what this might mean in terms of cultural policy. A radical cultural policy would have to go beyond the Old Left's aims of widening access if it is to challenge the authority of cultural producers and to alter what she regards as the present unequal terms of cultural citizenship. New modes of cultural experience, she suggests, are at present 'stabilized in the life-style discourse of an individuated self-realization, but are potentially available as resources for a more collective creativity', one in which the active engagement of the audience can feed into the process of cultural production. If this were to happen, the creative interplay and interpretation of new forms and performances would help to shape a more participatory, critical and just society.

Thus what is also involved in these papers is an implicit debate about the nature and meaning of cultural citizenship, and one in which the division between Right and Left is in some respects less significant than that between Old and New versions of each. For both the Old Right and Old Left being a good citizen was different from being a good consumer. In terms of culture, the good citizen aspired to appreciate the disinterested and dispassionate realms of aesthetic contemplation, and perhaps even entered the Temples of the Muses to see an art exhibition, watch a play, or listen to a concert. By counteracting the mundane and instrumental in life, the arts helped the citizen develop a full and healthy existence.

Both New Right and New Left have rejected this idealistic and cosy model. Both seem to welcome the weakening of producer authority, whilst the Old Right and Old Left distrust this shift of authority because of the danger, as they see it, of a loss both of standards and of a type of engagement which producer authority maintained through hard-earned critical knowledge, judgement, and discrimination, publicly expressed and mediated through institutions such as national museums.

As the New Right seeks to empower the consumer, the New Left seeks to wrest authority away from the cultural producers towards the audience. But whereas the former tends to assume that consumers will choose politically desirable options, the latter may hope that enough power will be available for consumers to grasp a sense of authority, play with it, subvert it, and ultimately transcend the Right's political programme. And whereas the New Right tends to define cultural citizenship in terms of an individualized model of consumer choices, the New Left remains committed to more collective, community-based forms of cultural democracy, and continues to harbour suspicions about the process of commodification (see Kershaw). As we shall see, similar political divisions in the understanding of citizenship also emerge in debates about the organization of public services.

CONSUMING PUBLIC SERVICES (PART THREE)

Along with the problem of spiralling state expenditure on health, welfare and other public services – the so-called 'fiscal crisis' – there had also emerged by the end of the 1970s, in Britain and elsewhere, a widespread sense that the organizational frameworks through which these services had traditionally been provided were failing to 'deliver the goods': that they were frequently inefficient, producer-dominated, unresponsive to the wishes or needs of their users, and providing poor quality services. As both Kieron Walsh and Richard Hugman note here, this perception was often shared by the political (New) Right and Left, despite their parting company on how these problems should be resolved. But it was the former's diagnosis and prescriptions for reform that dominated the consequent restructuring of public service provision during the following decade.

That diagnosis was based on the supposed virtues of the free market, as compared with centralized bureaucratic state structures, in empowering consumers through the effects of their actual or potential 'exit' behaviour on competing, profit-maximizing producers. As one sociologist neatly puts it:

> Customers can exert power (albeit limited) within a market through their purses, pockets and pouches, but this is denied to a client within a system of state provision. Clients can complain, can vote, can demand, but in the end they have nowhere else to go, and no choice but to accept what they are offered. They are, in short, *dependent* in a way that is never true of customers in a competitive market.
>
> (Saunders 1986, p. 345)

However, since a basic rationale for public provision of these need-related services has been that a free market economy inevitably makes access to its products dependent on people's (unequal) wealth and income, rather than their needs, any wholesale transfer of them to the private sector seemed still to be ruled out – though there were some exceptions to this in, for example, the encouragement of private health insurance and pensions, often supported, as Hugman notes, by appealing to the value of 'individual responsibility' (cf. Keat 1991); and as Oliver Fulton emphasizes, the over-arching concern of many government reforms has often been 'that someone else should pay'.

The task, then, was to find ways of reproducing the supposedly consumer-empowering (and cost-cutting) effects of the market whilst retaining the principle that these services, funded largely through taxation, should be free at the point of use/access. The solution consisted in introducing various kinds of partial analogues or parallels to standard elements of a free market system – including what are now often termed 'quasi-market' mechanisms – along with the techniques and 'outlook' of commercial management.

Perhaps the 'purest' (that is, with the closest analogy to the free market) quasi-market mechanism would be the use of state-provided vouchers, with which individual user–consumers can 'purchase' (at no expense to themselves) the services of competing providers, whose own financial resources will thus be determined by their ability to attract sufficient custom. But although something approaching this system is perhaps emerging in higher education (see Fulton), this device has remained largely untried (but see Hugman on Canadian experiments with welfare provision). More generally, as Fulton argues in the case of education, direct attempts to empower consumers by providing them with opportunities for 'exit' behaviour encounter serious practical difficulties about the availability of realistic alternatives, and of information about these, and tend to reinforce existing patterns of inequality amongst consumers.

Instead, as several contributors emphasize, the predominant forms of quasi-market systems have been based on the market principle of contract, and/or the introduction of an organizational split between 'purchasers' and 'providers': for example between health authorities and hospitals in the 'internal market' reforms of the health service, and in the contracting out of local government services such as refuse collection. Here the purchaser is expected somehow to represent or articulate the interests of users, specifying how these are to be met in its contracts with providers. Such systems, one might suggest, would be equivalent to a relationship between, say, food-retailers and food-suppliers, but where the former specifies the interests of food-consumers, rather than being subject to their actual purchasing decisions.

Walsh terms these (and related) kinds of arrangements 'surrogate consumerism', and like Fulton and Hugman raises several doubts as to their likely effectiveness in meeting user demands. He notes, *inter alia*, that attempts to monitor the behaviour of service providers through the use of performance indicators, inspection-systems, etc., tend to produce new forms of bureaucracy, and indeed centralization of control – often leading not so much to a straightforward reduction in (typically professional) producer dominance, as to the replacement of 'traditional' by 'new' professional groups (cf. Abercrombie in this volume).

But he also argues that attempts to specify standards of quality and so on for the services concerned encounter difficulties of a normative and not merely practical nature. In particular, one cannot simply assume that the preferences of individual users are sacrosanct here (that is, consumer authority): questions of value, and of policy, inevitably arise, that should be debated and decided by people acting collectively as citizens in the democratic, political domain, rather than as individual consumers in a quasi-economic one.[4]

However, this distinction between citizen and consumer is increasingly difficult to articulate in an unambiguous fashion. For, since the early 1990s, the newly empowered consumer–users of public services have been depicted in government policy as citizens, with their rights to decent standards of public service set out in a series of Charters – which tend to reproduce the discursive style and content of many commercial enterprises' customer-service guarantees.

This concept of citizenship was, of course, John Major's 'big idea', designed to differentiate his political position from its predecessor, Thatcherism – which itself, in its later stages, had also introduced a concept of citizenship, but of a very different kind: Douglas Hurd's 'active' citizens, involved in countless voluntary contributions to the well-being of their fellows, and thereby demonstrating that there was nothing intrinsically selfish about the ideal Thatcherite individual (see Heelas 1991).

To thus describe the consumer rights of public service users in terms of citizenship does not, of itself, imply that the rights of citizens consist in no more than this: in principle, at least, conceptual space remains for the articulation of other kinds of citizenship rights – political, civil, and so on. Yet there is clearly a possibility (and some would say a danger) that this space will in practice be filled by consumerist redefinitions of such non-market forms of citizenship – especially when, as one sometimes finds in current discussions, the market is itself presented as 'democracy at work', the sovereignty of the consumer being compared favourably, or even elided, with that of the citizen in the political sphere.

Tony Heward provides one illustration of this issue in the case of civil rights. In the course of his case-study of the Metropolitan Police's recent attempts to refashion their corporate identity, in response to a growing sense of breakdown in their relations with the public, he questions whether their new-found concern with 'customer-care' provides an appropriate way of dealing with the serious problems which affect, for example, the treatment and rights of suspected offenders. He also draws attention to the paradoxical situation of an organization that paradigmatically expresses the authority and power of the state ('the Police Force') taking on the commercially modelled rhetoric of the sovereign consumer ('the Police Service'). There are clearly some limits to user-friendliness here – and questions about who exactly are the 'consumers'.

What Heward's paper also illustrates is that the transformation of public service users into 'consumers' cannot be understood solely in organizational terms, for example through the introduction of quasi-market mechanisms into their systems of provision. For it is also, as Norman Fairclough argues here, a matter of the ways in which their users are discursively represented by the providers of these services; and to 'think of' them as consumers is typically to take over the kinds of 'promotional' discourses currently employed in commercial advertising, marketing, etc.

Thus for Fairclough, the 'discourse of the consumer' is not to be understood as the frequent use of the term 'consumer' and its cognates in discussions about the organization of public services, but rather as the growing deployment of specific discursive forms of the kind just noted. It is this phenomenon of discursive, rather than organizational, boundary-crossing – or indeed colonization – that Fairclough explores, in the context of a more general concern with the process of commodification.

What often emerges, he suggests, is a 'hybrid' discursive form: elements of the previously authoritative discourses – for example in university prospectuses, where institutions lay down their regulations and requirements for potential students – are combined, in an often uneasy relationship, with the promotional modes of address appropriate to customer-oriented discourses. Furthermore, the former elements are frequently partly concealed, or subordinated to the latter. Yet they remain – along, arguably, with the continuing power of these institutions to enforce such requirements on their 'sovereign' consumers.

Fairclough also draws attention to a specific feature of these promotional discourses, their increasing use of informal, 'conversational' styles. He suggests that, whilst the growing conversationalization of previously formal discourses has its roots in much broader social and cultural developments, this has in effect been appropriated by commercial enterprises and used for their own strategic purposes. Partly because of this, whether their use by public service providers – including their role in the communicative interactions between, for example, medical and counselling professionals and their clients – involves a genuine shift in previous asymmetries of power and authority, a form of 'democratization', is a complex question which he addresses in some detail.[5]

Hugman's paper is similarly concerned with the extent to which the 'consumerization' of public service users involves real changes in this respect; but, like Walsh and Fulton, his approach is organizational rather than discursive. He distinguishes between market and democratic forms of consumerism. The former is broadly equivalent to the consumerist conception of citizenship explored by Walsh, based on the use of quasi-market mechanisms. The latter involves a particular version of what Walsh refers to as a non-consumerist, communitarian view of democratic citizenship which, as both implicitly agree, has so far played a relatively minor role in constructing user-empowering alternatives to traditional forms of public service provision.

For Hugman, this democratic consumerism is best represented by the emergence of a wide range of service-user groups, whose members are concerned not just with ensuring the delivery of 'high quality' services to individual users, but with participating directly and collectively in the formulation of policy – with, in effect, the definition of what good services should consist in. In doing so they have not only challenged the authority of professionals to determine such matters, but also the nature of the relationships and interactions between professionals and clients involved in the actual 'delivery' of those services – a concern which, in terms of our earlier political mappings, might be seen as characteristic of the New Left.

Whilst emphasizing the need to distinguish different kinds of professional power and organization, Hugman also notes that a distrust of professional authority is also to be found in many advocates of non-democratic, market consumerism; and this is one of several elements he discusses in exploring the convergences and divergences between each of these forms of consumerism and political affiliations of Left and Right.

Fulton, too, considers how the New Right's distrust of professional authority and ability to escape the rigours of control by market forces has operated in educational reforms. But he also emphasizes the complexity and variety of political and sectional interests here, including the way in which free market ideology is often combined or allied with what he terms 'cultural restorationism', the desire to reinstate 'traditional' educational values and methods at the expense of 'progressive' ones.

Indeed one might suggest that many who propose market-based solutions to (supposed) educational problems, especially through the empowerment of parent-consumers, do so in the hope and expectation that these consumers' preferences will have a suitably 'traditionalist' character – just as, amongst promoters of the reform of cultural organizations discussed in Part Two, it may often be hoped and expected that consumer-audiences will display politically and culturally appropriate preferences. Their authority as consumers may thus be politically accepted only on the condition that it shows proper respect for more traditional forms of cultural authority.

NOTES

1 There is also the corresponding tendency for all kinds of goods and services, cultural exhibitions and performances, outcomes of educational processes, etc., to be represented as 'products'; but this is not the direct concern of the papers in this volume.
2 To talk simply of 'producer–consumer relations' involves a high degree of abstraction from the complexities involved in the actual social and economic processes of production and consumption: see Warde (1990) for a useful corrective.
3 We use this term here in a relatively broad sense, by contrast with more specific and theoretically loaded concepts such as 'consumer culture', which are discussed in several papers in Part 1.
4 A similar argument is presented by Sagoff (1988) in the case of environmental decision-making. More generally, the recent development of 'green' (and ethical) consumption (see Elkington and Hailes 1988, and Whiteley 1993) might be regarded as introducing elements of citizenship into the sphere of consumption, rather than, as New Right understandings of citizenship would seem to imply, reducing the 'public' role of the citizen to the 'private' one of the individual consumer.
5 Fairclough's paper is not exclusively concerned with the public services, and its mode of analysis brings together and develops many themes explored in Parts One and Two of this volume.

REFERENCES

Bagguley, P. (1991) 'Post-Fordism and enterprise culture', in Keat and Abercrombie (eds) (1991), 151–68.
Bauman, Z. (1988) *Freedom*, Milton Keynes: Open University Press.
Elkington, J. and Hailes, J. (1988) *The Green Consumer Guide*, London: Gollancz.
Heelas, P. (1991) 'Reforming the self: enterprise and the characters of Thatcherism', in Keat and Abercrombie (eds) (1991), 72–90.

Heelas, P. and Morris, P. (eds) (1992) *The Values of the Enterprise Culture: The Moral Debate*, London: Routledge.

Keat, R. (1991) 'Starship Britain or universal enterprise?', in Keat and Abercrombie (eds) (1991), 1–17.

Keat, R. and Abercrombie, N. (eds) (1991) *Enterprise Culture*, London: Routledge.

Sagoff, M. (1988) *The Economy of the Earth*, Cambridge: Cambridge University Press.

Saunders, P. (1986) *Social Theory and the Urban Question*, 2nd edn, London: Hutchinson.

Warde, A. (1990) 'Production, consumption and social change', *International Journal of Urban and Regional Research*, 14: 228–48.

Whiteley, N. (1993) *Design For Society*, London: Reaktion.

Part One

Social change and consumption

Chapter 1

Scepticism, authority and the market

Russell Keat

This chapter explores some philosophical issues raised by current debates about the desirability of protecting cultural practices from the effects of unregulated market forces. In particular, it considers the implications for these debates of relationships between forms of social authority and epistemological theories, that is, theories about whether, and in what ways, various kinds of knowledge-claims can be justified.[1]

I start by noting what strike me as some significant features of the theoretical and political alignments that often emerge in these debates:

1 Those who try to defend the special status of cultural practices, to exclude or protect them from the market domain, are frequently accused of being (cultural) *elitists*, of displaying a contemptuous attitude towards the tastes and judgements of 'ordinary consumers'. This anti-elitist rhetoric seems often to be used both by the bosses of multi-national media empires and by 'radical' cultural theorists who otherwise have little in common with them.

2 Many economic theorists, including those who are especially keen to promote the virtues of the market, are *subjectivists* about the epistemo-logical status of value-judgements (see Plant 1989, Roy 1989). That is, they regard such judgements – about ethical, aesthetic and similarly 'evaluative' matters – as no more than the expression of individual tastes or preferences, and hence as having no rational or objective mode of justification. In doing so they espouse a particular form of philosophical scepticism.

3 'Post-modernist' social theorists – by which I mean those who celebrate, rather than merely chart, the supposed emergence of a radically new form of social and cultural life, and are correspondingly disparaging about its predecessor, modernity – are sometimes accused of complicity with the (capitalist) market and/or its 'consumer culture' (see Jameson 1984, but cf. Selden 1991). Such theorists tend also to endorse the kind of scepticism about knowledge to be found in post-structuralist philosophy and literary theory; and one reason for their celebration of

post-modernity is their belief that the social 'authority' of such knowledge and its bearers in modern societies is now waning (see Bauman, 1987).

Whether or not these 'observations' are correct, they serve to indicate the main questions that will be explored in this paper. Do arguments for the exclusion of cultural practices from the market require the defence of certain forms of social authority for cultural 'producers', and a corresponding rejection of the authority or 'sovereignty' of consumers? Are such arguments undermined by scepticism about particular forms of knowledge or judgement? And does scepticism about values – commonly termed 'meta-ethical' scepticism – itself justify the use of the market for any products about whose value, according to such scepticism, no justifiable knowledge-claims can be made?

I shall now explore the first point in more detail, which may make its connections with the second and third, and its bearing on the questions just noted, a little less opaque. I shall then go on to examine what is involved in the ascription of sovereignty to consumers in orthodox economic theory, and to present a (partly) hypothetical example of how such sovereignty might be seen by cultural producers as challenging their authority. I shall conclude by sketching an argument for the protection of cultural practices from the market, and considering how this would be affected by meta-ethical scepticism.

ELITISM, AUTHORITY AND MODERNITY

When those who work in non-market cultural institutions try to resist their subordination to market forces, they often claim that the effect of this would be to compromise the integrity of their practices,[2] to distort their proper character, to undermine the quality of what would become their marketable 'products', and so on.

So, for example, academics often argue that the pressure to compete for students will undermine their conception of what is educationally worthwhile; television producers, that the deregulation of broadcasting will lead to a decline in the quality of programmes; subsidized theatre and dance companies, that the commercially modelled criteria for funding imposed by the Arts Council will inhibit artistic innovation; and museum curators, that being reduced to the status of a leisure industry will put at risk the proper purposes of their collections.

Such objections are often met with the charge of elitism. For surely, it is said, the essential feature of the market is the sovereignty of the consumer, and hence the exercise of control by the judgements of consumers over what is produced? If so, to resist such control can only indicate an elitist contempt for consumers' judgements, tastes, intelligence and so on, and a corresponding insistence that they should instead defer to the authority of a cultural elite.

Yet many who oppose the commercialization of cultural practices in these terms do not regard themselves as elitists. So how might they rebut this accusation? Clearly, a good deal depends here on how 'elitism' is defined; and although this term is often now used to convey little more than content-less political abuse, one can still identify at least two relatively clear and distinct senses of it, which I shall call 'elitism of access' and 'elitism of judgement'. In the case of cultural practices, the former might be expressed in the slogan 'high culture is only for us, the few', the latter in 'high culture is what we few who can judge these matters say it is'.

In more theoretical terms, the former concerns the potential social range of distribution of various valued forms of experience, appreciation, enjoyment and so on – the elitist of access claiming that this is necessarily, or at least desirably, highly limited. By contrast, the latter concerns the social location of the judgements which, as it were, confer value on such items – the elitism of judgement claiming that this too is necessarily or desirably limited to some specific social group.[3]

It seems clear that resistance to the market need not involve commitment to elitism of access. For whilst cultural practitioners may fear the effects of competition to satisfy existing consumer preferences, they may none the less believe that pretty well anyone who wishes to is potentially capable of experiencing and appreciating the 'products' of these cultural practices. What is more problematic is elitism of judgement: can the kinds of claims noted earlier about the potentially damaging effects of the market be made without commitment to this form of elitism? My answer to this is: 'Yes – but only if one is not an epistemological sceptic, and not without appealing to some form of social authority.'

That there is no necessary commitment to elitism of judgement might be argued as follows. The relevant judgements here can be supported by forms of reasoning and argument that are open to anyone to understand and evaluate; and the criteria by reference to which they are made can likewise be rationally justified, or at least intelligibly and openly contested. Hence they are not necessarily the judgements of an elite group which declares, in effect, 'these things are valuable, true, etc., just because we say so'. Indeed, it might be said, to reject this argument would imply that simply to believe that rationally defensible judgements are possible is elitist – and this is absurd.

This argument is quite persuasive as far as it goes. But it fails to engage with a further set of problems which are perhaps what those who make the charge of elitism (of judgement) often have in mind, even if their concerns are not best expressed through this particular concept. To see what may be involved here, I will briefly consider an apparently extreme example, that of science, and the judgements made by the members of a scientific community.

This case is 'extreme' in that, of all forms of intellectual inquiry – and also of cultural practices, if one may regard such forms of inquiry as belonging to this broad category – science can be seen as having the strongest claim to operate at least potentially in accordance with rationally justifiable criteria (via rules of evidence, hypothetico-deductive theory-testing, etc.), so that scientific judgements are open to essentially impersonal and objective standards of assessment.

Indeed it is precisely this feature of science that makes it the paradigmatic instance of *modern* knowledge. In particular – and the same story can be told of, for example, 'modern' philosophy – its practitioners typically represent this discipline as originating, historically, in the overthrow of all appeals to 'authority', that is of all attempts to justify scientific claims by reference to the beliefs or judgements of particular individuals, social groups, members of religious institutions, etc. Such appeals to authority were to be replaced by reliance upon canons of reasoning and the proper use of empirical evidence, regarded not only as the epistemologically relevant criteria for assessing scientific claims, but also – at least in Enlightenment thought, and closely related to its ideal of individual autonomy – as depending on, and made possible by, human capacities which everyone either possesses, or can in principle acquire and exercise.

Yet however convincing this account of modern science is epistemologically, it is potentially misleading sociologically. For both the conduct of scientific research, and even more obviously the education of scientists, require complex forms of social authority, in which particular individuals and groups are accorded, by virtue of their supposed expertise, training, etc., the right to make judgements about the merits of others' scientific work, and legitimate power to enforce these. Similar points apply to the ways in which the judgements of a scientific community are themselves accorded such authority when its 'knowledge' is practically employed or relied upon outside that community.

So even if it is true that 'anyone and everyone' can in principle reconstruct and evaluate for themselves the lines of reasoning and evidential support for any scientific claim, both the internal conduct and external role of science would be impossible if this were the social process through which the validation and application of such claims actually took place.[4]

At the risk of hasty generalization from this particular case, one might then suggest that every social practice which either depends upon, or issues in, knowledge-claims – whether these are scientific, aesthetic, moral, philosophical, etc. – requires some relatively coherent and effective forms of social authority. And, relatedly, one might also distinguish two different kinds of criticism that may be directed at specific exercises of such authority. First, it may be claimed that the authority has been *abused*, in that the judgements made fail to accord with the practice's own criteria as a result, for instance, of the intrusion of their authors' particular social interests.

Alternatively, however, it may be claimed that the authority in question is *ill-founded*, in that the criteria upon which these judgements are based are themselves defective in various ways. The most radical version of this second kind of criticism is the sceptic's, according to which there are *no* criteria by which these judgements can be evaluated, no way of justifying any claims to knowledge in this particular domain. Scepticism, that is, necessarily de-legitimates any form of social authority in the domain of knowledge to which such scepticism is thought to apply. The exercise of such authority must then appear as no more than the arbitrary exercise of power, as the concealed expression of its bearers' social interests.[5]

If this is so, and if what underlies current charges of cultural elitism is hostility to certain forms of social authority, one would expect to find a correlation between anti-elitist rhetoric and scepticism about the relevant form of knowledge or judgement. This seems to be confirmed by the current prevalence of such rhetoric in the aesthetic domain, where scepticism is probably at its strongest. One would also expect to find a tendency to regard anyone who is not an aesthetic sceptic as a cultural elitist – a view which, whilst conceptually somewhat confused, may none the less express a significant social insight.

Furthermore, this account may explain (if any explanation is necessary) why post-modernist social theorists, who tend to be sceptics about the possibility of 'foundations' for any kind of knowledge or judgement (except perhaps their own, which they often seem happy to impose on their students through their authority as academics) tend also to represent modernity and the Enlightenment as 'authoritarian' – a charge that scientists and others of a 'modern' frame of mind find especially distressing, for the reasons indicated above.[6] Again, whilst conceptually confused, this may have the virtue of encouraging such 'moderns' to acknowledge the necessary role of social authority within their intellectual practices – even if, rightly unconvinced by such scepticism, they continue to regard this authority as legitimate.

CONSUMER SOVEREIGNTY AND THE AUTHORITY OF CONSUMER PREFERENCES

I turn now to the concept of consumer sovereignty, and explore its relationship to the issues about scepticism and authority presented above. Although one is unlikely to find much explicit discussion of this concept in standard textbook accounts of a market economy, I shall suggest that its implicit role in these has considerable significance for arguments about what kinds of activities and goods are suitably located within the market domain. I begin with a sketch of how the free market system is supposed (that is, theoretically) to operate which, whilst highly simplified, is I hope recognizably related to neo-classical economic theory and to influential justifications for the market which draw upon this.

In a market economy, rival producers compete with one another in pursuing their overall aim of profit-maximization. Their success or failure in this task is ultimately determined by their relative ability to meet, in a cost-effective manner, the demands of actual or potential purchasers of their products: that is, to satisfy the wants or preferences of consumers, where these preferences are indicated by the consumers' willingness to pay for the products on offer. Consumers are free to choose between the producers from whom they will make such purchases; and thus the failure of any producer to satisfy these preferences is typically met by the 'exit' response of taking their custom elsewhere. Likewise, new firms are free to enter the competitive process at any point, and/or existing firms to develop new products, etc. But their success in doing so is always subject to their relative ability to satisfy the preferences of consumers.

This picture of how the free market is meant to operate is closely related to an influential justificatory account, that is, one that tries to show why the market is a better set of mechanisms, procedures, institutions, etc. than any other (for example than a state-controlled system, a feudal/guild one, a hunter-gatherer one, and so on). This consists in claiming that a market system is the most efficient, in the sense that for any given set of resources, it maximizes the total amount of preference-satisfaction that can be obtained from their use.[7]

But what exactly is meant by a 'preference' here? The brief answer is *anything*, or at least anything that may incline someone towards the acquisition of a product, and is expressed by their willingness to pay for it. Both the specific character and possible bases of such preferences are matters of complete indifference on this account of the market: that is, there is no concern about either what they are preferences for, or what if any reasons might support these preferences.

This conception of consumer preferences is sometimes taken to imply that they are to be seen as 'mere' or even 'arbitrary' in character. But this is potentially misleading. The use of such terms would normally imply some contrast with, say, well-founded or reflectively formed preferences. But consumer preferences are not necessarily 'mere' or 'arbitrary' in this sense, either in (economic) theory or in practice. Rather, the concept of preference should be understood in an essentially neutral or 'agnostic' way, so that it can refer both to 'mere' and 'not mere' preferences, without any distinction being made between these (cf. Sheffrin 1978, and Norton 1987: ch. 1).

This use of the concept is related to the way that economists see it as no part of their business to make any 'value-judgements' about consumer preferences – in any way to 'discriminate' between them on the basis of their aesthetic, moral or political character, of the soundness or otherwise of the reasons which may underlie them, or indeed of the extent to which their satisfaction contributes to the consumer's own well-being, a point to which I shall return in the penultimate section.

The refusal to make such judgements is typically justified by an appeal to the methodological ideal of value-freedom or value-neutrality, together with the claim that, to the extent that one is concerned only with constructing predictive and/or explanatory theories of the market, there is no need to discriminate in this way between preferences. But it is often further supported by invoking some form of scepticism about value-judgements: claiming, in effect, that these are purely 'subjective', indeed themselves no more than the expression of (in this case necessarily) 'mere' preferences.

Further, this lack of concern by economic theorists about the possible character and basis of consumer preferences is, as it were, shared by the market itself, according to their account. For in a market system, consumers do not have to provide any rationale for their purchasing decisions, and their access to products is not dependent on any assessment by others of the preferences they expect such products to satisfy. Indeed, that the market is one of the few spheres of social life in which one is not required to render an acceptable account of one's actions may be seen as an additional virtue of it.

What *is* required of consumers, though, is that they should know *what* their preferences are, and *whether* they have been satisfied by a particular purchase. But such knowledge, it is typically assumed – and perhaps necessarily, if the justification for the market noted above is to be plausible – is something of which every consumer is capable. After all, it consists essentially in people's 'first-person' knowledge of their desires, beliefs, etc., that is in the kind of knowledge for which everyone has indisputable 'authority' in his or her own case – perhaps the only kind of knowledge which needs no special structure of social authority to produce or validate. 'It's true because I say it is': this is the authority of the consumer with respect to first-person knowledge claims about their preferences and/or the satisfaction of these. No one else knows any better, and hence no one else has the right to challenge such claims, or to replace them with others 'more' authoritatively made.

But it is precisely the fact that this is pretty much all that the consumer is required or expected to know that may well concern those who oppose the subordination of cultural practices to the market, and who regard the forms of social authority required for the integrity of these practices as potentially undermined by the sovereignty of consumers, that is, by their ability to determine what is produced on the basis of judgements whose authority holds only with respect to their preferences. In the following section I shall illustrate the nature of such concerns through a particular example. But first I want to contrast this kind of objection to the market with another.

The claim that the market succeeds in maximizing the satisfaction of consumer preferences is often criticized on the grounds that, at least in practice, its operation may not achieve this goal. For, alongside more technical issues about 'market failures' in the case of externalities and public goods, it may be argued that there are also many ways in which consumer preferences may fail to control producer decisions – for instance, by the power of producers to prevent or inhibit consumer access to relevant information (see Winward in this volume), or indeed by influencing the character and formation of preferences themselves.

Thus according to this kind of criticism – which has been a central theme in socialist objections to the market, together with issues of distributive justice – the idea of consumer sovereignty is essentially a myth, since market economies leave consumers too vulnerable to the power of producers. By contrast, it seems, the defenders of non-market cultural practices fear that consumer sovereignty might be a reality, which would make cultural 'producers' too vulnerable to the power of consumers – too vulnerable since the only kind of authority that consumers have, that is about their own preferences, may be seen as an inappropriate basis for the control of cultural production. The market thus threatens the authority of cultural practitioners – a characteristically 'conservative' fear, though one that also, I would argue, has a proper home in socialist thought.

CULTURAL PRACTICES AND CONSUMER SOVEREIGNTY

To explore what is at issue here, I will now consider the case of a hypothetical university department faced with the kind of quasi-market situation that is increasingly characteristic for higher education institutions in Britain: that is one in which, although students do not (as yet) actually pay for their degree-courses, a significant proportion of the financial resources available to a department depends on its ability to attract students (consumers) in competition with other departments elsewhere. Each department's viability thus depends on its relative ability to satisfy the preferences of its student-consumers.[8]

Of course, since this example is drawn from the educational sphere, it is not altogether representative of other kinds of cultural practices: public service broadcasters, for instance, are not vested with the authority to examine or certify their viewers' performance or competence. None the less academics are, *inter alia*, participants in cultural practices, which have much in common with more typical cases; and I shall try here to abstract from those features of the example specifically related to the validating authority of educational institutions.

A basic concern of academics in this quasi-market situation is, I suggest, typically this: given the potentially arbitrary character of their students' preferences, judged in terms of the criteria internal to the relevant academic discipline, the competitive pressures of the market may lead to a loss of control over what counts as a genuine education in that discipline, and hence, in the longer term, over the nature and development of the discipline itself. Hence the authority that they regard themselves as legitimately possessing, with respect to the meaning and character of their intellectual work, is seen as vulnerable to the sovereignty of their newly enthroned consumers.

To illustrate this concern I shall consider two of the most obvious strategies that, say, a department of philosophy might adopt in competing for student-consumers. The first is to adjust the content of its degree courses so as to eliminate those elements which, on past experience, they suspect are unattractive to students, and replace them with others that are less so.

So, for example, the department might abandon its existing requirement for students to take courses in formal logic, introducing in their place an alternative option on reasoning in everyday contexts; and/or it might adjust the content of its courses in continental philosophy, so that, say, the less immediately accessible, metaphysical aspects of Sartre's and Heidegger's work are replaced by a focus on their claims about bad faith, authenticity and 'the human condition'; and similarly oriented changes might be made in other courses.

For the purposes of this discussion, I assume that these changes are made despite being at odds with (members of) the department's own judgements of what is an essential element in the discipline, of what aspects of a philosopher's work must first be grasped if others are to be understood and evaluated, and so on. I am not claiming that in other contexts, there could be no good reason for introducing these particular changes. But here, they are introduced solely to acquire a competitive advantage over other departments, by enhancing its relative ability to meet student preferences.

In this respect, therefore, the department is likely to be seen by others as unscrupulous, opportunistic, lacking in integrity, etc. But the nature of the market system is such that they, now placed at a competitive disadvantage, may well be 'forced' to follow suit, unless they display considerable 'altruism': they can no longer afford the costs of acting in accordance with their convictions (see Keat 1991, and O'Neill 1992). The ethics of their actions are thus significantly different from those of the initiating, 'rogue' department; though as the market situation develops over time, it will become increasingly difficult to make such a distinction.

This ethical distinction is related to a more general point about the sense in which, in this kind of competitive situation, cultural producers might see themselves as unduly vulnerable to their consumers. For this vulnerability arises, not directly from the power of consumers, but rather from the willingness of those who will initially be regarded by others as 'rogue' producers to 'confer' this power upon them – by meeting their preferences in ways that other producers had previously been unwilling (and regarded as unjustifiable) to do. It is thus the openness of the market to new producers, or to producers with new products, that makes this potential vulnerability realizable.

There is, however, a second competitive strategy available here. This is to develop a degree that appeals to a specific section of the 'market' (in a different sense of this term) for philosophy, rather than trying to compete with others in catering for the 'general' student's preferences. Indeed ideally this group of potential students will be one that no other, rival department is targeting, since the rationale for this strategy is typically to avoid direct competition – though there is no guarantee that this can be sustained over time, since direct competitors may re-emerge, and the department will find itself either forced back on the first strategy, or needing to find a different, and possibly more specialized market niche.

For example, a department might reckon that there is an untapped demand for a philosophy degree that consists entirely of practical ethics, with an array of courses on medical and business ethics, environmental issues, animal rights, and so on; or for a degree which caters for Channel 4 viewers who find contemporary developments in post-structuralist philosophy and the aesthetics of post-modernist architecture especially exciting, with courses on the history of philosophy seen through exclusively Nietzchean eyes; or for one that appeals to students with an interest in humanistic psychology and 1960s-style counter-culture, who already believe that all forms of mind–body dualism are misconceived, and will go elsewhere if this belief is not reflected in their courses.

Again, I assume here that these degree-schemes are regarded as philosophically illegitimate by the department that introduces them. Yet it may find itself in a situation where its inability to enforce its own authoritative judgements about the nature of the discipline make this perceived loss of integrity difficult to avoid. It thus finds itself losing control over the nature of the 'product' that it has to offer. And it resents the fact that control is being ceded to those whose preferences for certain kinds of philosophical products it regards as having no authority. On this anti-market view the student is, after all, seen essentially as an *apprentice*, not as a sovereign consumer: as someone who is required to accept the authority of this cultural practice's members as a condition of entry into it.

However, as soon as one presents such concerns about the possible effects of the market in these terms – of 'losing control over the nature of the product', etc. – one is bound to be struck by how odd it would be if similar concerns were (at least openly) expressed by commercial firms operating in a standard market situation.[9] Why is this so? And more importantly, are there any good grounds for distinguishing the two cases so radically, so that the former concerns are justifiable whilst the latter are not? In the next section I will present one possible way of giving a positive answer to this question. But first I will introduce an additional element to the philosophy example.

So far I have been assuming that philosophy is a single, relatively monolithic academic discipline, in the sense of there being a strong degree of consensus amongst its practitioners about, for example, what counts as a genuinely philosophical problem, what would constitute a possible solution to such a problem, the canon of philosophical texts, the ways in which the different specialized areas within 'the' discipline relate to one another, and so on. Yet this is far from actually being the case – even if one puts aside the existence of differing 'national traditions'. (In this respect philosophy is, at least nowadays, like many other disciplines in the humanities and social sciences, and many non-academic cultural practices – though arguably unlike the natural sciences.)

There is, in other words, a certain kind of plurality 'within' philosophy, which means that there is no single, agreed set of authoritative judgements about the proper nature of this form of intellectual inquiry, and hence about what constitutes a proper education in it. This is not to say that there is no actual or possible dialogue between these various 'schools' or conceptions of philosophy; nor that philosophers are themselves pluralists, in the sense that they all agree on the desirability of this situation. But this fact of plurality does complicate my earlier account of the two competitive strategies since, roughly speaking, what is a 'rogue department' from one philosophical standpoint may be an exemplary department from another; and what some philosophers see as the unprincipled exploitation of a market niche may seem to others the fortunate existence of a market for their particular conception of philosophy.

Further, anyone who regarded such plurality as itself desirable might regard 'the subordination of philosophy to the market' as a useful way in which this pluralistic ideal could be realized, with each conception of philosophy establishing its own niche market amongst the plurality of consumers which is itself, according to some social theorists, an increasingly evident feature of contemporary, 'post-modern', societies. Thus, far from being seen as a threat to the authority of the discipline's practitioners, this pluralized form of consumer sovereignty would serve to undermine the imperialistic tendencies of any one conception of philosophy; and it might be especially attractive to those whose own conception of the discipline was at present marginalized by its dominant form.

But this kind of optimism – or opportunism – about the market might well prove illusory. First, there is no guarantee of a correspondence between the plurality of consumer groups and that of conceptions of philosophy: such a pre-established harmony could arise only if conceptions of philosophy were themselves directly consumer-generated. Second, and more importantly, there is nothing to prevent the problems noted earlier for the first competitive strategy being reproduced for the practitioners of each of these different 'philosophies', since they cannot prevent what they would regard as 'rogue' producers competing 'unscrupulously' with them in what had initially been their own market niche.

Thus even a pluralistic view of philosophy will still involve claims to authority on the part of each group of practitioners within the overall plurality. Their internal standards of judgement etc. may not be shared by other philosophers; but they may well, like them, find themselves wanting to reject the sovereignty of their consumer-students. (Postmodernist academics, beware!) The pluralists' rejection of monolithic authority does not imply the rejection of authority *tout court*.

CULTURAL PRACTICES, WELL-BEING AND SCEPTICISM

But even if cultural practitioners are right to regard the market as threatening the integrity of their practices for the kinds of reasons just presented, this does not by itself establish the case for forms of public support that would protect these from the unregulated effects of market forces.[10] To show this one must also present some positive justification for the existence of such practices – over and above, that is, the benefits that may accrue to their own members. I will now sketch out one such possible justification, and consider the bearing upon this of the issues about scepticism and authority explored earlier.[11]

Cultural practices, I suggest, can be justified in terms of their potential contribution to the well-being of what I shall term their 'audiences' (that is viewers, listeners, students, visitors, spectators, etc.). The well-being of individuals may be thought of as consisting in the extent to which they are able to realize their own conceptions of the good, that is to live in a way that conforms to their sense or judgement of what is valuable, worthwhile, desirable, fulfilling and so on.[12] Further, such conceptions of the good are rarely homogeneous: they typically include a variety of heterogeneous 'goods', of different kinds of activities, relationships, and experiences with distinct, and possibly incommensurable values.

If public support for non-market cultural practices is to be justified in terms of their contribution to human well-being thus conceived, it must first be shown that such well-being may at least arguably consist in something more and/or other than the satisfaction of consumer-preferences – assuming, for these purposes, that the market is the most efficient way of achieving this aim. This does not mean showing that consumer satisfactions make *no* contribution to human well-being; only that they may perfectly well not be the sole such contributors.

But this should be a fairly easy task. First, one should remember that at best, the market only maximizes the satisfaction of consumer preferences 'as they happen to be', that is whether or not they involve the kinds of critical or reflective processes upon which, ideally, individuals might wish to base their judgements of what is valuable to them. Second, there is considerable empirical evidence that people's sense of their own well-being is not directly and positively correlated with the extent to which their preferences as consumers have been satisfied (see Sagoff 1988: Ch.5).

Finally, it seems clear that a central concern for many people is precisely with how large a part should be played in their lives by the pursuit of consumer satisfactions – as compared, for instance, with the value of friendships and family relationships, engagement in political or community activities, and so on (see Anderson 1990). This concern would make no sense – and my argument requires only that it should be intelligible – if human well-being and consumer-satisfaction were wholly and unarguably identical with one another.

Turning now to the potential contribution of cultural practices to well-being thus defined, one can note, first, that the quite commonplace concern just described is one that may itself be addressed in their various 'products' – in novels, soap operas, philosophical treatises and the like. And it seems plausible to argue that, both in this case and more generally, people's ability to develop their own sense of what is valuable, and of the relative value of different life-activities, will be enhanced by their access to cultural practices in which the tensions and conflicts between various conceptions of the good for humans, and hence of their well-being, are thematized and explored in both discursive and non-discursive forms. To deny this would be to assume that individuals' conceptions of the good are best developed in a social and cultural vacuum, an assumption supported only by the most extreme and implausible forms of individualism.

Second, and perhaps more typically, cultural practices may be seen as attempts to sustain and develop specific 'forms of the good', that is forms of experience and activity which may constitute at least part of what their audiences come to regard as valuable, fulfilling, and so on. That is, cultural practices themselves embody (and often in a 'pluralistic' manner – see the previous section) various conceptions of the good; and so they collectively provide, as it were, a sourcebook for ways of understanding and practising what may be of value to human lives, and which, through their audiences' access to them, may thus contribute to the latter's well-being.

This does not imply that cultural practitioners are primarily motivated by their desire to contribute in these ways to the well-being of their audiences – as if they were 'cultural altruists', sacrificing their own interests to the task of providing others with ways of understanding and exploring the nature of the good for humans. My argument here is compatible with a variety and mixture of practitioner motivations, including straightforward enjoyment of their engagement in the cultural practice concerned, some belief in its value – that it may well constitute some part of the good for humans – and indeed, a recognition that the practice is itself radically incomplete in the absence of an audience.[13] But this does not mean that their primary aim is to enhance the good of others.

Neither does this justification for the support of non-market cultural practices imply their members being invested with the authority to determine what the good for humans consists in, or to legislate for others how their well-being is to be achieved. Rather, the account that I have outlined is quite consistent with the *autonomy* of all those concerned, that is with the moral 'right' of individuals to decide for themselves their own conceptions of the good, and hence what their well-being may involve. Indeed it is arguable that such autonomy, if it is thought of as something more than the mere ability of individuals to say 'this is what I think', or 'this is what I value', itself requires access to the substantive possibilities of the human good, and the resources for reflection upon these, that can be provided by a flourishing range of cultural practices (see Kymlicka 1989).

The authority required here is of a different kind (cf. Winch 1967). Consider, say, the (highly pluralistic) cultural practice of music. My argument does not imply that musical practitioners should have the right to 'tell' their potential audiences that a life without (this form of) music is not worth living, nor the authority to prescribe, for example, what part such music should play in people's lives. Their authority is, rather, of an 'internal' nature: it concerns their special relationship to the concepts, criteria and skills involved in the practice, and their acquired ability to evaluate particular attempts to realize these, and hence at least implicitly to determine what count as genuine, admirable or other such instances of the practice. Such authority is not, of course, unchallengeable, either internally or externally; nor is it one that cannot or should not be shared in certain ways with an audience. But it is difficult to envisage any cultural practice without it; and if the argument in the preceding section is plausible, such authority is always potentially vulnerable to the effects of the market.

Furthermore, I suggest, if potential audiences are to benefit from their access to cultural practices, they need to approach them in a way that at least initially recognizes such authority, since they will otherwise not be in a position to understand, and hence judge for themselves, its possible value to them, nor to enjoy the specific human good it may represent. In

other words, a certain attitude or mode of engagement is required –
which is not to say that it can or should be enforced. This is not an
attitude of deference or passivity, but of (potentially critical) respect;
without it, there is nothing that can be learnt, and hence little that can
be enjoyed.[14] The market can in no way be relied upon to encourage or
sustain such an attitude amongst consumers, at least partly because it
often gives rise to justifiable suspicions amongst them about the integrity
of producers, though it does not necessarily prevent its existence.

To illustrate what is involved here – and to reinforce my earlier account
of the typical concerns of cultural practitioners about consumer sovereignty – one can consider the partly analogous case of tourism, where
'another culture' is the equivalent of a cultural practice. Of course, there
are disanalogies between the two cases, including the 'non-voluntariness'
of members' involvement in their own culture, which provide additional
reasons for the tourist's 'respecting the authority' of the visited culture's
members. But, putting aside these specifically moral considerations, it can
be argued that a certain mode of engagement with another culture is
necessary if its potential to enrich or develop one's own conception of
the good, and hence potentially one's own well-being, is to be realized.

For example, it should not be approached exclusively as a means of
satisfying an existing set of preferences, whose content and rationale bear
no relation to the 'local' meanings and values of that culture, and which
are not open to reflective change as a result of this encounter (cf. Norton
1987 on 'transformative values'). Further, some attempt must be made to
comprehend it 'in its own terms', rather than simply to impose or project
upon it a prior set of meanings, or to constitute it as meaning whatever
it is that comes into one's head, and so on. And clearly, 'unscrupulous
producers', such as tour operators and local businesses, can all too easily
act in ways that are destructive of the culture, by empowering tourist-
consumers to treat it not in its own terms, but as the object of their
'arbitrary' preferences. For preferences, in effect, serve to define the
meanings of their objects, not merely to select between objects independently defined: the only relevant features of their objects are those picked
out, or even created, by preferences, and hence by consumers.

Following through this proposed analogy, one can then move on from
'other cultures' to 'popular' culture; to sports, festivals and games; to
broadcasting and the media; and then on to the arts, academic disciplines
and 'high' culture. By putting these kinds of cultural practices in this
particular (rhetorical) order I am trying to suggest that the argument I
have presented is not just another conservative plea for the protection of
high culture against the incursions of mass culture; and likewise, that the
kind of authority of cultural practitioners which I am defending is not
open to the charges of elitism considered earlier.

SCEPTICISM AND THE MARKET

But what of the sceptical challenge to any forms of authority that depend on claims to knowledge or judgement whose possible justification the sceptic denies? Although the argument for non-market cultural practices that I have presented does not involve attributing to cultural practitioners authority with respect to the good or well-being of others, a thoroughgoing scepticism would undermine this argument at various points.

First, scepticism in its extreme, individual-subjectivist form, would rule out even the 'internal' authority of practitioners' judgements within each cultural practice. Indeed, it is probably incompatible with any mode of social practice – though this may not be so of more moderate forms of pluralistic, socially grounded relativism. Second, scepticism about the interpretation of meanings is broadly antithetical to the 'mode of engagement' which, I suggested, is necessary if cultural practices are to contribute to their audience's potential well-being. For if there is no way of showing that one account of a cultural object's meaning is better justified than another – if 'anything goes' when it comes to interpretation, and hence understanding – the idea of respect for a cultural practice loses its basis.

Finally, the concept of autonomy is also undermined by scepticism, since it reduces people's conception of the good, and hence also their judgements of their own well-being, to the expressions of unjustifiable, arbitrary preferences. It is thus unable to make sense of, for example, the ways in which individuals see themselves as learning through their experience of different conceptions of the good, and hence as replacing their previous beliefs by others which they come to regard as better justified. Thus, far from scepticism providing support for autonomy (as it is sometimes thought to) by protecting individuals from the supposedly 'coercive' possibility that their own beliefs might be mistaken, whilst those of others are correct, it instead renders unintelligible what is presupposed by autonomous judgement.

But although in these ways scepticism undermines the kind of justification for non-market cultural practices I have presented, it does not follow that scepticism provides positive support for the use of the market in these or other areas. Meta-ethical subjectivism, for example, as a purely epistemological thesis, is arguably consistent with any substantive ethical or political position, including many that would be highly antithetical to 'market' values.

However, if one moves from this strictly philosophical level of analysis to consider how sceptical beliefs may actually operate in specific cultural contexts, the situation is more complex. For nowadays, I suspect, the adoption of such scepticism is typically associated with – even, though mistakenly, thought to support – a kind of 'tolerant', loosely 'democratic' standpoint, according to which 'no one has the right to impose their views on anyone else' (since none can be justified anyway), and 'everyone's values should be given equal status'.

And from this standpoint, the market is bound to seem an attractive means of making social decisions about what kinds of goods and services are to be produced, even if it is not necessarily the only means – provided, of course, that it works as its neo-classical proponents say it does, and one ignores inequalities of wealth and power. For if there are no 'objective' ways of judging the value of such products, what 'fairer' solution is there than to allow them to be judged by their consumers' preferences (that is by their *value*-judgements)? All that such consumers need to know is their own desires; and their first-person authority with respect to these – their authority as consumers – is the only kind that is likely to survive the sceptical attacks which undermine the forms of authority that would be necessary for at least some, and possibly any, alternative, non-market means of economic organization.

This line of thought is far from conclusive, but neither is it altogether implausible. More importantly, perhaps, it has a powerful contemporary appeal. Here I return to some of my remarks at the outset of this paper. Those who celebrate the advent of post-modern society tend to value such phenomena as the 'transgression' of previously accepted, and authoritatively 'enforced' boundaries; the displacement of serious, fixed and authorial meanings by the playful fluidity of readers' meanings; and so on. This does not, in logic, commit them to a celebration of the market. Yet arguably in reality this is indeed their greatest ally – the most powerful transgressor of boundaries, the most active dissolver of meanings, the most radical challenger of social authority.[15]

It is for such reasons that conservatives have always viewed the effects of the unbridled market with such concern. But whilst socialists have been happy to accept the destructive effects of the market on certain (typically pre-modern, hierarchical) forms of authority, their egalitarian conception of human well-being also requires, if not the elimination of the market, then at least the construction of clear boundaries around it, and the flourishing of social practices which can only be sustained by non-individualistic (yet autonomy-enhancing) patterns of authority.[16]

NOTES

1 'Knowledge-claims' here include claims to justified beliefs, whether actually true or not. Correspondingly, I take scepticism to deny the possibility of justified beliefs, not merely of true and/or conclusively justified ones.

2 My use of the term 'practices' involves an implicit reference to Alasdair MacIntyre's specific conceptualization of these, though much of the time it can be understood in a more theoretically neutral sense: see MacIntyre (1981),

especially ch. 14, and my discussion of this in Keat (1991), which forms the background for much of the present paper.

3 One reason for distinguishing these two is that, at least on the face of it, the latter does not entail the former.

4 It is Thomas Kuhn's emphasis on such features of scientific practice that partly gives rise to his criticisms of Karl Popper's 'Enlightenment' view of science: for a brief account of the two, see Chalmers (1982). But like other conservative thinkers, Kuhn also denies that scientific judgements are, even in principle, wholly reconstructible in terms of impersonal criteria of rationality: see Kuhn (1977), and also Ravetz (1971) for a brilliant account of the delicate social mechanisms required for the 'quality control' of scientific work, conceived as a craft practice.

5 One might speculate that (the perception of) recurrent abuses of authority generates cynicism, and that cynicism makes people more susceptible to what might otherwise appear to be rather bizarre forms of philosophical scepticism.

6 Hence the hostility of more orthodox philosophers of science to Paul Feyerabend's Humean and/or post-modernist scepticism, and to his view of scientific rationality as oppressive, which lead him to propose the 'disestablishment' of science – if 'anything goes' there can be no justification for scientific authority: see Feyerabend (1988).

7 Here I ignore more technical issues about Pareto-optimality etc.: on these see Buchanan (1985), and also for a distinction between 'ethical' and 'efficiency' justifications for the market.

8 Such fears may of course prove unfounded, if students' preferences are themselves shaped by respect for existing academic authority (see Fulton in this volume). Here as throughout I am concerned mainly with the *possible* implications of consumer sovereignty, whose actual effects will depend *inter alia* on the culturally specific ways in which consumers conceive of their relations with producers, discussed elsewhere in this volume.

9 This is not to say that commercial producers never 'think' in such ways about their consumers, only that the theory (and ideology) of the free market renders such thoughts unacceptable – and market mechanisms are intended to render them ineffectual.

10 What forms such support or protection might take is an issue I shall not consider here.

11 The following account draws on the work of several social philosophers who have recently tried, in effect, to develop a version of Aristotelian ethics consistent with certain features of modern liberalism – for example Kymlicka (1989), O'Neill (1993) and Raz (1986), especially ch. 12 – together with that of MacIntyre (1981). All reject a purely 'want-regarding' conception of well-being: see Barry (1965).

12 This may or may not include a concern with the well-being of others: my account is neutral on this question, though I believe such concerns form part of most people's conceptions of the good.

13 My remarks about practitioner–audience relationships are deliberately, though unfortunately, highly abstract: for useful antidotes, see Ang (1991) and Mulgan (ed.) (1990).

14 See Whiteley in this volume. This argument for 'the right mode of engagement' needs to be complemented by an account of how cultural practitioners should conduct themselves if they are to merit such respect; and my argument here should not be taken to imply that actual cultural practitioners typically do so.

15 Alternatively, of course, it may be argued that the market only has such effects

when it is itself allied with independently generated processes of cultural change.
16 Thus here as elsewhere socialism and conservatism have much in common: see Keat (1981). On the problem of market boundaries, see Walzer (1983: ch. 4), Anderson (1990) and Keat (1993).

REFERENCES

Anderson, E. (1990) 'The ethical limitations of the market', *Economics and Philosophy*, 6: pp. 179–205.
Ang, I. (1991) *Desperately Seeking the Audience*, London: Routledge.
Barry, B. (1965) *Political Argument*, London: Routledge & Kegan Paul.
Bauman, Z. (1987) *Legislators and Interpreters*, Cambridge: Polity Press.
Buchanan, A. (1985) *Ethics, Efficiency and the Market*, Oxford: Clarendon Press.
Chalmers, A. (1982) *What is this Thing called Science?* 2nd edn, London: Open University Press.
Feyerabend, P. (1988) *Against Method*, 2nd edn, London: Verso.
Jameson, F. (1984) 'Postmodernism: or the cultural logic of late capitalism', *New Left Review*, 146.
Keat, R. (1981) 'Individualism and community in socialist thought', in J. Mepham and D.-H. Ruben (eds) *Issues in Marxist Philosophy*, IV, Hassocks: Harvester Press.
—— (1991) 'Consumer sovereignty and the integrity of practices', in Keat and Abercrombie (eds) (1991), 216–30.
—— (1993) 'The moral limits of the market', in C. Crouch and D. Marquand (eds) *Varieties of Capitalism*, special issue of *The Political Quarterly*.
Keat, R. and Abercrombie, N. (eds) (1991) *Enterprise Culture*, London: Routledge.
Kuhn, T. S. (1977) 'Objectivity, value-judgment and theory choice', in *The Essential Tension*, Chicago: University of Chicago Press.
Kymlicka, W. (1989) *Liberalism, Community and Culture*, Oxford: Oxford University Press.
MacIntyre, A. (1981) *After Virtue*, London: Duckworth.
Mulgan, G. (ed.) (1990) *The Question of Quality*, London: British Film Institute.
Norton, B. (1987) *Why Preserve Natural Variety?*. Princeton: Princeton University Press.
O'Neill, J. (1992) 'Altruism, egoism and the market', *The Philosophical Forum*, XXIII: 278–88.
—— (1993) *Ecology, Policy and Politics: Human Well-Being and the Natural World*, London: Routledge.
Plant, R. (1989) 'Socialism, markets and end states', in J. Le Grand and S. Estrin (eds) *Market Socialism*, Oxford: Oxford University Press.
Ravetz, J. (1971) *Scientific Knowledge and its Social Problems*, Oxford: Oxford University Press.
Raz, J. (1986) *The Morality of Freedom*, Oxford: Oxford University Press.
Roy, S. (1989) *Philosophy of Economics*, London: Routledge.
Sagoff, M. (1988) *The Economy of the Earth*, Cambridge: Cambridge University Press.
Selden, R. (1991) 'The rhetoric of enterprise', in Keat and Abercrombie (eds) (1991), 58–71.
Sheffrin, S. (1978) 'Habermas, Depoliticization and Consumer Theory', *Journal of Economic Issues*, 7: 785–97.

Walzer, M. (1983) *Spheres of Justice*, London: Martin Robertson.
Winch, P. (1967) 'Authority', in A. Quinton (ed) *Political Philosophy*, Oxford: Oxford University Press.

Chapter 2

Authority and consumer society

Nicholas Abercrombie

INTRODUCTION

> In our days men see that the constituted powers are crumbling down
> on every side; they see all ancient authority dying out, all ancient
> barriers tottering to their fall, and the judgment of the wisest is
> troubled at the sight; they attend only to the amazing revolution that
> is taking place before their eyes, and they imagine that mankind is
> about to fall into perpetual anarchy. If they looked to the final conse-
> quence of this revolution, their fears would perhaps assume a different
> shape. For myself, I confess that I put no trust in the spirit of freedom
> which appears to animate contemporaries. I see well enough that the
> nations of this age are turbulent, but I do not clearly perceive that
> they are liberal and I fear lest, at the close of those perturbations,
> which rock the base of thrones, the dominion of sovereigns may prove
> more powerful than it ever was.
>
> A. De Tocqueville, *Democracy in America*, 11: 314, quoted in Nisbet
> (1967)

People often complain of the collapse of authority and have done so in
western societies for some considerable time. The quotation from De
Tocqueville above might stand for many nineteenth-century discussions
of the topic; traditional patterns of authority are being eroded by the
new spirit of democracy and the spread of individualism. Desirable or
otherwise, these changes leave a vacuum into which other forms of
authority, despotic, arbitrary and even more unaccountable, may step.
Similar concerns are raised in the twentieth century, even if the language,
and many of the themes, are different; influential figures bemoan the loss
of respect for authority, a decline in traditional institutions like the family,
a consequent growth in crime, and a generalized sense of unease and
disorder.

The continuity of complaints about the erosion of proper authority
over a long period raises a number of questions. It may well be that the
complainants have only a partial view of the matter and their worries are

a kind of special pleading. Thus they may be exercised about the decline of authority only because it is the authority of a particular social group or class, of which they are members or spokesmen, that is in decline. They see in their own decline that of society as a whole. In contemporary society this may be particularly the case for older members. The middle-aged or elderly, who are beginning to lose their power and status, are particularly prone to see the young, who are beginning to gain theirs, as failing to respect authority, and simultaneously as constituting sources of disorder. Even if these diagnoses of the erosion of authority are correct, there are questions about the kind of explanation that is appropriate. Thus, these could be commentaries on a long-term change in patterns of authority – secular changes. Or, the complainants could simply be witnessing short-term adjustments in the kinds of social groups that hold authority without serious alteration to the structures of authority – cyclical changes. Perhaps more seriously, generalized claims about the collapse of authority – 'constituted powers ... crumbling down on every side' – tend to obscure the way that everyday life is constituted by very *many* spheres of authority, perhaps overlapping, some of which may indeed be in decline, while others are hale and hearty.

This chapter attempts to contribute to this debate by discussing a particular social relationship – that between producers and consumers – in terms of the distribution of authority between the two parties. This relationship too is often said to be undergoing profound change, particularly in the period since the second world war and most especially since about 1980. Producers of commodities have, it is said, a greatly different view of their own activities. Instead of producing what they think ought to be produced, or what is most technologically advanced, they produce what the consumer wants or is assumed to want. Even more important, this prioritization of assumed consumer preferences is extended beyond the production of commodities to the provision of professional and public services. The wishes, needs and aspirations of the consumer of legal, banking and accountancy services become crucial matters; students, patients and travellers become consumers buying services as they might buy goods in a high street shop. There has, in other words, been a progressive tendency to widen the scope of the idea of the consumer. In more and more aspects of their lives people are expected to behave as consumers and it is similarly expected that they will be treated as consumers. The construction of people as consumers is further often associated with other processes. Not only are the denizens of modern society consumers, they are also consumer*ist*. Their lives are organized around fantasies and daydreams about consuming; they are hedonists, primarily interested in pleasure, and sensual pleasure at that; they are individualists, largely pursuing their own ends and uncaring about others.

Even if this constitutes an exaggerated way of characterizing the importance of consumption in everyday life, consumerism, hedonism and individualism are potentially undermining of traditional ways of behaving. They involve a stress on pleasure rather than the duties of work, on the rights of the individual to decide on courses of action, and on the centrality of consumer desires to the conduct of life. Above all – or perhaps beneath all – the spread of market relations is corrosive of traditional authority. When everything can be bought and sold, all human relations reduced to those of producer and consumer of commodities, then other forms of sovereignty become difficult to maintain. As Marx and Engels pointed out in the *Communist Manifesto*, the market 'has stripped of its halo every occupation hitherto honoured and looked up to with reverent awe' and has swept away 'all fixed, fast-frozen relations, with their train of ancient and venerable prejudices and opinions'.

DOMINATION, POWER, AUTHORITY

In looking in more detail at the changed authority relations between producers and consumers, I begin with a set of classical distinctions – classical that is to the sociological canon – between domination, power and authority. In a general sense, both power and authority are forms of domination; they are both ways in which the will of one person, or group of persons, is exercised over others. Weber proposes more specific definitions. He suggests that domination is the 'likelihood that a command within a given organization or society will be obeyed'. Power is 'the probability that one actor within a relationship will be in a position to carry out his own will despite resistance'. Authority is a sub-type of power in which people willingly obey commands because they see the exercise of power as legitimate.

For Weber then, authority is legitimate power. But what does legitimacy mean here? Weber seems to think that legitimacy is a function of belief. If subordinates – and those claiming authority – *believe* that exercises of power are legitimate, then they are. An assessment of the legitimacy of an authority is therefore a question of reporting the beliefs of those involved. As Beetham (1991) points out, however, subordinates may have all sorts of bad reasons for holding the beliefs that they do; they may be mistaken about the actions of the authority or, worse, their beliefs may be manipulated in various ways. Beetham further argues that, even if subordinates could give good grounds for their belief that an authority was legitimate, it would still not follow that that regime was legitimate; the whole enterprise of defining legitimacy in terms of belief is largely mistaken for two main reasons.

First, it misrepresents the relationship between legitimacy and belief. An authority relationship is not legitimate because people believe it is so, but because it can be justified in terms of those beliefs. A particular regime will lose legitimacy, for example, not because people have stopped believing in it, but because the actions of that regime do not conform with the values and standards of proper political behaviour current in that society. Second, it does not take account of aspects of legitimacy that are nothing to do with belief – actions, for instance. For example, consent to the authority of a regime is often given by actions such as voting. Voting does not imply a belief in legitimacy necessarily; it can proceed from all sorts of motives. What it does do, however, is to confer legitimacy on a regime.

In the sociological literature on power, authority and legitimacy, the examples chosen are usually drawn from the analysis of the political relations of governments or states or, at the other end of the scale, from more personal relationships between pairs – a subordinate and a superordinate. Many of the relationships of authority which are of greatest interest are, however, in between the macro- and micro-scales. These are interesting because the means by which legitimacy is maintained do not depend so much on legality (as in the case of political regimes) or on coercion (as in the case of more personal relationships) but, typically, on more subtle forces. Expertise, for example, can be a basis for the maintenance of legitimacy of an authority relationship. Expertise does not confer legitimacy simply because people believe that an authority – a doctor for instance – has expertise. It is also required that the expertise is manifested in certain actions and that it is consonant with general principles and skills (those of scientific method, for instance) current in society.

Indeed, most human relationships that are structured, generalized and institutionalized involve relations of authority. They are structured in that they become repeated and patterned over time; generalized in that a particular relationship of one type can become generalized to all relationships of that type – for example, the particular relationship of a pupil to a teacher is generalized to all teacher–pupil relationships; institutionalized in that they become normatively organized. I will call these *authority contexts*. Examples of authority contexts include the relations between parents and children, between teachers and pupils, and between men and women as well as that between state and citizen. Clearly the relationship *between* authority contexts is a major issue and it would be an unusual authority context that did not overlap with others so that positions, roles or persons dominant in one context are dominant in another.

There are a variety of mechanisms that maintain a particular distribution of authority. Again, much sociological attention concentrates on the large-scale authority contexts such as nation-states. Contexts such as these will be maintained by force or legality, mechanisms less likely to apply to smaller-scale contexts. There are a number of smaller-scale mechanisms but four are of particular importance.

1 **Expertise**. Certain authority contexts are maintained by the greater knowledge and/or skill of the superordinate. So, it may be widely recognized in a society that certain positions require expertise acquired through a period of training. Claims to expertise only have legitimacy to the extent that incumbents of positions of authority actually do deploy their expertise successfully in the ways recognized by both superordinates and subordinates. Clearly, this recognition breaks down from time to time, undermining the basis for authority. In contemporary society this seems to happen to many professional relationships, especially teachers.

Carter + Reagan vs. Clinton on tob.

2 **Deference**. The persistence of particular qualities of authority relations has often been explained by appeal to feelings of deference on the part of subordinates and of superiority on the part of superordinates. For example, the industrial behaviour, attitudes and voting patterns of a North Lancashire town is explained, partly at least, by the deference of the workers towards the family that owned the bulk of the industry and had a substantial stake in local politics. 'The family adopted a patriarchal role within the community, a role endorsed by many but not all other members of the community; a quasi-feudal dependence relationship evolved, compounded of domination, generosity, and deference' (Martin and Fryer 1973: 32). The result was that authority contexts, particularly in work and politics, were maintained in a manner unusual for the region. Voting patterns, for instance, were much more conservative than was characteristic of similar nearby towns of comparable demographic, industrial and class structure.

3 **Taboo**. In some authority contexts, the feeling, on the part of both sub- and superordinate, that the boundary between them is semi-sacred and cannot be crossed, violated or not recognized, without serious consequences, is important to the maintenance of the boundary. These are feelings often associated with the symbols of disease, dirt, danger or otherness – and with deference (Douglas 1966). Taboos of this kind may be particularly obvious in contexts that involve public ceremony – those of royalty, the aristocracy or offices of state. However, I would argue that most relations of authority invoke, and are protected by, feelings of this kind.

4 **Meaning**. In many authority contexts, superiors succeed in imposing their definitions of the (joint) situation on subordinates. They define the meaning that all people in an authority context give to that context. At its most fundamental and extreme, this involves superordinates being able to define what kind of human beings subordinates are. As Foucault (1977) pointed out, the disciplinary power of modern societies stems largely from the ability to define *identity*. This can only happen if the conditions, particularly the means by which meaning is transmit-

ted, are appropriate and, generally, that is most likely to happen in smaller-scale authority contexts (Abercrombie, Hill and Turner, 1980).

In actual practice, all four of these mechanisms will contribute in varying degrees – and in association with legality and force – to the maintenance of authority contexts. In the teacher-pupil relationship, for example, the context is sustained by the accepted expertise of the teacher, occasional deference, taboos, as are present when, for instance, the pupil ventures to the staff room door, and the definition of meaning provided by the teacher that is almost the essential characteristic of the role. In addition, the position of the teacher is supported by certain legal requirements and, though decreasingly, by the threat, or actual administration, of force.

Defining authority in terms of legitimacy, even if not a belief in the legitimacy of an authority, can be taken to imply, unfortunately, an active, permanent and unvarying consent to all exercises of authority in an authority context. This is misleading, for authority is almost always contested in some way; authority may be legitimate in the senses discussed by Beetham but this does not mean that it is not resented. Many sociological accounts make it difficult to get at the idea of resistance to *authority* because they are more usually concerned with resistance to *power*. There is no reason not to extend the idea of resistance to authority since its exercise will always involve a restriction of the material interests or the freedom of subordinates.

There are a number of different modes of resistance which do not necessarily vary in intensity with varying degrees of legitimacy. At one extreme, the least serious, are strategies such as gossip. By such means resentment is expressed *and* shared. At certain times, and in certain authority contexts, gossip of this kind can be quite disruptive. Another characteristic mode of resistance which deserves greater attention is that of play. In many types of authority context, subordinates adopt behaviour which is non-serious, makes fun of authority, or they refuse to take the regimes of everyday life seriously. The archetypical case of play-as-resistance is the relationship between parents and children. However, all work situations are characterized by 'fooling about' and it is perhaps revealing that such behaviour is often described by a disapproving authority as childish. Authority emphasizes order and seriousness; subordinates emphasize play. At the other extreme of resistance strategies are those that seem to involve a breakdown in legitimacy, or at least the beginnings of it. Various forms of non-compliance in industrial organizations illustrate this form, including absenteeism and the deliberate sabotage more common than is often thought.

Resistance may take a different form for each of the four supports of authority mentioned above. Expertise, for example, may be challenged by the development of alternative bodies of knowledge. So the authority-through-expertise of the doctor might be contested actively by the development of alternative medical practices or, more passively, by the use of commonsense or traditional practices and remedies. Similarly, the attribution of meaning and identity can be less seriously disputed by the playful transformation of the original use of commodities (Hebdige 1979) by youth subcultures or, more seriously, as when schoolchildren deliberately take up deviant roles within the school culture (Willis 1977).

Perhaps as an outcome of resistance, authority can move from one party to the other as these props of authority are undermined. Authority is not either/or; people can have more or less of it. Therefore, claiming that there is a shift of authority within an authority-context does not mean a reversal – subordinates becoming superordinates. It simply means that superordinates' judgements are *less* authoritative, are more insecure and more likely to be contested. Authority is shared out more equally. This suggests that an hydraulic image is most appropriate for changes in the balance of authority in a context. As the mechanisms that support an authority context weaken or strengthen, so authority *flows* from one pole to the other – and back again.

So far, I have treated authority contexts as independent of one another. It is however clear that they are – or can be – connected. In some societies, contexts are best seen as overlapping circles in which a social group dominant in one context is also dominant in another or, at least, has close connections with another group that is. The obvious case here is domination by a particular social class, whose authority can be hegemonic because it succeeds in connecting up different authority contexts. In traditional societies, authority may be all-pervasive in this way. As Nisbet (1967: 107–8) argues, in these societies authority may not even have a separate identity: 'Deeply embedded in social functions, an inalienable part of the inner order of family, neighbourhood, parish, and guild, ritualized at every turn, authority is so closely woven into the fabric of tradition and morality as to be scarcely more noticeable than the air men breathe.' Even by the nineteenth century authority no longer had this hegemonic quality and in the twentieth there is even less to hold the authority contexts together.

So, there can be movements *within* authority contexts and the disappearance of links *between* them. These can happen independently, which makes an overarching sociological account very difficult. It is furthermore important to note that changes in these patterns of authority can be cyclical and not necessarily secular, a point to which I will return.

CONSUMERS, PRODUCERS AND AUTHORITY

The relationship between producers and consumers is potentially an authority context. At first sight it seems rather odd to say this, since we think of producers and consumers as equal parties to a contract which serves both of their interests.

As a rough and ready definition, producers are those who are responsible for creating a good or service which is offered, transferred, given or sold, in a relationship of exchange, to someone else, a consumer, who directly selects, appropriates and uses the good or service. Clearly there are many different kinds of producer–consumer relationship. The modal type might be the purchase of goods in a shop, but there are many others, from the purchase of services like transport or telecommunications to others reviewed in this book, like teaching, policing, watching a film or looking at pictures in a gallery.

The relationship is one of authority; that is, it involves *legitimacy*. The mechanisms that support authority vary from one kind of producer–consumer relationship to another although several may be present in varying degrees in different relationships. In some, doctor–patient, or artist–audience, for example, expertise or skill is of the greatest importance, while in others, police–criminal perhaps, legality is more relevant. Even in the least likely territory, the purchase of a commercially produced good or service, issues of expertise and deference or loyalty are potentially present, though to a lesser extent than in contexts of public service. However, in all of them, I would argue, control of *meaning* is particularly significant in contemporary societies; that is the authority of the producer is sustained by the capacity to define the meaning of the transactions involved and is lost as consumers acquire that power.

To develop this point I turn to an argument (Campbell 1987) concerning the special nature of modern consumption. Campbell argues that consumption in traditional societies is organized around the satisfaction of the senses. Modern consumption, on the other hand, is built around fantasizing and daydreaming. Modern people speculate, fantasize, think about, dream about what they are about to consume. They form images of what they want to be, what they want to experience, which will be brought about by a purchase or an act of consumption. It is almost as if we do not consume things or services, but only the images of things that occur in fantasy – and this will apply, not only to the purchase of a video-recorder, but also, if to a lesser extent, to a visit to the doctor. At this point, Campbell's argument is very similar to the more general doctrine that the essential quality of modern, or post-modern, society is its domination by images. Baudrillard (1983), for example, argues, following Marx, that the development of capitalist society has seen a gradual change away from use-value to exchange-value, that is a transition from producing goods and services for one's own use to producing solely for sale on the market. He goes further, though, to suggest that in late capitalism, commodities take on sign-value, such that their utility to consumers consists in the meanings, signs or images that they convey. Eventually a simulational culture develops in which images and reality become confused (but, for a contrary view, see the papers by Winward and Warde in this volume).

Baudrillard's may be an extreme view, but if images are at the centre of modern consumption and of the producer–consumer relationship, then the control of their *meaning* is similarly central to the distribution of authority in that relationship. What counts is how meaning is decided. As Keat argues (this volume), the authority of the producer lies in the capacity to define the meaning of that which is consumed. Producers have more authority to the extent that the meaning or value of an object or service is defined by how the producer understands, interprets, judges it in terms of what it does for him/her, or of its particular significance for him/her, or of how it relates to his/her particular projects, aims, needs; or the meaning of the object or service is given by virtue of its position in relation to a certain tradition.

Contemporary consumption, in sum, is largely about meaning, and producers face a substantial task in trying to control the ascription of meaning. As with any authority context, there are struggles between subordinates and superordinates. Struggles between producer and consumer are not, therefore, only about what is produced and at what price, but also about meaning and the commodification of meaning. Producers try to commodify meaning, that is try to make images and symbols into things which can be sold and bought. Consumers, on the other hand, try to give their own, new, meanings to the commodities and services that they buy. The best examples of this process come from cultural commodities, especially those of popular culture. Much innovation in popular music, for instance, comes from the way that consumers interpret and change the music that they are commercially offered. After a while, the music industry sells these innovations back to the consumer.

Related to this question of struggle over meaning is the issue of order and play raised earlier. Modern consumption is not only about images, it is also about play, especially play with meaning. Consumption is not primarily concerned with satisfying primary needs but is more to do with unserious playful pleasure. Producers, on the other hand, in making meanings into commercial objects by rationalized production processes, necessarily emphasize order and seriousness. In the struggle over meaning between producers and consumers, therefore, play is a strategy in the hands of consumers. Some sociologists have argued that this process goes as far as playing with *identities* (Featherstone 1991). Contemporary consumers, especially young people, will experiment with different identities, by ignoring the way in which class, gender and race construct the boundaries of identity. As I argued above, a resistance to a particular ascription of identity is one of the most fundamental ways of contesting authority.

FROM PRODUCERS TO CONSUMERS

In contemporary societies, especially since the second world war, there has been a loss of authority from producers to consumers. Many of the papers in this volume illustrate this trend in very different ways. A. Lury, for example, documents the way that advertising has for some time been consumer- rather than producer-driven; the advertiser asks the consumer what he/she thinks of the product or service and then constructs the communication around these feelings. However, the consumer–producer relationship is changing and advertising needs to reflect the change. Future advertising will reflect the assumption that the consumer is an equal and is, furthermore, a knowing equal, media literate and experienced. Heward describes a change within the police force towards treating those who come into contact with the service as consumers. This is, admittedly, a contradictory phenomenon, as the police have to reconcile the need to regulate the public with the wish to be responsive to them as consumers. None the less, when a very senior police officer suggests that not only the victims of crime, but also the perpetrators – 'the abusing husband, the foul drunk' – should be seen as 'customers', there is a real, if partial, shift of authority to the consumer. Winward points to the conflict between producer and consumer and argues that, in two respects, the consumer is gaining in authority within the relationship. First, the consumer is not passive and, in particular, is not passive in being forced to attach particular meanings to items of consumption; 'consumers are fully aware that they are the targets of advertising, and are prepared to resist it' (p. 88). Second, within this process of resistance, consumer organizations are beginning to play an important role. These organizations may not be equivalent to political parties which contest particular distributions of authority, but they are none the less significant in representing and informing consumer interests. As I have already argued, the struggle between consumer and producer is, to a very large extent, a struggle over meaning. Two linked processes are responsible for the greater control over meaning by consumers. It is often argued that modern life is 'culturally drenched' (see, for example, Featherstone 1991). Everyday life is 'aestheticized', invested with symbolic value, and infected with considerations of style. A growing aestheticization of everyday life gives to the consumer a greater power to decide on the particular meaning to be bestowed. At the same time, a parallel process, the de-aestheticization of art, takes authority over meaning away from the producer (see Whiteley, this volume). The objects of art are no longer given a semi-sacred quality and they are no longer seen as deriving from the unique talent of the artist. Instead, the objects of everyday life acquire artistic status and are displayed in museums as art objects. The aestheticization of everyday life and the de-aestheticization of art conspire to transfer authority in this area from producer to consumer.

My argument is then that there is a gradual loss of producer authority, a loss of legitimacy. Expertise carries less weight, taboos function less well, deference is less marked, even the legal powers effectively deployed by teachers (via certification), or doctors, or social workers, are undermined.

THE BOUNDARY BETWEEN PRODUCERS AND CONSUMERS

If I am right that there is a shift of authority from producers to consumers, and this shift is best conceived as a flow of authority, then an examination of the marginal changes at the boundary between producers and consumers should be illustrative of many of the processes that I am discussing. To show how this works, I turn to an analysis of hot-rodding – the racing of specially prepared cars over short distances – undertaken by Moorhouse (1991).

Moorhouse is interested in the economic and social structure and functioning of hot-rodding as an *enthusiasm*, a hobby or activity which mobilizes peoples' intense interest, or, literally, enthusiasm. He suggests that the hot-rodding enthusiasm has the following layers. First, there is the core of professionals who make their living from the enthusiasm, those who build and drive the cars. Associated with this core in the economy of hot-rodding are the 'experts' of all kinds – the promoters, officials, suppliers of parts. Also making their living from hot-rodding are the communicators, the writers and commentators, who own or work for the various hot-rod magazines, a vital part of this enthusiasm, as for so many others. The next layer consists of amateur enthusiasts, for whom hot-rodding is a central life-interest but who earn their living outside the enthusiasm. They can be in conflict with those in the inner layers involved in the economy of hot-rodding in that they may, from time to time, emphasize the non-commercial values of the enthusiasm. Related to the amateur enthusiasts is a layer of the interested public, 'a heterogeneous group consisting of dabblers in the focal concerns, mere consumers of symbols, novices and new entrants, state bodies concerned with control, big businessmen seeking opportunities, the mass media looking for stories . . .' (Moorhouse 1991: 22). The interested public will have a more detailed knowledge of hot-rodding than the next layer, the general public, the members of which will have only a passing interest and relatively little knowledge. It is important to make the obvious point that the membership of these categories is not static and people will readily move from one to the other.

Like many enthusiasms, hot-rodding started as a purely amateur sport and gradually acquired its own economy and entrepreneurs. Moorhouse points out, however, that it is dangerous to see this as a simple process of commodification – the taking over of innocent pastimes by commercial interests. Of course, there is a commercial centre to the enthusiasm that consists of small-scale enterprises, like specialized parts dealers, and large organizations, like the magazine empires and the major car manufacturers. However, there is a perpetual tension between this commodification and the virtues of amateurism which are loudly proclaimed by the non-professional. Even more important, the intellectuals of the movement, those writing for the much-read magazines, insist on the values of community, hard work and skill, as opposed to those of the market. 'To this end, they warned their readers of the hollowness of the interest shown by big business, of the perils attendant on all-out economic exploitation and the danger of the constant encroachment of dull bureaucracies' (p. 226). Lastly, the professionals of hot-rodding are critically dependent on the enthusiastic amateurs. This is not because of the market that the amateurs provide, but because of the innovations that come from the non-professionals; consumers, in other words, cross the boundary to become producers.

This brings me to the central issue to be derived from this case-study. In situations where authority lies with producers, they also have a monopoly, or near monopoly, of expertise, skill and knowledge. Consumers are relatively passive. As the *Daily Telegraph* (16 September 1989) reporting an investigation by the Henley Centre for Forecasting, said, 'passive consumers still believe they are at the mercy of manufacturers, and according to Mr. Michael Willmott, assistant director of Henley, "tend to accept anything that they are told by manufacturers" '. On the other hand, as consumers acquire skill and knowledge, so also do they acquire authority; they become *active* consumers able to assert their authority against producers. It is clear from Moorhouse's study that the non-professional hot-rodding enthusiasts do have very considerable levels of skill and knowledge. The emphasis throughout the enthusiasm is on the values of planning, hard work, risk, competition, learning by doing, scientific knowledge, understanding the engine, backyard experimentation and design skills. The importance of technical knowledge and skills is mirrored in the very high technical level of the articles in the hot-rod magazines. Moorhouse further argues that the preservation of skills amongst the enthusiasts is actually necessary to the commodification of the enthusiasm. If it all becomes too easy, there is the risk of

> incurring the wrath of the core devotees or losing its promise to all layers of enthusiasts that at least somewhere in modern life they can find an interesting world separate and distinct from the general grey, that they will be expert about something 'real' and 'useful' and will be associated with some activity through which they are likely to be able

to gain status in whichever of their 'communities' their skill is relevant. Some complex core task and some body of knowledge has to remain for the devotees to practise and learn or the whole enthusiasm will lose its weight.

(p. 226)

In sum, hot-rodders have a great deal of technical skill and knowledge relevant to their enthusiasm. Because of this reservoir of expertise, there is movement across the boundary between producer and consumer and there is relatively less authority attaching to producers. These are characteristics not restricted to hot-rodding; they are also present in other enthusiasms, in other producer–consumer relationships. Laing (1985) and Willis (1990), for example, point out how much expertise about music there is amongst young people and how often this is used in performance of various kinds and contributes to innovation in the rock music industry. McRobbie (1989) advances similar arguments about fashion. It could be argued that these are all leisure industries in which the barriers to entry are relatively low, which may encourage consumers to develop the expertise they need to become producers. Such a view would, however, underestimate the degree of expertise wielded by consumers in general. Studies of television watchers, for example (Morley 1986; Taylor and Mullan 1986; Buckingham 1987), show how aware audiences are of how television programmes are produced. These are not trivial skills or exercises in mere cynicism either. Audiences can deploy a sophisticated knowledge of acting and actors, the deficiencies of scripts, camerawork, and can relate what is shown to their everyday lives. At a more general level, ethnomethodologists often point out how skilful everyday life is, a fact obscured by the taken-for-granted nature of the skills (Garfinkel 1968).

Any explanation of changing distributions of authority will necessarily be complex (see Abercrombie 1991) and there is not the space to discuss the possibilities here. However, there is one preliminary issue that it is useful to mention by way of conclusion to this essay.

In many discussions of social change, both technical and everyday, it is common to find the assumption that the changes are secular, that is, very long-term and almost inevitable. Thus, for example, diagnoses of the ills of contemporary society offered in the media and discussed in everyday life, often compare the present with some golden age in the past when all was well. The assumption is that some fundamental change has taken place – for the worse – that is continuous and irreversible. More technically, the Marxist idea of commodification makes similar assumptions. This is the proposition that the capitalist mode of production, driven by the forces of competition, is an ever-expanding, ever-innovating, overwhelming system of social relations. In its expansion, it is forced to look for new ways of realizing value. As a result, more and more things, services, even human relationships are commodified, that is, are given a monetary value so that they can be bought and sold in a market. This process is seen as secular and as reversible only by revolution, an entire restructuring of society.

A process of commodification might be one way of explaining a shift of authority from producer to consumer. In order to maximize sales, producers will become more orientated to the needs and wishes of consumers and less organized around their own concerns. An alternative explanation, however, might be that the change in the distribution of authority is cyclical not secular, and reflects a struggle between producers organized as conflicting social classes or class fractions. A rising producer group will attempt to diminish the authority of a dominant producer group. A short-run effect of this struggle will be an apparent transfer of authority to consumers. However, when one producer group emerges, or re-emerges, as dominant, authority will return to producers. In a struggle between producers, commodification makes a useful weapon, for commodification, the intrusion of market relations, is corrosive of all traditional or existing authority relations. One may therefore expect rising groups of producers to advocate, and try to introduce, market relations in an effort to disrupt the authority of existing dominant producers, an effort which will have the temporary effect of empowering consumers.

REFERENCES

Abercrombie, N. (1991) 'The privilege of the producer', in R. Keat and N. Abercrombie (eds), *Enterprise Culture*, London: Routledge.
Abercrombie, N., Hill, S. and Turner, B. S. (1980) *The Dominant Ideology Thesis*, London: Allen & Unwin.
Baudrillard, J. (1983) *Simulations*, New York: Semiotext(e).
Beetham, D. (1991) *The Legitimation of Power*, London: Macmillan.
Buckingham, D. (1987) *Public Secrets: Eastenders and its Audience*, London: BFI Publishing.
Campbell, C. (1987) *The Romantic Ethic and the Spirit of Modern Consumerism*, Oxford: Blackwell.
Douglas, M. (1966) *Purity and Danger*, Harmondsworth: Penguin Books.
Featherstone, M. (1991) *Consumer Culture and Postmodernism*, London: Sage.
Foucault, M. (1977) *Discipline and Punish*, London: Allen Lane.
Garfinkel, H. (1968) *Studies in Ethnomethodology*, Englewood-Cliffs: Prentice-Hall.
Hebdige, D. (1979) *Subculture: the Meaning of Style*, London: Methuen.
Laing, D. (1985) *One Chord Wonders*, Milton Keynes: Open University Press.
McRobbie, A. (1989) *Zoot Suits and Second Hand Dresses*, London: Macmillan.
Martin, R. and Fryer, R. H. (1973) *Redundancy and Paternalist Capitalism*, London: Allen & Unwin.
Moorhouse, H. (1991) *Driving Ambitions: An Analysis of the American Hot Rod Enthusiasm*, Manchester: Manchester University Press.
Morley, D. (1986) *Family Television*, London: Comedia.
Nisbet, R. (1967) *The Sociological Tradition*, London: Heinemann.

Taylor, L. and Mullan, B. (1986) *Uninvited Guests*, London: Chatto & Windus.
Willis, P. (1977) *Learning to Labour*, Farnborough: Saxon House.
—— (1990) *Common Culture*, Milton Keynes: Open University Press.

Chapter 3

Consumers, identity and belonging

Reflections on some theses of Zygmunt Bauman

Alan Warde

INTRODUCTION

One feature of accounts of social change in the last decade has been the centrality of processes of consumption. One of the most radical and ambitious interpretations is offered by Zygmunt Bauman, who has developed a distinctive, insightful and challenging understanding of changes in the role of consumption in advanced societies. He puts it at the very centre of the operation of the social world today, the cement that links the social system, its institutions and the everyday experiences of individuals in the lifeworld. His general thesis is that a new epoch of western society, characterized by the cultural attributes of post-modernity, is now established. This chapter reflects on those aspects of Bauman's analysis directly relevant to understanding the consumer in contemporary society. Bauman implies that there is a new consumer, and that though the consumer does not have complete authority, at least s/he has, through the use of markets, usurped authority from the state and from traditional arbiters of cultural correctness.

Bauman's position is presented in subtly different formulations in several of his recent works.[1] He begins from a distinction between two broad social categories, the seduced and the repressed. The seduced are thoroughly incorporated into consumer culture and their lives are in significant part devoted to the acquisition and display of commodities. The repressed are those who, lacking resources, are excluded from the market and whose lives therefore become intricately entangled with state institutions. The paramount motivation of the individual consumer is a search for self-identity, and consumer choice becomes a major arena of liberty for most of the population of the advanced societies because it is a channel of autonomous self-expression. Concentration on the 'self-assembly' of the individual consumer does not indicate how the purchase of goods and services contributes to group membership, however. Therefore Bauman introduces concepts of neo-tribe and life-style in an attempt to capture the link between identity and belonging. These considerations constitute the basic elements of a theory of consumption.

The development of Bauman's position illustrates some of the dilemmas involved in understanding contemporary consumption. His is an ambivalent, bitter-sweet interpretation of consumer behaviour. He exhibits his customary concern with moral aspects of the contemporary human predicament, characterized by the counter pressures of individual freedom and social membership. Hostile to state control and disaffected with class as a progressive political bond, Bauman struggles to envisage an institutional nexus that might generate both tolerance and moral obligation. His project is admirable, his diagnosis largely pessimistic. However, I believe the analysis is mistaken in certain respects and his pessimism thereby somewhat misplaced. It has three major defects which successive sections of this chapter discuss. First, the distinction between the seduced and the repressed is hard to sustain, being dependent on a stark, overdrawn antinomy between the state and the market. Second, the restless pursuit of self-identity through consumption is a one-sided appreciation of the rationale of consumer behaviour. Third, having constructed the individual consumer in such a fashion, inhibits the development of a plausible account of the role of consumption in securing group membership and a sense of belonging.

THE SEDUCED AND THE REPRESSED

Bauman developed the distinction between the seduced and the repressed towards the end of *Legislators and Interpreters*, his study of the changing role of intellectuals in western culture. There it contributed to the argument that previously intellectuals, bolstered by convictions of scientific certainty, had pronounced confidently, after the fashion of law-makers, on the way the world ought to be; however, the radical doubt of the postmodern period (compare Lyotard 1984) renders them mere interpreters, intermediaries in cultural communication between social groups with diverse meaning systems. The growth of culture industries and the proliferation of the consumer culture eliminated the role of the intellectual as legislator. For where markets operate 'There is no site from which authoritative pronouncements could be made, and no power resources concentrated and exclusive enough to serve as the levers of a massive proselytising campaign' (1987: 167). In such circumstances, Bauman argues, citing Bourdieu, the mode of domination in society alters, the new one distinguishing itself 'by the substitution of seduction for repression, public relations for policing, advertising for authority, needs-creation for norm-imposition. What ties individuals to society today is their activity as consumers, their life organised around consumption' (1987: 168). However, Bauman criticizes Bourdieu for failing to realize that there are still some people subjected to repression. Not everyone is allowed as a full member into the club of consumers; the excluded, the poor, are also the product of consumer culture. Thus exists a world of two nations, not of exploiter and exploited, but 'of the seduced and the repressed; of those free to follow their needs and those forced to comply with the norms' (1987: 169). This is presented as the major division in contemporary society.

Bauman's focus in *Legislators and Interpreters* is consumer culture and the way that increasing commodification operates systemically to establish a relationship between a majority of happy shoppers and a minority subject to state surveillance and control. Though not referred to as such, this is one way of restating the argument for the emerging importance of consumption cleavages. But it has a harrowing twist. For Saunders (1986) and Dunleavy (1979), being dependent on the state allocation of services tended to result in a poor quality product. For Bauman, such people are deprived of liberty and expressiveness, for the world we inhabit is one where 'Individual needs of personal autonomy, self-definition, authentic life or personal perfection are all translated into the need to possess, and consume, market-offered goods' (1987: 189). Those without access to market goods are, therefore, denied the means to develop their human potential.

In Bauman's view, the seduced are incorporated, free to make decisions in the market arena, and in the process they thereby enter into society and exercise a freedom in civil society beyond the surveillance of the state. Those who cannot be contained through consumption have to be policed, presumably both by coercive means and by state surveillance through the regulations governing social security payments, state provision of services, etc. However, it is hard to imagine the mechanism that generates repression. Determined that the mechanism is not class (Bauman is very circumspect, in the sense of never mentioning capitalist accumulation as a background to this harmonious social system), and going beyond the view that it is simple poverty, he has no explanation of disprivilege. The state surely does not want such a group and would never have sought to create it. The state would rather it were not there, for it is expensive and embarrassing. It would be a far-fetched conspiracy thesis to suggest that the state has to create this group in order to get the consent and routine obedience of the seduced. Yet Bauman has no other recourse: in the absence of a mechanism for generating economic disprivilege, there is no satisfactory explanation of the socio-genesis of this group.

The implications of this distinction are considerable, suggesting both a highly limited oppositional role for the subordinate group and that the individuals within it are permanent members. It is dubious analytically (as opposed to rhetorically) to identify two nations and, even if this were appropriate, questionable whether it is proper to call the second nation 'the repressed'. The consequences of intensified commodification do not seem to be well grasped by the strict division between the seduced and the repressed. There is no clear, mutually exclusive, division between these groups; rather, a continuum exists, with position marked by financial resources. In many ways the category that Bauman is describing might be better understood simply as the poor. Poverty studies have usually maintained that people slip in and out of poverty over the life course, though in periods of economic recession the duration of periods of distress for persons of working age is more prolonged. The mechanisms for keeping individuals in these categories are unspecified. In fact, the flow into and out of unemployment is very considerable. It is not a structural boundary. Conceivably there has been a structural transformation in the character of poverty in recent years, but that remains to be demonstrated. The operation of power supposed to have erected the boundary is implausible and the culpability of the state exaggerated. The state does not create the boundary between the seduced and the repressed, though, of course, for other reasons, it may indeed deal differently with people temporarily on different sides of that boundary.

Many sociologists who glimpse the benefits of the market and fear the potential repressive power of the state have recently tended to exaggerate the efficacy of markets. A decade of Thatcherism and the collapse of East European communism is reflected in social theory as the disparaging of state intervention. State power in all its forms is identified as the main enemy of human freedom; market processes, pluralistic because not amenable to central control, are deemed preferable to administrative allocation. However, advocates of the market readily forget the extent to which it is state regulation and the contractual aspects of civil society that make it possible for the market to operate at all. Moreover, in the recent past, state intervention and regulation has reduced undesirable and unjust outcomes in terms of distributive justice. Rejecting state-based political solutions to such injustice requires very careful deliberation. For present purposes, though, what is important is the implication of this analysis for an understanding of consumers. First it creates a very strong sense in which the consumer might be said to have authority. If the state has deprived the repressed of self-development and control over their own lives, then those who, by contrast, have the resources to be involved in the consumer culture must have some real power. Consumer freedom becomes more than a slogan. A second corollary is that we are permitted to think of consumption in individual terms, to begin sociological analysis from the point of view of the individual consumer. This shift to examining the individual consumer is the main transition between *Legislators and Interpreters* and the analysis offered in *Freedom*.

SELF-IDENTITY

In *Legislators and Interpreters*, Bauman displayed affinities with the critical theory of the Frankfurt School, exhibiting a predominantly negative attitude toward consumer culture, disinclined to approve of commodification despite being concerned to expose the deficiencies of states, and little disposed to depict explicitly the motives of the consumer. The consumer as a 'type' was said to be guided by 'the principle of comfort' (1987: 192), and the concept of the consumer society was deemed 'a description which pinpoints, as the paramount feature of the new historical period, the advent and the (at least numerical) dominance of the consumer' (1987: 193). Bauman was unsympathetic to consumerism, not for puritanical reasons but because he saw it as part of a process of societal rationalization which entailed an end to utopias and the entrenchment of privatization. In *Freedom*, commodification and markets are much more positively assessed and the choices of individual consumers given a more prominent and acceptable role. The book seeks to explain how the consumer culture is sustained through the objectives and intentions of individual actors, suggesting links between structure and agency.

Freedom explicitly links together consumption and liberty. It is a philosophical and historical account of the character of human freedom. Bauman notes, first, that there are historical variations in the character of freedom and that it has always been the case that if some people are to be free others must be unfree. Second, he observes that the pure condition of individual freedom could only exist if there were no other people around. Not only is this empirically absurd, it would be unsatisfactory because, Bauman maintains, the human condition contains both the need for freedom and the need for social interaction. In practice, individuals must compromise between these needs.

Freedom is a double-edged condition, and while being 'free of oppression' is a good thing, its corollary, being 'responsible for choices', may be stressful. With the historical decline of traditional ties, individuality emerges as a problem: the individual is under-socialized because there are no universal, overarching grounds for obedience, but over-socialized because, as a result, other people and explicit social regulations have to intervene endlessly to ensure satisfactory behaviour. Bauman conceives the predicament of individuality as a problem of self-identity: modernity, or post-modernity, is seen to demand that individuals construct their own selves. No longer are people placed in society by way of their lineage, caste or class, but each must invent and consciously create a personal identity. This construction of self involves, in great part, appropriate consumer behaviour. In this context, one of Bauman's remarkable insights is his stress on the individual responsibility incurred when faced with consumer choice. The authority that accrues to the individual consumer by the very situation of being able to choose may often generate anxiety. Shopping confidently in this sense is an accomplishment, a task that requires considerable skill. Perceptively, Bauman notes that one function of advertising is to comfort the beleaguered shopper in the moment of decision.[2]

The proposition that a key objective of consumption is the securing of self-identity might be endorsed by a number of other writers (for example, Giddens 1991; Featherstone 1991). Bauman, however, following Baudrillard, proceeds to argue that as choice of goods comes to be governed primarily by sign-values rather than use-values, a new arena of social competition over symbols emerges. Such competition, in contrast with competition in the sphere of capitalist production, is benevolent and without tendency to monopoly. For Bauman, consumer freedom is not a zero sum game, largely because 'Identities are not scarce goods' (1988: 63). It is not self-annihilating competition. Therefore, people can be left to choose, free from regulation. Any insecurities they might have (regarding confirmation of the self-identity that they have constructed) are assuaged by expert advice, primarily from the advertising industry, on what to buy. Consumer freedom is therefore the most successful form of freedom ever for most people; it is more real than that associated with the entrepreneurial age of capitalism where competition was destructive. Consumer freedom consequently produces self-contentment, social integration and system reproduction:

> The consumer market is therefore a place where freedom and certainty are offered and obtained together: freedom comes free of pain, while certainty can be enjoyed without detracting from the conviction of subjective autonomy. This is no mean achievement of the consumer market; no other institution has gone this far towards the resolution of the most malignant of the antinomies of freedom.
>
> (1988: 66)

Bauman, once again, insists that the consumer culture is an ambivalent one. Consumer culture has a disturbing other-side. It excludes 'the repressed' who, subjected to the disciplinary social control of the state, are excluded from the realm of freedom. Even the lucky two-thirds, 'the seduced', only experience this freedom at one remove, for the system ultimately determines the form of their behaviour too. For the organization of consumption depoliticizes societies as a whole, particularly the seduced who, happy in their pluralistic consumer arena, are denied wider democratic self-control and encouraged to view the plight of the excluded as a matter of indifference. As Bauman sums up the account:

> for most members of contemporary society individual freedom, if available, comes in the form of consumer freedom, with all its agreeable

and not-so-palatable attributes. Once consumer freedom has taken care of individual concerns, of social integration and of systemic reproduction (and consumer freedom *does* take care of all three), the coercive pressure of political bureaucracy may be relieved, the past political explosiveness of ideas and cultural practices defused, and a plurality of opinions, life-styles, beliefs, moral values or aesthetic views may develop undisturbed. The paradox is, of course, that such freedom of expression in no way subjects the system, or its political organisation, to control by those whose lives it still determines, though at a distance. Consumer and expressive freedoms are not interfered with politically so long as they remain politically ineffective.

(1988: 88)

This is a brilliantly suggestive thesis, but it has three defects. First, it gives a one-sided description of the consumer's motivations. Second, the hierarchical social effects of competitiveness between consumers are underestimated. Third, though aware that the concepts of economics are rarely entirely appropriate to sociological analysis, Bauman imports key aspects of the economists' abstract model of 'the consumer' which help shore up a tendentious notion of consumption as a sphere of freedom.

Bauman's consumer, whose primary social objective is the search for self-identity, is but one model of the contemporary consumer among many currently circulating in the sociological literature. Colin Campbell (1987) conceives the modern consumer as a dreamer whose pleasure derives from anticipating the possession of objects, a never-ending process since actual possession is unsatisfying. John Winward (this volume) conceives of consumers as more rational beings, requiring information with which to make decisions guided by careful calculation of the usefulness, appropriateness and comparative cost of particular items. Grant McCracken (1988) identifies yet another alternative process that he discusses in terms of 'Diderot-unity' and 'the Diderot-effect'. Diderot, given a new red dressing-gown, changed all other objects in his study because they looked drab and out of place in comparison. He thus turned a familiar and comfortable place into something which he subsequently neither identified with nor liked. 'Unity' arises from having products complement each other. This might explain some of the perpetual spiralling upwards of expenditure and of the failure ever to gain pleasure through consumer durables (compare Hirschman 1982): something new at the margin is always required, yet its acquisition creates further disharmony.

All these constructs have a certain plausibility and probably many people on many occasions engage in each type of purchasing incident. But all are one-sided. It might be that there is a tendency for one model to become more prevalent in current practice. If that could be demonstrated it would enhance Bauman's argument for the emergence of a new consumer type. But this remains to be established. No evidence is advanced to this effect: rather, the word of Baudrillard and general consistency with the post-modernity thesis are the main foundations of Bauman's construction of the consumer.

There is reason for doubting that the pursuit of self-identity is the paramount goal of consumption. Almost all recent accounts of consumption exaggerate the part that establishing self-identity plays in the activity. There can be no doubt that this is one important part of consumption, but the question arising is how important it is in relation to other purposes. The idea that identity-value has entirely supplanted use-value and exchange-value as consideration in consumer decision-making seems to me misjudged (see Warde 1992). If self-identity is the paramount value in consumer behaviour, if it is inherently anxiety-provoking and if the possession and display of material objects is the principal means of handling distress, then it might be anticipated that whole populations of western societies would be constantly in the throes of individual crises. The implication, however, would be a considerable growth of psychiatric problems among the most affluent consumers, since they have most choice of identity. This is not the case, largely because the displaced and disembedded *persona* proposed by the model is misperceived. Rather more often, being socially acceptable is the goal and the means of allaying anxiety.

Bauman maintains that people compete over the construction of self-identities. It is not entirely clear that self-identity can be the object of a competition. Perhaps a narcissist might consider the achieved self as a statement in some kind of imaginary contest with others; but only just. That aside, and more controversially, Bauman implies that consumer competition is harmless. Probably the single-minded pursuit of pure difference in appearance is less harmful than many other known forms of competitive behaviour. However, many forms of consumer competitiveness, and those previously identified in sociological studies, are less innocuous. Many would say that consumer competition is a source of divisiveness, a basis for conflict and exclusion. Pierre Bourdieu (for example, 1984) implies this in maintaining that consumption practices are a display of, and a way of acquiring, cultural capital. Cultural capital is a source of power in its own right and may also be converted into economic power. Consumption is an integral element of reproducing social hierarchies and locating people in them. Similarly, sociological inquiries in the 1960s suggested that competition over commodity possession was a virulent source of division and envy. Emulation entailed 'keeping up with the Joneses', a disquieting, privately oriented obsession, where the display of objects substituted for traits of good character in establishing reputation, so that people came to be measured by their possessions rather than by their virtue, which engendered a petty social divisiveness.[3]

Consumer free choice may not be such a profound instance of liberty, partly because more gross, or less image-directed, objectives are integral to it. People also use consumption to exercise power, to express indifference to others and to manipulate social situations in accordance with personal ambitions.

The account in *Freedom* is excessively individualistic in that it fails to specify the effects of competition on comparative status. The sense of individual symbolic struggle addressed by Bauman probably emphasizes too much the pluralistic aspect of consumer culture to the neglect of its hierarchical element. This error, it seems to me, arises partly from his overall view of post-modernity and partly from a certain complicity with the concept of the consumer derived from economics.

In the last decade, economic concepts have come to play a prominent role in sociological analysis and Bauman is one of the many who frequently deploy the concepts of 'the consumer' and 'the market'. The consumer is an abstraction of economics and it is not easily, nor should it readily be, imported into other areas of social science. The abstract individual of neo-classical economics is not the burdened, worried, haunted, embedded, memory-infested, befriended kinsperson who stalks the social stage.

To an important degree talking of 'the consumer' is merely to dignify the term 'shopper'. The consumer is the abstract individual required in a commodified world where money is the main instrument of economic exchange. For economics, a consumer is just somebody who buys something, but economic theory doesn't tell us why any particular good is chosen. The concept of 'revealed preference' provides the syllogistic reasoning that passes for an economic theory of consumption; people want the things that they buy and you can tell they want them because they bought them. For certain accounting purposes this is a perfectly reasonable axiom, but it is sociologically unilluminating. There are no generalizations that one can sensibly make about the consumer.[4] The use of the term 'the consumer' signifies an undersocialized actor; it exaggerates the scope and capacity for individual action. In doing so, however, it authorizes the view that consumers choose freely simply because they are not forced to purchase anything in particular.

It is anomalous that, for Bauman, consumers are both free and seduced. In ordinary language these terms are not synonymous! Nor, to be fair, are they used in exactly the same way by Bauman, for he considers consumers free as individuals but systemically seduced. Without legitimation from economic theory the sense in which consumers are free would be much harder to convey.

The very notion of the individual consumer prevents us from being able to appreciate the constraints people face in their consumption practices, as embodied persons rather than ghostly abstractions of economics. Implicit reliance on the idea of the consumer leads Bauman to ignore his own axiom that opportunity for engagement in social interaction is a fundamental need. That which is sociologically interesting happens in the space between responsibility for one's own actions and the classification procedures of social groups. The social world is differentiated by the groups to which a person belongs and has on-going interaction. Other people are co-participants, not just an audience, as is implied in the logic of consumer self-identity. The mechanisms whereby consumption secures a sense of belonging are poorly developed; people belong to groups that have a collective history of consumption and, thus, do not enter the department store naked. For this reason Bauman subsequently explores the concepts of neo-tribe and life-style.[5]

BELONGING

In most of Bauman's work the problem of belonging resides at the centre of the contemporary human predicament. Being as belonging, practising mutual responsibility, searching for a tolerant community, are major objectives of, for instance, his magisterial study of the Holocaust (1989). His moral project, to find an institutional basis for tolerance and solidarity, is about the human right to belong to the group that one chooses – from which one derives security, approbation, meaning and context – without thereby being treated by others in a demeaning, condescending, dismissive or hostile fashion (see Bauman 1991). It is therefore vital that the links between 'individual self-assembly' and group membership be thoroughly analysed. *Freedom* failed to specify adequately the basis for belonging in the process of the individual consumer trying to secure self-identity. Bauman implicitly acknowledges this in *Thinking Sociologically* where his position is further developed.

In *Thinking Sociologically* Bauman returns to the process of consumption in the context of analysing 'going about the business of life' (1990: 195–213). He observes that we depend heavily in our practical everyday activities on commodities that incorporate expert knowledge in the form of a technological sophistication which we scarcely understand, cannot repair, yet cannot do without. Electricity supplies, word processors, washing machines and so forth are indispensable but not within our personal capacities to secure except through market exchange. We are disabled and de-skilled in that sense, but we compensate (to differing degrees!) through learning the art of shopping. This fosters 'the consumer attitude' – which involves seeing life as a series of problems which have to be solved and believing that the means to their solution (objects or recipes) can be bought – through which the art of living becomes 'the effort to acquire the skill of finding such objects and recipes, and gaining the power to possess them once found' (1990: 204). This becomes the way of individually acquiring a personal identity, the models for which are available on the market. 'The models come complete with all the bits and pieces one needs to assemble them, and with point-by-point instructions on how to put them together: genuine "DIY identikits" ' (1990: 205). Illustrating with reference to the nature of life-style advertisements (see Leiss *et al.* 1990), Bauman asserts that: 'What is being sold is not just the direct use value of the product itself, but its symbolic significance as a building block of a particular cohesive life-style – as its indispensable ingredient' (1990: 205).

Bauman then briefly redescribes life-style in terms of membership of 'neo-tribes'. Acknowledging that different styles are differentially attractive in different social circles he then asserts that: 'There is no more, or almost no more, to my making myself a member of that group than sporting such signs: wearing the group-specific dress, buying the group-specific records [etc.]. I may "join the tribe" by buying and displaying the tribe-specific paraphernalia' (1990: 206). He describes the neo-tribe as informal, without authority, and non-exclusive, except for the obligation to take on the identity-symbols of the tribe. However, he goes on to observe that there is one gatekeeper in the process, the market: 'Neo-tribes are in essence *life-styles*, and life-styles, as we have seen, boil down almost entirely to *styles of consumption*' (1990: 207). In a world where life-styles are thoroughly public, those who are prevented from acquiring a prestigious one are likely to feel frustrated and inadequate. Inaccessible to those with limited resources, the deprived are not 'self-made persons': they cannot choose who they will be, cannot enter a new life-style when it appeals to them. The proliferation of life-styles suggests an equality between consumers, promoted by advertisements implying the universal availability of all styles to any consumer, but that is belied by the fact that people come to markets with unequal resources. He is thus pushed to admit that this may have a class basis:

> At the end of the day, it transpires that with all the alleged freedom of consumer choice the marketed life-styles are not distributed evenly or randomly; each tends to concentrate in a particular part of society and thus acquires the role of a sign of social standing. Life-styles tend to become, one may say, class-specific.
>
> (1990: 211)

This account of the business of life modifies the earlier ones but is also somewhat deficient in its manner of connecting individual consumer behaviour to social belonging. Introduction of the concept of neo-tribe is not pursued very far, partly because it does not easily support the argument. If neo-tribalism is intended to capture the nature of, for instance, adolescent style-groups, then it is contestable whether belonging is so limited a commitment or so easy to achieve. Only in situations akin to the impersonality of the urban crowd – situations that recent urban sociological research would suggest are a relatively small part of everyday life even in the metropolis – can the uninitiated individual pass for a member. True, anyone with the necessary resources can become equipped with the clothes, haircut and records that constitute the tribe's insignia. But the ensuing display is most meaningful only in the company of other adherents. This entails standards of acceptability in face-to-face interaction which depend on other features, such as accent, language, posture, norms and values. Moreover, the company in the new milieu will usually have highly refined capacities for discrimination within the group, such that the novice will easily be identified and subjected to judgement about appropriateness for continued membership.

It is perhaps then unsurprising that Bauman reverts to the more familiar concept of life-style. Yet the concept of life-style, now widely used, is a far from precise notion. There are at least five different senses of the term in use, with substantially different implications for an understanding of the operation of consumption.

1 Market research uses the term to indicate market segments, that is groups of people with a higher than average probability of purchasing particular kinds or qualities of goods.
2 It may refer to the identifying characteristics of a status group, as was the case in the classical conceptual formulation of Weber (see Weber 1978; also Turner 1988).
3 It can describe a set of practices – consumer behaviour, activities, body language, speech, etc. – which reflects a shared set of material circumstances and social class positions (for example, Bourdieu 1984).
4 The term may indicate a consumerist life-project, the pursuit by certain 'heroic consumers' of a coherent, comprehensive and highly stylized pattern of activities and possessions (see Featherstone 1991: 83–94).
5 Finally, it can imply pursuit of an ethical and principled way of life, irrespective of the purchase of commodities and shared class or demographic characteristics. This conception has affinity with the concept of neo-tribe, which has its origin in Maffesoli.

These senses of the term have some things in common but nevertheless have quite different implications for an understanding of everyday life in consumer culture. Bauman moves inconsistently between these, starting from the market research sense, moving through the neo-tribe and ending with the class attribution. This is not helpful conceptually. Moreover, the application of the term life-style is in important respects incommensurate with the model of the consumer as a free-floating agent, voluntarily choosing among commodities in the market with a view to creating a distinctive and individual self-identity. The notion of life-style indicates constraints, imposed by group belonging, on individual choice. Though necessarily aware of the styles associated with neo-tribes, the consumer chooses the group as much as, and probably more than, the style; and membership of the group commands a certain path through the enormous number of commodities on sale. Belonging comes before identity.

The abstract consumer does not belong; individual competing consumers do not belong; competition does not, in this field, generate belonging. *The* free consumer makes choices that are personal and instantaneous at the point of purchase. Belonging, by contrast, implies inter-personal and constrained decisions. However, once one belongs to a consumption niche, a subculture or whatever, the logic of the market paradigm no longer prevails. Social, group-solidaristic, considerations enter into play; it is no longer a case of a consumer buying cheaply – witness the logos and brands of the fashion industries – but one of acting in accordance with the logic of group membership regardless of cost or, probably, ideas of self. People seek the insignia of membership, irrespective of its market price or established personal taste, because of its role as a marker.

Ironically, Bauman's reasoning leads him back to a concern with class, abandoned in his *Memories of Class* (1983), where he argued that class was no longer a major social division in contemporary society and that work and occupation had been relegated to a minor role in people's life concerns, opportunities, self-identity and political consciousness. Apparently with reluctance, since otherwise he never links consumption to class, Bauman reintroduces the concept, driven by the need to explain the source of unequal financial power. But it is debatable whether accounts of neo-tribes are consistent with explanations of the class basis of life-style. The only way in which this would be possible, and it is not suggested by Bauman, would be if neo-tribes were class-specific, if they resided *within* classes, their members belonging to the *same* class.

Class matters because it is a partial explanation of how people come to have the resources they have when they step out to the shops. But class also matters to the extent that Bourdieu is correct in saying that consumption reproduces social hierarchy and class cohesion. Neo-tribes merely express difference; if they are truly voluntary and can be joined and left with the wave of a credit card then they are clearly not a fixed part of, nor grounded in, a social hierarchy. Observers of any given neo-tribe will be unable to place it in a system of social inequality. There would therefore be no basis for systematic material resentment, for patronizing attitudes, or for struggles over resources. The neo-tribe attribution is consistent with Bauman's view that consumer styles generate endless, but harmless, competition between individuals and with his central moral vision of tolerance without indifference. However, it is weakly defined, somewhat implausible, and certainly not consistent with a class-based account of consumption. Ultimately, it is difficult consistently to hold to the model of the consumer that he has devised while also properly appreciating the group dynamics of consumption.

CONCLUSION

The train of Bauman's successive arguments is instructive for the difficult task of developing a theory of consumption. Consumer purchasing poses awkwardly the classic sociological dilemma, of explaining individual action that is in one sense highly autonomous, but where there are nevertheless powerful inter-individual patterns. Many millions of consumers, each discretely making many purchases daily, without direct formal regulation, legal restraint or political direction, do not behave arbitrarily or unpredictably. If they did, not only would market research fail but so too would the mundane but vital activity of social identification in impersonal situations. The inadequacies of Bauman's solution derive from accepting a thesis about the overwhelming importance in post-modern times of individually distinctive visual appearance and its autonomy from material hierarchies. This has consequences for the political analysis of the role of the state, the model of the consumer and the interpretation of belonging.

By identifying the poor as repressed Bauman implies that the state is responsible for the unpleasant condition of the subordinates – it is the state that is repressive. However, if shortage of resources is the problem, then it is surely market relations that are to blame, since as we know, the market does not distribute rewards equitably nor, indeed, even in accordance with minimum conditions of survival. In the past the state has intervened in order to redistribute wealth because the market is incapable of securing a sufficient degree of social justice.[6] To call the poor 'the repressed' shifts the blame from market to state for the existing injustices. What the poor need most is more money, and no institution except the state is remotely likely to organize systematically the meeting of such a need.

Reliance on models of '*the* consumer' is unhelpful. By operating with his particular model, which is 'the consumer' as described by neo-classical economics embellished with an additional, but narrow, set of social motivations directed towards self-identity, Bauman distorts the features of consumer culture. He understates the hierarchical element of consumption practices while exaggerating the extent to which today's consumers are distinctive, self-centred and uniform in their objectives. An over-individualized and under-socialized consumer is portrayed, an impression partly confirmed by the difficulties that arise in handling questions of belonging.

The sharing of paraphernalia is a weak basis for membership or solidarity. Urban ethnographic research since the time of the Chicago School has identified multi-faceted ties of belonging that lie beneath, and serve to maintain, common surface appearance. Group identification requires more than accoutrements: specialized language, affirmation of authenticity through talk and interaction, nonchalant familiarity with a practical culture and shared judgement serve to distinguish members from pretenders. I doubt whether post-modern, consumer culture has eroded such norms of association, bases of co-operation or roots of obligation.

Zygmunt Bauman portrays a consumer culture uniform and universal in its effects. However, the seduction is not consummate: belonging is more secure, narcissism less entrenched; incorporation is conditional, permanent exclusion politically unfeasible. Choosing in the market place is a partial and limited means to empower people or to protect individuals against the power of producers. The general appreciation that freedom is achieved and protected in major part through collective action does not, hopefully, escape the ordinary citizen to the extent that Bauman fears.

NOTES

1 The main sources are: *Legislators and Interpreters* (1987: 149–187), *Freedom* (1988: esp. 19–98), *Thinking Sociologically* (1990: 195–213), *Intimations of Post-modernity* (1992: 49–53, 97–8, 197–8).
2 However, this is somewhat one-sided. On other occasions the effect of advertising is precisely to generate anxiety; adverts for cosmetics and slimming foods are notorious for creating or exacerbating people's anxieties about the adequacy of their bodily appearance. There are many other ways in which uncertainty in the face of choice is managed, which imply a different view of the consumer. The enormous membership of the Consumers' Association (see Winward in this volume) must be in significant part due to the fact that it offers objective information directed towards making rational and instrumental decisions when planning purchases. Indeed, consumer organizations are, in general, much more likely vehicles for expressing the authority of the consumer. Not only does their advice reassure the consumer, but their capacity for attracting public attention enhances the possibilities of exerting some systematic influence over large producers who seek to protect their reputation.
3 This scenario was probably partly based on a false impression of the homogeneity of poor communities in the past (compare Young and Willmott 1957 with Cornwell 1984).
4 The consumer has very few properties:

a) The consumer chooses to buy something, but *nothing in particular*.
b) The consumer wants to buy that something, '*cheap at the price*'. This in no sense means that the consumer wants to spend a small amount of money, indeed there are lots of reasons for wanting to spend lavishly. But the consumer's interest is to get a good deal.
c) Whatever thing the consumer wants must be *available for sale*. It is sometimes said that everyone and everything has its price. But this is doubtful. Moreover, it may be that even though something is for sale the potential purchaser cannot find out where, or who is the current owner, or cannot get through a traffic jam to peruse the required object, or whatever. Whether

one can get access to what is wanted is a constraint on the consumer. The consumer's interest is that whatever is wanted can be bought.

d) The consumer must have (if not lots) *sufficient money* with which to purchase whatever.

These are the necessary conditions for being that abstract entity the individual consumer.

5 For similar reasons other sociologists have also deployed terms like style group, status group and subculture.

6 Of course this is not to deny that state allocation of services may be demeaning, inconsiderate or inefficient.

REFERENCES

Bauman, Z. (1983) *Memories of Class: the Pre-history and After-life of Class*, London: Routledge & Kegan Paul.

—— (1987) *Legislators and Interpreters: on Modernity, Postmodernity and Intellectuals*, Cambridge: Polity.

—— (1988) *Freedom*, Milton Keynes: Open University Press.

—— (1989) *Modernity and The Holocaust*, Cambridge: Polity.

—— (1990) *Thinking Sociologically*, Oxford: Blackwell.

—— (1991) 'Postmodernity: chance or menace?', Lancaster University, Centre for the Study of Cultural Values Occasional Paper no. 2.

—— (1992) *Intimations of Postmodernity*, London: Routledge.

Bourdieu, P. (1984, 1989) *Distinction: a Social Critique of the Judgement of Taste*, London: Routledge & Kegan Paul.

Campbell, C. (1987) *The Romantic Ethic and the Spirit of Modern Consumerism*, Oxford: Blackwell.

Cornwell, J. (1984) *Hard-Earned Lives: Accounts of Health and Illness from East London*, London: Tavistock.

Dunleavy, P. (1979) 'The urban basis of political alignment: social class, domestic property ownership, and state intervention in consumption processes', *British Journal of Political Science* 9: 409–44.

Featherstone, M. (1991) *Consumer Culture and Postmodernism*, London: Sage.

Giddens, A. (1991) *Modernity and Self-Identity*, Cambridge: Polity.

Harvey, D. (1989) *The Condition of Postmodernity*, Oxford: Blackwell.

Hirschman, A. (1982) *Shifting Involvements: Private Interest and Public Action*, Oxford: Blackwell.

Leiss, W., Kline, S. and Jhally, S. (1990) *Social Communication as Advertising: Persons, Products and Images of Well-being*, 2nd edn, London: Routledge.

Lyotard, J.-F. (1984) *The Postmodern Condition: A Report on Knowledge*, Manchester: Manchester University Press.

McCracken, G. (1988) *Culture and Consumption: New Approaches to the Symbolic Character of Consumer Goods and Activities*, Indiana University Press: Bloomington.

Saunders, P. (1986) *Social Theory and the Urban Question*, 2nd edn, London: Hutchinson.

Turner, B. (1988) *Status*, Milton Keynes: Open University Press.

Warde, A. (1992) 'Notes on the relationship between production and consumption', in R. Burrows and C. Marsh (eds), *Consumption and Class: Divisions and Change*, London: Macmillan, 15–31.

Weber, M. (1978) *Economy and Society*, Berkeley: University of California Press.
Young, M. and Willmott, P. (1957) *Family and Kinship in East London*, London:
   Routledge & Kegan Paul.

Chapter 4

The organized consumer and consumer information co-operatives

John Winward

The literature on consumption has been mainly unfavourable to consumption as an enterprise and (often casually) dismissive of the potential of consumers to create themselves as an organized political force. At the same time, 'consumer movements' have developed on a significant scale throughout the world. Consumer groups take many forms, but it is notable that, in most advanced capitalist countries, independent organizations have developed along roughly the same lines as Consumers' Association in the UK: non-profit-making, funded by subscription to one or more magazines (which do not take advertising), primarily devoted to the publication of comparative test data on goods and services, but with a wider lobbying role. Such organizations appear particularly significant because they are funded by consumers themselves, and act on behalf of consumers as a group.

THE PLEASURES (AND DISPLEASURES) OF CONSUMPTION

Moral denigration of consumption appears to be coeval with the literature on economic development itself (Leiss 1983). In many areas of social and political commentary, indeed, the strength of hostility revealed in the literature (and from left-inclined critics in particular) can be positively disconcerting. An early book of essays with the promising subtitle 'Social and economic problems from the hitherto neglected point of view of the consumer' could begin by describing consumers as having 'some of the characteristics of a mob. . . . This [mob] instinct displays itself openly in bargain-hunting at sales, in mass-response to "cheap lines" and in the innumerable coupons, prize-giving, and debt-creating schemes degrading to trade' (though the author concedes that 'there we touch the lower levels . . .') (Co-operative Wholesale Society 1930: 4).

A number of distinct concerns appear to underlie this type of distaste. First, consumption (some consumption, at least) is viewed as wasteful. This currently finds expression mainly through the 'scientific' model of environmentalism, but certainly predates it. Commentators have expended much effort seeking to build distinctions between 'real' and 'unreal' needs, or 'natural' and 'unnatural' needs, and thereby to differentiate between 'essential' and 'frivolous' consumption. The left has been particularly assiduous in this, and the task of the socialist has often been to do away with the frivolous consumption thus identified (see, for example, Mort's (1989) observations on the 1949 budget of Sir Stafford Cripps). Consumers are accused of being manipulated in their choice of pleasures (Galbraith and others), of having the *wrong kind* of pleasure (the Frankfurt School) or obtaining *less pleasure than they imagine* (the earlier Baudrillard). It is hard to escape the feeling that behind these criticisms lies a 'horrified prudery' about pleasure itself (Leiss 1983).

But it is two further assumptions about consumption that we wish to consider here: that consumers as a group are incapable of self-organization: 'again, we see the heedless, unorganized, cumulative force of the mob' (CWS 1930: 4), and that consumption is necessarily a passive and uncreative process.

ARE CONSUMERS ORGANIZED?

The premise of the disorganized consumer has often been used to contrast consumers unfavourably with workers as a potential political force: 'consumers, as such, are unconscious and unorganized, just as workers may have been at the beginning of the nineteenth century' (Baudrillard 1988: 55). Yet active consumer organizations – often of quite considerable size – exist throughout the world.

Consumer organizations take many forms, and have many objectives; as a crude measure, over a hundred organizations are affiliated to the National Consumer Congress of the UK as 'consumer members', and can therefore be assumed both to define themselves as consumer organizations, and to be accepted as such by the Congress Committee. Such organizations range from the single-issue to the generalist, from the entirely self-funded to the entirely government-funded, from the local to the national, and so on. If there is an 'ideal type' of middle-to-late-twentieth-century consumer organization, however, it is the self-funded 'information co-operative', of which Consumers' Association in the UK and Consumers' Union in the US are examples.

Though they differ in detail, such organizations share the following characteristics:

- they are funded wholly or mainly by payments from their members;
- that revenue comes wholly or mainly through subscriptions to a magazine or magazines (*Which*? and its sister publications in the case of CA), which take no advertising;

- the central plank of the magazines is the comparative testing of goods and services;
- they are non-profit-making, but use 'surpluses' generated by magazine sales to campaign for changes in the law, or to give help and advice to individual subscribers;
- they act in a representative role on behalf of the generality of consumers at both national and international political levels, for example by giving evidence to parliamentary or governmental inquiries; by suggesting and even initiating pieces of legislation (in the UK, often through the Private Members' Bill mechanism); by participating in the work of standards-making bodies; and by contributing money and resources to bodies like the International Organization of Consumer Unions.

They take as their aims:

- to research – using a wide variety of techniques from engineering to social research in order to collect comparative data on the performance of competing (and even monopolistic) goods and services;
- to inform – publishing information through their own magazines and other channels to help consumers optimize their choices between the goods and services currently available;
- to improve the quality of goods and services available – both by providing information in competitive markets, and by lobbying for changes in the law, or improvement in the way that monopoly services and public goods are supplied.

Although the field of 'consumer activism' has always been under-theorized, there clearly is a paradigm of consumption, and of economic systems, from which the consumer organizations work. It is implicit rather than explicit, but includes the following beliefs:

- that free markets are a highly exploitable mechanism for individual consumers to use, but that most markets exhibit significant imperfections;
- that it is possible for use-values and exchange-values to diverge significantly, so that within the market place there will be, at one and the same time, both 'bargains' and 'rip-offs' on offer;
- that consumers as a group stand in a clear, and often oppositional, relationship to a recognizable 'producer' grouping, and that the latter often unites (against consumers) groups which might in a different context be in conflict – for example managers and workers, manufacturers and retailers, managers and shareholders, etc.

THE FAILURE OF MARKETS

Even the most enthusiastic proponents of economic markets accept that they can 'fail' in a variety of ways. Two particular assumptions about the structure of markets are most relevant to this discussion. Standard economic models assume, *inter alia*, that:

All buyers and sellers have perfect information about all the products on sale in the market.
The products on sale are homogeneous.

(adapted from Ramsey 1984: 15)

Clearly, all real markets diverge significantly from this 'ideal' state, most obviously in respect of the 'perfect information' rule. At first sight, this offers a temptingly straightforward way of slotting consumer organizations into standard economic theory: as arbitrage agents, operating a secondary market in information itself. On closer examination, this proves insufficient to explain the rationale for consumer organizations.

The most simple and obvious piece of consumer information is price. In a 'real-world' application of the perfect information model, it is only held to be necessary that a minority of 'marginal consumers' arm themselves with sufficient price information to penalize sellers whose prices are above those of the cheapest. The 'market perfecting' effect of these consumers is then expected to force prices to cluster (Schwartz and Wilde 1979). In practice, there is empirical evidence that prices diverge considerably in local markets (see, for example, Kirman and Vignes 1991). Yet, despite the potential for arbitrage, consumer organizations place much more emphasis on measuring and comparing the different characteristics of competing brands and models than they do on collecting and disseminating pure price information.

Up to a point, consumer ignorance about quality differences between different brands and models can be characterized simply as a further information failure. It is, however, rather different in nature to information failures about price, and reflects the fact that the goods on sale are rarely completely homogeneous, from the point of view of the consumer.

Curiously, this has received little attention in the literature of economics; traditional demand theory ignored the actual characteristics of goods – an omission which led Lancaster to observe that 'Someone with no economic background, studying the economist's theory of demand, might well find the ... exclusion of properties of goods a strange one' (Lancaster 1971: 2). Outside the mainstream of economics, the treatment has often been even more cavalier. A significant part of the academic discussion of consumption seems to be based on the assumption that the goods and services which are consumed are, on the practical level at least, unproblematic (or if problematic, essentially unimprovable). Fromm

(1973: 79) is not untypical in stating, as an aside, that all brands of goods are 'virtually identical'; it is unclear whether he views them as identically good or identically bad. Closer to the mainstream, Lancaster and others concluded that demand theory should begin to consider the underlying properties of goods, rather than the goods themselves.

We should be clear that two quite separate issues are at stake here, the implications of which are significantly different. There are certainly circumstances in which we might conclude that there is a simple information failure in a market. Where it is clear that a single 'underlying property' is the *only* one which consumers are likely to value (an example might be the energy efficiency of a water heater), it would be reasonable to assume that a product which performed better on this dimension could command a higher price than competing models. If the quality difference is *not* captured in the price charged, it seems clear that the market has failed.

This, however, is rather a special case. More typically, a consumer purchase will offer a *range* of characteristics, the relative merits of which will be valued more or less highly by different consumers. The decision by Lancaster and others that demand theory should begin to disaggregate goods into underlying characteristics immediately raises much deeper issues about the nature of consumption – and, indeed, calls into question the view of consumption as a passive activity.

CONSUMER ORGANIZATIONS: INFORMATION FOR HOUSEHOLD MANAGEMENT

Questions about the 'satisfaction' gained from consumption have been discussed extensively by writers from a variety of disciplines, notably economics, anthropology, social psychology, sociology and cultural studies; each discipline has its own very distinct model (or models) of consumption and its meaning. As noted above, economics has generally reduced consumer demand to a simple issue of choice between identical competing alternatives, driven by the single measure of price. Once attention is shifted from the purchased product as the object of consumption to the underlying 'commodities' from which satisfaction is created, the model which emerges treats households as centres of production, rather than of passive consumption. In Lancaster's words, 'We assume that consumption is an activity in which goods, singly or in combination, are inputs and in which the output is a collection of characteristics' (1966a: 133).

In Stigler and Becker's (1977) even broader model, 'market goods' are viewed as simply one resource among many that consumers apply to the productive activity. In the consumption of 'music appreciation', for example, one of the resources being brought to bear is the individual's training and other human capital. This approach to consumption has similarities with a body of literature in the fields of sociology and cultural studies which emphasizes the way in which consumers engage with the 'products' of culture to alter and subvert their meaning. Bourdieu, for example, proposes a 'labour of appropriation'; that 'the consumer helps to produce the product he consumes, by a labour of identification and decoding' (Bourdieu 1989: 100). There are, it should be noted, some very fundamental divergences between the views of Lancaster and Bourdieu on the *uses* of consumption, which have significant implications for the formation of consumer organizations, and to which we return below.

In models like these, both the selection and use of consumer goods is an active process. For example, consider the case of a household (or individual) setting out to 'manufacture' social prestige. Many different market goods could be applied to that manufacturing process (jewellery, cars, fashionable clothes), or the entire field of market goods might be substituted by human capital (education, 'taste'). It follows that 'A firm can have many perfect substitutes in the commodity market even though few other firms produce the same physical product' (Stigler and Becker 1977: 84). Conversely, a single market good contains many characteristics (for example, different cars offer different combinations of speed, comfort, economy, etc.) so that 'the simplest consumption activity will be characterised by joint outputs' (Lancaster 1966a: 133). The act of choosing and applying consumer goods is now seen to be a complex act, with 'managerial' characteristics.

It is in this context that the first role of consumer organizations – as providers of information to help the process of household production – can best be understood. The very first issue of *Which?* magazine explained its purpose as 'the giving of accurate factual information about the goods and services you buy', in order to 'enable people to get better value for their money'. Consumer testing organizations view the provision of information in both a wide and narrow sense. In the wide sense, it is hoped that the injection of consumer information will improve the workings of the market place and lead to the refinement of goods and services available to *all* consumers (not just those who directly receive the information). However, they also accept that the provision of such information is a *direct benefit to consumers in itself* – empowering them to make better choices.

A CONSUMER HABITUS

What can we say about the habitus – the basic, deeply interiorized master patterns of a group's collective unconscious (Harker *et al.* 1990) – from which consumer information co-operatives have grown? What would we look for if we attempted to take that group which chooses to subscribe to a consumer organization, and '. . . name the principle which generates all [its] properties and all [its] judgments' (Bourdieu 1989: 170)?

Some social recognition of the rights of consumers (for example, laws regulating trade) appear to be as old as human society, but the specific form of consumer organization here being discussed arose in a very distinct historical period: it is a twentieth-century project. The first organizations emerged in the US, with Consumer Research and, shortly afterwards, Consumers' Union. In a direct or indirect sense, all the current consumer information co-operatives can be seen as offshoots of Consumer Research. Consumers' Union was formed when founding staff split from Consumer Research. Consumers' Association of the UK was founded in 1957, based explicitly on the CU model and with a founding grant from CU. The first US models appeared in a specific context, and during a particular phase in the development of capitalistic production and sales, the most prominent aspects of which were the rapid spread of mass-manufacturing techniques (specifically the production-line methods associated with Ford) and a shift in the emphasis of marketing. In two straightforward technical senses, the comparative testing programmes on which the groups were founded could only have developed in the world of Fordist production. First, because they were predicated on testing the type of commodity-form which Fordism produces: standard, branded, widely available and quality controlled products. Second, because developments in the technical sphere made it possible, for the first time, to establish reasonably robust comparative test methods (Thorelli and Thorelli 1974: 439).

Perhaps of more significance, though, was the emergence, with Fordism, of new class fractions and a new world view. The new production methods were closely associated with new forms of social organization which started within the factory but spread beyond it; in particular the scientific management theories of Taylor and others.

Many of the techniques which comprise scientific management were applied long before the twentieth century. In the seventeenth century, for example, William Petty's theoretical writings on 'political arithmetic' and his organization of the 1654 survey of Ireland show him to be a Taylorist *avant la lettre* (for a description of Petty's works, see Strauss 1954). However, the very widespread interest in the ideas of scientific management in the early part of the twentieth century mark it out as a new type of social phenomenon. Several observers have noted that the model of Taylorism came to be applied far more widely than to the field of factory organization. It has been linked to the growth of the political party, the organization of American football, and even the classical ballet ('Diaghilev was a Taylorist in dance' – Murray 1990). More generally, Merkle argues that Taylorism became 'an important component of the philosophical outlook of modern industrial civilisation' and describes it as a 'mental revolution' that became widely adopted as a social philosophy (Lash and Urry 1987: 164). The emergence of Taylorism was associated with the ascendancy of new class fractions, notably the industrial manager and the industrial engineer.

The key to Taylorist organization (in its narrower sense) was, of course, the detailed specification, specialization and subdivision of work. One of the factors facilitating the spread of Taylorist methods was the impact of the first world war which, among other things, led to the enormous extension of state purchasing of standardized products (Lash and Urry 1987: 167). The impact of this is seen, of course, in the rapid extension of mass production. It also, though, required the introduction of Taylorist purchasing methods on the part of government agencies.

It was this rationalized and Taylorized procurement that was used as the model for the development of consumer testing organizations. In their book *Your Money's Worth*, Chase and Schlink observe that 'Skilled chemists, physicists, engineers, research workers ... are passing continually and relentlessly upon the relative quality of the goods which the purchasing agent proposes to buy', and ask, 'Why cannot this technique be extended to aid the consumer at large ...?' The authors went on to form an independent testing agency, Consumer Research, with Schlink as Director and Chase a member of the Board (Thorelli and Thorelli 1974: 439). As noted above, Consumer Research was the direct precursor of both Consumers' Union and Consumers' Association.

DISTINCTION AND POST-MODERNISM – SOCIOLOGICAL CHALLENGES TO CONSUMER ORGANIZATION

The 'household production' model proposed by economists such as Becker and Lancaster was an attempt to extend the concept of 'use-values' to subsume the more ineffable notion of 'tastes' as specific to a particular individual or group, and thereby open such issues as addiction to a formal and rationalistic analysis. It is easy to fit the information-providing consumer organization into this model (and Lancaster (1966b) explicitly does so). It is rather more difficult to square the idea of consumer organizations with the – at first sight similar – models offered by sociologists and cultural theorists, for two closely linked reasons.

First, such theorists present the purpose of consumption as that of creating distance or distinction between social actors. Bourdieu himself is highly critical of economists (unnamed, but he clearly means Lancaster) who hypothesize that products possess objective, 'technical' characteristics which, once revealed, would allow all consumers to rank the decisive attributes of competing goods in a consistent way. In Bourdieu's view, 'objects, even industrial products, are not ... independent of the interest and tastes of those who perceive them' (Bourdieu 1989: 100). Second, in analyses such as Baudrillard's more specifically semiotic approach, use-values (or even exchange-values, as traditionally described) become ever more remote from the purpose of consumer goods, which now perform as elements in a linguistic system, used as signals of the taste of individuals or social groups and to secure territory in a war of position.

While much in this latter approach is familiar – economic analysts from Adam Smith onwards have recognized that the exchange-value of goods includes the additions to social status which ownership conveys – nevertheless the model of exchange which Baudrillard and others describe is potentially threatening to the practices, or indeed the very existence, of consumer organizations. If structural changes in the productive base now mean that 'the value of commodities is seen to derive less from the laws of economic exchange . . . or from the ability of products to satisfy primary needs as from the way they function culturally as signs within coded systems of exchange' (Hebdige 1989: 81), then the approach and methods of most existing consumer organizations are patently meaningless. Beyond that, if 'a need is not a need for a particular object, as much as it is a "need" for difference (the desire for social meaning)' (Baudrillard 1988: 45), then the very idea of general consumer solidarity is surely an absurdity. For in what sense could consumers combine, if the whole purpose of consumption is to divide? It appears to be this theoretical consideration that drives Baudrillard to the conclusion that consumers cannot undertake collective action.

The problem is not so much that of deciding whether social functions are to be attributed to consumer goods (the answer seems self-evidently that they are). The key questions are first: are such functions now to be considered the primary attribute of goods – and if so, which range of goods? and second: is there a 'post-modernist' form of semiotic exchange which is different again from the older conception of exchange-value, and which is progressively replacing it? The literature offers little help with the first of these questions, in large part because the authors concentrate on a restricted range of examples – essentially cultural goods (or goods with a high 'cultural content') and luxury goods. Bourdieu, for example, cites specifically a 'work of art' as an extreme object of this labour of appropriation, in which such labour may 'constitute the whole of the consumption' (Bourdieu 1984: 100). In the more routine fields of the consumption of goods (for example the 'staples' and 'technology' sets, to borrow Douglas and Isherwood's (1979) typology), it seems less plausible that such a form of symbolic reconstruction is central to the act of consumption. Interestingly, Baudrillard himself does specifically mention a more routine product: the washing machine, which he describes as *serving* as equipment and *playing* as a sign (of comfort, prestige, etc.) (Baudrillard 1988: 44 – his emphasis).

Information as cultural capital

The world of goods also provides a field for the acquisition and display of 'cultural capital'. There are, again, two aspects to this. One is directly related to the 'household production' model: as novel products enter the market, consumers need to be educated about them. In an obvious sense, they need information about the performance of the product (what does it do?). Further, though, the acquisition of consumer information can be seen as a social asset in its own right: 'the mastery of the cultural person entails a seemingly "natural" mastery not only of information (the autodidact "memory man") but also of how to use and consume appropriately and with natural ease in every situation' (Featherstone 1991: 17). Knowledge of a product can be seen to add to the ways in which that product can *play* as a cultural item.

However, we would differ with Featherstone's analysis on two points. First, the acquisition of consumer information need not be made to appear 'natural' at all. Second, there is a 'political' dimension to consumer information; it is seen (by some consumers at least) as conferring power in an oppositional relationship with producers and retailers.

The first of these points reflects the fact that consumer magazines themselves are products, with the ability both to perform and to play. Featherstone assumes that cultural capital must seem to be effortlessly acquired. On the contrary, the access to an independent source of information is one that can be exploited for social purpose:

> In fact, you can be quite a celebrity amongst your peers. You can say, hang on a minute I'll look in my *Which?* and tell you.*

> It's all in conversation, if someone comes in and says I'm going to buy a video at the weekend, I say 'get one of those' and they say 'why?' I say 'because *Which?* thinks they're great'.*

Secondly, Featherstone neglects the oppositional relationship between consumers and producers. Consumers wishing to demonstrate 'mastery of information' consciously do so in a world in which advertising is providing privileged information. Although advertising, shop assistants and so on are seen as being a valuable source of information, they are recognized as unreliable. This aspect of consumer information emerges strikingly in research among *Which?* subscribers. As part of the process of resistance, subscribers to consumer magazines can be typified as information seekers. Information is gathered from a variety of sources, but that from the consumer magazine (alongside, often, that from friends and relatives) is valued more highly for being independent of commercial interests:

---

* All starred quotations are from unpublished research carried out on behalf of the Consumers' Association between 1988 and 1991.

I don't know anywhere else I can go to get an unbiased opinion of things.*

I can't buy anything without consulting [*Which?*]. I am terrible, I just don't believe any of the salesmen in the shops.*

Advertising clearly plays a part in maintaining this oppositional relationship. While consumption was becoming more 'Taylorized' and 'rationalistic', advertising was moving in the opposite direction. Until the first decade of the century, advertising itself had taken a rationalistic model of human nature, and advertising material had been largely of an educational nature, describing the characteristics and properties of the advertised goods in some detail, and appealing to the rational consumer by stressing the durability, reliability, etc., of the advertised goods. However, mass production requires mass consumption, and by the second quarter of the century, advertising was shifting to an irrationalist model, playing more on suggestion and appeals to the senses (Leiss 1983). For a group actively wishing to add to a specific form of cultural capital in the field of consumer goods, advertising became less useful. Moreover, to a group which placed high store on the 'rationalistic' aspects of consumption, such advertising would create negative value.

If you don't watch out you can end up more confused than helped, because they all say this is the best thing since sliced bread.*

We're in a world that throws a lot of gloss and hype at us. We need *Which?* to clarify it for us.*

Consumer organizations: Lobbying on behalf of consumers

It is this oppositional relationship that gives consumer organizations their wider social role, acting on behalf of consumers against producer interests, and is the reason that all consumer organizations, to a greater or lesser extent, perceive themselves as political organizations. In expending resources on lobbying governments, producer groups and others, consumer organizations recognize that many consumer problems are impossible to resolve at the level of the individual. Some consumer organizations (for example, the National Consumer Council, UK) deal only with issues of this sort. Typically, the self-funding organizations apply surpluses generated from sales of magazines to this purpose, and have described this as their 'dividend to shareholders'. Normally, the membership is not directly involved in the process of campaigning (though they might be invited, for example, to write letters complaining about particular practices and supporting the organizational line). However, the campaign is very often backed by large-scale survey research among the organization's members, and this is held to increase greatly the legitimacy of the case presented by the officers of the association.

Survey data suggests that the campaigning/lobbying role of the organizations is understood and supported by their members. It is also interesting to consider the comparative success of more and less politicized consumer organizations. In both the UK and the US, rival consumer testing organizations grew up side by side. In the US, the Consumers' Union split off from Consumer Research (see above). In the UK, the British Standards Institution launched a comparative testing magazine (*Shopper's Guide*) at the same time as the creation of *Which?* (1957). In both cases, one organization adopted a 'radical' stance, the other a less aggressive one. Consumers' Union was 'sparked by more social zeal than Consumer Research, was markedly more committed to political and economic reforms to alleviate the plight of the consumer' (Thorelli and Thorelli 1974). In the UK, the Moroney Report noted that *Shopper's Guide*'s 'dependence on BSI – and thus, indirectly, on manufacturers – has restrained the vigour of *Shopper's Guide* comments, and has caused consumers to mistrust its independence'. In each case, the more 'radical' of the testing publications was significantly more successful than its less radical rival. Many different factors have played a part in this, of course, but it does not, at the very least, suggest that an 'unpolitical' stance is attractive to potential members.

On the other hand, 'direct action' by members is rare. There is a modest history of consumer boycotts, particularly in the USA and 'refusal to pay' campaigns (for a European example, see Cherki and Wieviorka 1980). Generally, however, physical participation has played a minor role in the work of the consumer organizations. One major caveat needs to be added: by simply declining to buy particular products which are identified (by consumer organizations) to be unsafe, unnecessary, or simply a poor bargain, consumers may have a very powerful influence on their environment. Surprisingly, perhaps, the actual effect of consumer advice on consumer markets has been little studied, though anecdotal information suggests that it might be considerable. In other words, 'exit' provides a more powerful weapon in consumer transactions than 'voice'.

ARE CONSUMERS ORGANIZED? SOME CONCLUSIONS

The simple existence of the consumer organizations described here, and the existence of international networks of such groups, suggests that the organized consumer exists as a social fact. Moreover, these groups (and other social forces) have succeeded in creating an inter-articulation between the state and the 'consumer movement' at a number of levels. This has included the establishment of government-funded consumer institutes (for example the National Consumer Council in the UK), but the independent bodies themselves are widely recognized as representatives of consumers on official bodies, as well as being consulted by government, by Select Committees and agencies such as the Monopolies and Mergers Commission. They have also sponsored (via Private Members' Bills), supported and fought against specific pieces of legislation.

It is less obvious that membership of such organizations is perceived as an act of solidarity. The methods of the consumer organizations do not (normally at least) offer any prospect for the type of physical solidarity that would lead to the emergence of a traditional Marxist 'class-for-itself' (Marx 1900). Consumers are not, on the whole, geographically organized; attempts have frequently been made in the UK to set up voluntary groups of consumers who would act together at the local level. These have largely failed, at least in comparison to organizations like CA, though local consumer groups do appear to flourish elsewhere in Europe. It is not, however, obvious that forms of action nearer to the traditional labour strike would be effective, and evidence from the US suggests that consumer boycotts do *not* produce stable, long-lived groups of activists (Herrman *et al.* 1988).

This physical disorganization of consumers currently provides, perhaps, less of a contrast with the labour movement than would once have been the case. The relative fragmentation of consumers could be read off as a precursor to the post-modernist collapse of other 'grand narratives' and the decline of the Fordist political structure. This, though, might be seen more as a loss to the worker than a gain to the consumer. But is even the present state of consumer organization sustainable? Four specific postulated characteristics of the 'post-modern' condition would be (if they do indeed become generalized) threatening to the existence of the consumer organizations considered here:

1 Radically 'post-Fordist' methods of production (with every item virtually custom-built for the individual consumer) would render the stock-in-trade of the testing organizations both impossible (only mass-produced commodities can be comparatively tested) and perhaps otiose (if every individual consumer becomes a niche market, there is no need for choice).

2 The decline of the modernist belief in the military/technical metaphor (Hebdige, 1989: 87) would threaten, and might destroy, the extended Taylorist *mentalité* on which we have argued the audience for comparative testing be constructed.

3 The (related) ending of commitment to the meta-discourse of 'truth' would, at a deeper level, render the consumer information project impossible, by removing the privileged position on which the consumer organizations stand.

4 If the use-values and even the exchange-values of goods are indeed
replaced by 'symbolic values', the problems of comparative testing will
become intractable in practice. Moreover, if such values are exclusively
to be deployed in the competitive creation of distinction between social
actors, it seems unlikely that publicly disseminated comparative information could retain much merit.

Perhaps fortunately for consumer organizations, the post-modernists'
announcement of the death of traditional consumer values seems prema-
ture. Even if symbolic values are becoming, and continue to become,
more significant in the selection of goods, we would suggest that traditional values may have some way yet to run, for use-value and symbolic
value interpenetrate in complex ways. At the very least, it is implausible
that a particular model of car (for example) could either 'serve' as a
means of transport or 'play' successfully as a symbol of comfort or prestige if it was constantly breaking down. If objects are acting as symbols,
they must be free to carry the full range of meanings which natural
language can convey; that includes conveying the idea that a particular
purchaser has been 'suckered' – which is hardly likely to act as a positive
sign of prestige.

Even straightforward use-values seem to have some life left in them.
The markets for cars and motorcycles – both fields with high levels of
cultural association – seem to illustrate this. Triumph and Harley David-
son, for example, both enjoyed very strong cultural associations with their
products, yet one was wiped out, and the other almost so, by competition
from the less glamorous, but better designed and engineered Japanese
products. Similarly the US car industry was severely damaged by the
gasoline price hikes of the 1970s.

What is left unexplained (or unconvincingly explained) in the post-
modernist analysis is the social process by which consumer goods become
suitable vehicles for meaning, if not through some reference to their
actual performance. It is rare for an entire class of goods to carry the
same social meaning (and then it is usually only a temporary phenomenon, while simple possession is itself a sign of economic distinction):
more normally, different brands or models carry very different meanings
(for example Skodas and BMWs are both cars, but convey utterly different social meanings in contemporary society). It often seems to be
assumed that a particular meaning can unproblematically be attached to
a particular product (almost at random) by manipulative techniques such
as advertising. Yet consumers are fully aware that they are the targets of
advertising, and are prepared to resist it. Within this process of resistance,
the consumer organizations constitute a major force, both as providers of
oppositional information and as promoters of structural change. 'Every
new product' may be, as Marx declared, 'a new potentiality of mutual

deceit and robbery' (Marx 1982). That is not to say that consumers cannot, or will not, organize themselves against deceit and robbery by producers and distributors.

REFERENCES

Baudrillard, Jean (1988) *Selected Writings*, ed. Mark Poster, Cambridge: Polity Press.
Bourdieu, Pierre (1984, 1989) *Distinction. A Social Critique of the Judgement of Taste*, London: Routledge.
Chase, Stuart, and Schlink, F. J. (1927) *Your Money's Worth: a Study in the Waste of the Consumer's Dollar*, New York: Macmillan.
Cherki, Eddy and Wieviorka, Michel (1980) 'Autoreduction movements in Turin' in *Italy Autonomia*, ed. Sylvere Lotringer and Christian Marazzi, 111 (3), New York: Semiotext Inc.
Co-operative Wholesale Society (1930) *Self and Society. The First Twelve Essays*, ed. Percy Redfern, Manchester: CWS.
Douglas, Mary and Baron Isherwood (1979) *The World of Goods*, Allen Lane.
Featherstone, Mike (1991) *Consumer Culture and Postmodernism*, London: Sage Publications.
Fromm, Erich (1973) *The Crisis of Psychoanalysis, Essays on Freud, Marx and Social Psychology*, Harmondsworth: Pelican Books.
Harker, Richard, Mahar, Cheleen, and Wilkes, Chris (1990) *An Introduction to the Work of Pierre Bourdieu. The Practice of Theory*, London: Macmillan.
Hebdige, Dick (1989) 'After the masses' in *New Times*, ed. Stuart Hall and Martin Jacques, London: Lawrence & Wishart.
Herrman, Robert O., Walsh, Edward J., and Warland, Rex H. (1988) 'The organizations of the consumer movement: a comparative perspective' in *The Frontier of Research in the Consumer Interest* ed. E. Scott Maynes and ACCI Research Committee, Columbia: American Council on Consumer Interests.
Kirman, A. and Vignes, A. 'Theoretical considerations and empirical evidence from the Marseille fish market' in IEA conference proceedings no. 98, ed. K. Arrow.
Lancaster, Kelvin (1966a) 'A new approach to consumer theory', *Journal of Political Economy*, 74.
——(1966b) 'Change and innovation in the technology of consumption', *American Economic Review*, 56.
——(1971) *Consumer Demand; a New Approach*, New York: Columbia University Press.
Lash, Scott and Urry, John (1987) *The End of Organized Capitalism*, Cambridge: Polity Press.
Leiss, William (1983) 'The icons of the marketplace' in *Theory Culture and Society, Consumer Culture*, 1 (3).
Marx, Karl (1900) *The Poverty of Philosophy with a Preface by Friedrich Engels*, trans. H. Quelch, London: Twentieth-Century Press.
——(1982) *The Economic and Philosophic Manuscripts of 1844*, London: Lawrence & Wishart.
(Moroney Report) (1962) *Final report of the Committee on Consumer Protection*. Cmnd 1781, London: HMSO, 25 April.
Mort, Frank (1989) 'The politics of consumption' in *New Times*, ed. Stuart Hall and Martin Jacques, London: Lawrence & Wishart.

Murray, Robin (1989) 'Fordism and post-Fordism' in *New Times*, ed. Stuart Hall and Martin Jacques, London: Lawrence & Wishart.

Ramsey, Iain (1984) *Rationales for Intervention in the Consumer Marketplace*, London: Office of Fair Trading.

Schwartz, G. and Wilde, L. (1979) 'Intervening in markets on the basis of imperfect information; a legal and economic analysis', *University of Pennsylvania Law Review*, vol. 127.

Stigler, G. J. and Becker, G. S. (1977) 'De gustibus non est disputandum', *American Economic Review*, vol. 67 (March).

Strauss, E. (1954) *Sir William Petty – Portrait of a Genius*, London: The Bodley Head.

Thorelli, Hans and Thorelli, Sarah (1974) *Consumer Handbook; Europe and North America*, New York: Praeger.

Chapter 5

Advertising
Moving beyond the stereotypes

Adam Lury

I am writing this from the point of view of a practitioner who believes that, in order to have a real understanding of the dynamics of advertising, it is important to understand the background and motivation of the people involved.

Advertising has a small 'legacy' – there is no formal industry-wide training scheme and very little knowledge is formalized. The most powerful influences are myth and oral history. Any study of advertising and advertising research methodology needs to take this 'invisible history' into account and I intend to outline some of the major forces and show how they affect advertising and how it is produced and measured.

THE CULTURAL STATUS OF ADVERTISING: FEAR AND LOATHING

Most people who currently hold power in advertising agencies and who are directly involved in the production of advertising are university educated. They will have come through universities when there was a considerable academic contempt for advertising (my philosophy tutor on hearing my choice of career responded with 'I don't care if you sell your body but for God's sake don't sell your mind!') Advertising practitioners have internalized that contempt and feel a deep sense of conflict and shame about their profession. But I believe that this shame will disappear gradually as 'cultural studies' and its attendant interest (and consequent legitimization) continues and its graduates and their peers find their way into media careers.

However, there are two key implications for current advertising of this internalized shame and guilt. The first is that it creates the need for public/consumer acceptance. The thinking runs along the lines of 'I'll get by if I can make you laugh or entertain you.' The phrase 'The uninvited guest in the living-room' haunts advertising people and the apology or plea for acceptance is the capacity to amuse. The second implication of the internalized shame is that advertising people accept the premise that advertising is not intellectually worthwhile. This underpins the Pilate-like approach to discussion of the social influence of advertising, often expressed as 'Advertising can't change society, it can only reflect it.' Remember that many of these people were not taught the critical constructs that allow them to ask 'Whose view of society?' 'Which part of "society's" view?' or to see that 'reflecting' society is a positive act of reinforcing one particular view of society.

CODES OF PRACTICE

The second key factor driving the production of advertising is the influence of the voluntary codes of practice set up and monitored by the regulatory bodies. These codes institutionalize a view of society that can be summarized as white, male and middle class: the fundamental precepts are based in a 1950s and 1960s view of mass communication in which advertising was the ultimate brainwash that somehow had to be controlled.

The concepts and conceptual power of feminism and anti-racism were marginal at best when the codes were originally designed. As a result, the codes cannot incorporate the huge and relatively recent change in views about the portrayal of groups of people in the media. This is why so much sexist and racist imagery persists in getting through the approval procedures. The best the codes can do is include clauses such as 'No advertisement may offend against good taste or decency or be offensive to public feeling and no advertisement should prejudice respect for human dignity.' There is no recognition that advertising can serve to perpetrate harmful stereotypes and therefore should be monitored carefully. Yet although the codes themselves are unwieldy and out of date, the people working at the regulatory bodies concerned do their best to move advertising into the nineties; they are always sympathetic and constructive.

THE CREATION OF 'QUALITY' AND THE AWARD SYSTEM

The advertising industry also has an awards industry within it. The theory is that groups of those at the top of their profession (heavily skewed in favour of the 'creative' skills – copywriting, art directing, TV production) meet and 'judge' ads on the basis of their 'creativity'. Creativity is never defined but has increasingly come to mean 'entertaining' – unsurprising given the factors influencing the production of advertising. As awards are a key determinant of perceived success and salary, the judgement of the award juries can make or break the career of those who write and make advertising. It is not surprising therefore that the 'standards' of juries are internalized and reproduced by those aspiring for their approval. The key point here is that the awards juries do not incorporate market-place effectiveness into their judgements *in any form whatsoever*. The judgements on the 'quality' of an advertisement are made independently of any evaluation of its prime purpose. This can only hold water if it is assumed that a consumer-type evaluation (funniest/best) has a connection with effectiveness in selling what is advertised.

ADVERTISING AS ASPIRATION

Advertising practitioners all accept as fundamental the premise that advertising is 'aspirational'. Now, at one level this appears to be obvious – most advertising is about making people want something (a favourite expression is 'advertising doesn't sell, it makes people want to buy'). For most practitioners this leads to the assumption that the values contained in advertising and its portrayal of life-styles must be aspirational – somehow better than those held by the consumer (one of the many paradoxes for a profession that merely 'reflects' society). This belief is the basis for the argument that everything in advertising must be attractive, expensive and exotic.

This is one of the assumptions behind the impression that advertising is a 'glamour' business. Whilst 'aspiration' may in the past have been important for a number of product categories, it is by no means applicable for all product categories. People on the whole quite simply do not 'aspire' to soap powder, canned soup, microwave snacks or a current account that pays interest. Changing economic circumstances and attitudes mean that the target market for such products takes such things for granted. They may look for and appreciate differentiated offerings, but they do not see the purchase of a microwave snack as intrinsically aspirational. Advertising people find this hard to accept, as communication predicated on the consumer as partner would require a radical reappraisal of the dynamics of communication.

COMMUNICATION AS A LOGICAL PROCESS

The 1950s saw the creation of the 'Unique Selling Proposition (USP)' – the idea that advertising should feature a logical (and tangible) product promise. This theory that advertising is at its core a logical, measurable process can be seen as a product of its time. Manufacturers looked at consumers as a 'mass' of identical consumers – a suitable audience for their mass production of identical units. What mattered was the number of units produced, messages made, and consumers reached. This underpins much of the language of advertising today – 'impacts', 'ratings', 'targets'. This value system assumes that everything in communication can be understood in quantitative terms and is correspondingly measurable. Even attitudes, values and feelings can be isolated and measured with great precision. It is the intellectual legacy of the Ford era, its methodology exclusively quantitative.

Whilst they still predominate, these assumptions have eroded slowly over the last twenty years with the emergence of qualitative research as a marketing tool which can give the consumer more direct input into the production process.

THE INCORPORATION OF THE CONSUMER INTO THE ADVERTISING PROCESS

A major innovation in the production-consumption cycle was the introduction of the concept of marketing. This is best described in Levitt's article 'Marketing Myopia' and at its core is an astoundingly simple thought. In a world where everyone was selling what they want to make, it made competitive sense to ask your customers what they want to buy and then make that. Marketing is about trying to incorporate the customer into the production process in order better to satisfy them and thereby increase your chances of making a profit. In the jargon of the business it is a shift from being product-led to being consumer-led. In advertising agencies this marketing philosophy found an expression in 'account planning'. Stephen King of JWT and Stanley Pollitt of BMP are both credited with having 'invented, created or introduced' the concept in the late 1960s. Fundamental to the discipline of account planning is the belief that the planner is the 'consumer's representative' within the agency. Again the principle is simple – the planner asks consumers what they feel about a product or service, builds the communication around those feelings, and then helps to construct a message that meets with consumers' approval.

A new concept needs a new methodology and qualitative research (predominantly focus or discussion groups) came into its own. This gave the consumer an active voice and one that was not shaped by the methodological assumptions of quantitative research. The incorporation of this approach led to a long methodological struggle with the result that now most agencies and clients apply a 'bit of both' to their processes – with qualitative research favoured for the development of ideas and quantitative research favoured for the testing and measurement of effect. The 'quant-qual' debate raged in the academic trade press (which has very little effect on mainstream agency behaviour) and has now all but disappeared with a 'different strokes for different folks' attitude.

However, the introduction of account planning was critical in the creation of a whole body of user-friendly advertising. It has led to the production of a body of advertising that is liked and approved by customers – commonly referred to by consumer and producer alike as 'good' advertising. British agencies were the first to incorporate the planning process into their production and it is this lead that has meant that

British advertising is generally acknowledged to be the 'best in the world' (for which read 'the most likeable/enjoyable').

It is important to note here that the use of these value judgements – 'good' and 'best' – refers to a (consumer-based) feeling about the advertising. It does not in any way relate to other aspects of advertising such as effectiveness. The assumption is that likeability leads to communication which in turn leads to persuasion.

THE END OF AN ERA

This then is a brief description of the status quo in advertising today. Advertising, despite all the hype and glamour, is a deeply conservative, angst-ridden business where, despite the presence of a number of clever people, there has been little real thinking done over the last thirty years. Much of the real thinking was done when mass communication was in its infancy. The thinkers of that period – David Ogilvy and Bill Bernbach, for example – dominate because, since then, no one has been able to articulate a world view of equivalent stature.

The consequent amalgam of values, attitudes and beliefs has served the industry reasonably well to date, but I believe that we have reached a point where they are exhausted and where advertising needs to adopt a new approach if it is to continue to provide clients with an effective, competitive marketing weapon.

The result of the pressures I have outlined is that advertising today is *passive* – a series of comic set pieces; *reflective* – reiterating the same old jokes and value systems; *explanatory* – lecturing the consumer on a whole raft of features; and crudely *aspirational* – working to a model that assumes that a consumer's life will be vastly improved with the acquisition of a particular product.

The market of the 1990s is radically different to the market of the 1950s and 1960s. Whilst adaptations of the philosophy of the first two decades moved with the market, in the 1970s and 1980s we needed a new start in order to build a dynamic and effective model for advertising in today's market place. This is as a result of a number of factors that I propose to discuss briefly.

A WORLD OF REFLECTING MIRRORS: CONSUMER RESEARCH TODAY

Conducting consumer research is a fascinating business. You can lose yourself in the traditional games of bluff and counter-bluff – are they telling you what they think or what they think you would like them to think? Do they mean what they say or is it the result of group/interviewer/ methodological dynamics?

Whilst these are important questions, I am operating as a practitioner who has to make judgements daily in order to progress. So although I recognize the validity of the concerns I have outlined, and incorporate the learning from the study of those issues into my work, I have to let go of the purely theoretical concerns at some time. I start from the assumption that the people I interview are there because they are interested and that they want to help me. The people I talk to are not afraid of advertising or of the processes involved (they have all been interviewed before or know someone who has been interviewed).

What I have found is that the consumer is no longer the 'tabula rasa' that she/he once was. People are no longer passive data bases revealing 'pure' or straightforward feelings about advertising. (The previous system was based on the belief that people's feelings about a particular advertisement are immediate, not premeditated and so are 'pure, direct responses'.)

Today's consumer has *internalized the value system* that I have outlined above. There are a number of reasons for this, including the marketing of advertising itself, evident in newspaper coverage and TV programmes, the widespread experience of the research process and, not least, the experience of thirty years of TV advertising. This means that some of the standard research issues are no longer appropriate. When you access today's consumer – *what they think, and what they think you want them to think, are often one and the same.* If you ask people what makes a 'good' financial services advertisement for example, they will tell you that it is an advertisement that tells you that the organization doing the advertising is 'big, warm, friendly and careful with your money'.

Why is this? Is it because people want financial institutions to project an image of being big, warm, friendly and caring or is it because financial institutions have spent the last ten years telling people that they are big, warm, friendly and caring? The answer is both. Ten years down the line it is impossible to say which came first – the chicken or the egg. We are like Rita Hayworth in Orson Welles' *Lady from Shanghai* – lost in a world of reflecting mirrors. This does not lead to a win–win situation for advertisers but rather a lose–lose situation. Strategic consistency becomes strategic parity, and, if the consumer is incorporated directly into the process, the result is that all advertisements look and sound the same, losing any potential competitiveness. How has this situation come about? The answer lies in the way in which all agencies have incorporated the consumer into their production processes – all in the same way.

THE PLANNING HEGEMONY

The importance of being liked

If you believe that you are the consumers' representative and you conduct or commission qualitative research over a long period of time, a strange thing happens – you begin to seek the approval of the consumer you access. Remember that as a traditional practitioner you have (at best) ambivalent feelings about your profession. Consequently being liked by those you feel you are manipulating is attractive – it soothes the conscience. As a planner you feel best about advertisements that are liked the best.

I am arguing that as a result of this desire for approval over the years, an implicit model of advertising has grown up which is: *comprehension and approval (likeability) = persuasion.* Now in the past this held good. In a world of producer-led 'soap powder' advertising, likeable advertising often did communicate better and more persuasively – and as a result gave the client a competitive advantage in the market place. Further, those few agencies that incorporated the consumer into their production processes via planning produced better advertising – advertising that was both likeable *and* effective.

However, what was an innovation twenty-five years ago is now standard practice. All agencies now incorporate the consumer into their production. All agencies aim to produce comprehensible, likeable advertising – often saying exactly the same thing. The result is that the old model no longer holds true. Instead: *comprehension and approval = acceptance.* Increasingly, that is, approval has come to mean 'meets my expectations of a good ad' – a response usually made in a research environment. Reactions, however, in the market place (full of similar advertising) will be very different.

The tyranny of the orthodox

As I have remarked, it is a feature of the industry that there has been no fundamentally different world view of advertising articulated for the last thirty years. This has led to an (unwritten) intellectual orthodoxy that pervades the whole industry. Account planners, clever and sensitive individuals on the whole, have been schooled in the planning orthodoxy and have used the authority of the consumer to gain authority for themselves in the production process. Innovative thinking was stifled in the process of assimilation into the mainstream and of copying by competitors. The innovating agencies failed to innovate further, believing that their competitive advantage was structural. Planning became a process in itself and was not seen or understood for what it originally was – a way of giving an agency's clients a competitive advantage. The planning profession preoccupied itself with 'angels on a pin' questions whilst going through a period of rapid growth. (If planners were so much in demand, why innovate?)

This made sense in an era where a company could enjoy a substantial 'lead time' from an innovation. However, in the world of the 1990s where innovations are copied overnight, the process of innovation has to be constant – no company can afford to rest on its laurels (Tom Peters and Robert Waterman chart this change in their move from *In Search of Excellence* to *Thriving on Chaos* and *The Renewal Factor* – arguing that the company that stands still, however excellent at the time, is dead). Quite simply the planning process is at crisis point because *everyone is doing it in the same way*. It is no longer competitive – it no longer works. Planning needs to adapt to the new market conditions of the 1990s – competition, change and complexity.

THE SHIFTING BASIS OF COMPETITION: VALUES NOT PRODUCTS

We live now in an age of product and service parity. The nature of competition has changed radically over the last twenty years. First the *volume* of competition has changed. Twenty years ago IBM was estimated to have 20 competitors – now the number is closer to 5,000! Second the *speed* of competition has changed – what took a competitor a year to copy can be done in some industries in seconds, while in other industries parallel production processes mean that similar products hit the market at the same time. This means that competitive insulation has disappeared. Third, most products in many categories have a surfeit of features. Compare cars, audio equipment or even tomato soup to discover a whole range of features incorporated in what seems to be a basic offering. Comparison becomes a long-winded and extremely difficult basis for making a choice.

The consequence of all this for advertising is that competitive communication can no longer be predicated on a feature-based approach. The Unique Selling Proposition was a tangible, specific product-based claim. This, quite simply, is no longer news and no longer competitive. The basis of competition has to shift – and it is my belief that it will shift further back in the production process. What will become important as a basis for competition is the company value system. It is this that is unique, competitive and sustainable. The how and why of production will be more important than the what. The rise of the importance of 'service-based businesses' also adds impetus to this move.

Competitive advertising based on company values as opposed to product features requires a different model of communication and makes different assumptions about the consumers receiving the messages.

I will now outline five driving forces of the new advertising. As will be apparent, they represent a radically different view of the consumer, and whilst they may mean less direct incorporation of the consumer into the production process, they make key assumptions about the consumer's expertise and experience in the field of advertising.

Future advertising needs to be provocative

Today's consumer is overwhelmed by communication. People receive between 1,300 and 6,000 commercial messages a day depending on which estimate you choose. The *only* survival strategy is to edit – the brain simply cannot process and spend time on all these messages and continue with daily life. The media-literate and experienced consumer of the 1990s can decode and deconstruct the messages she/he receives and is highly familiar with particular selling modes. Advertising that meets expected norms will not evoke a response – it will be coded as normal or expected and dismissed as 'noise'. In order for advertising to be registered and for it to evoke a response it must be provocative – it must be unusual and challenge the standard advertising methods. It must *stimulate* the consumer not *reflect* the consumer.

Future advertising must tackle new areas

Advertising has for too long remained stuck in the middle-class kitchen of the 1950s. It has allowed itself to focus on the 'aspirational' and to play in 'sit-com land'. In the future, advertising will deal with issues that are called 'social' by the critics – such as discrimination, one-parent families, prejudice, conditions of employment. It will no longer be able to claim (disingenuously) that the world it has presented is above social issues. Recent campaigns for Fuji film and Bisto gravy featuring discrimination and one-parent families respectively are leading the way. Advertising will be more about the world the consumer of today lives in and will therefore broaden the range of its subject material.

Future advertising will talk to the consumer on an equal footing

The implicit model in old-fashioned advertising has been parent–child. 'We know what's best for you. Buy this product and improve your life.' The assumption is that passive consumers are sitting there anxiously waiting to be told about ways in which their lives can be transformed. Future advertising will work from a different assumption – that of the consumer as an *equal*. The consumer as equal partner in any communication means that the strategies, approaches and advertising devices will have to change.

A recent campaign for *Exchange and Mart* involves the presenter explaining that he buys goods from *Exchange and Mart* because they're cheaper than in the shops and ends with him saying, 'But you don't have to do that. You can spend as much money as you like. No skin off my nose.' This 'take it or leave it' approach is shocking in advertising as it forgoes any overtly aspirational positioning in favour of a 'we both know what's going on here' approach.

Future advertisers will take on the role of the public persuaders

The whole process of advertising and selling is now a part of contemporary culture. Papers have a regular column on advertising. TV series are made about it and feature films refer continually to it. In addition many workforces now have their company's advertising presented and explained to them. The consumers of today actively seek information on advertising and enjoy talking about it.

Advertising is part of everyday conversation. It is not feared and loathed. Surveys show it is actually respected! All this means that the era of the 'Hidden Persuaders' is well and truly past. In the new era of Public Persuaders advertising people can share their 'games' with a knowing audience. In a recent campaign for Britvic Citrus Spring the presenter is the 'client' who updates the viewer on his difficulties in getting the recalcitrant agency to do his product justice. Another campaign, for the Vauxhall Astra, gives a behind-the-scenes look at the launch of the new car model – including the creation of the end line.

It is standard practice for old-fashioned critics to worry that these are somehow 'in-jokes', understood by only a few. This worry is a legacy from the hidden persuaders era and betrays a blinkered view on the influence of advertising in today's consumer culture.

Future advertising will show more 'real' people

Casting in advertising has always been a problematic issue. In a largely male-dominated industry, working to the maxim 'date her, don't cast her' would change the look of advertising overnight. Working on the 'aspiration' assumption, the principle behind casting has often been one of showing the most attractive people possible. This is one of the main driving forces behind the 'glamour business' myth and, like the world of fashion, can be extremely seductive. It assumes a basic insecurity on the part of the consumer and, by projecting idealized examples, aims to constantly reinforce it.

Today's consumers may still have insecurities but they resent the projection of them on to the small screen. The approach is beginning to become counter-productive. Impossibly attractive models (and sets) are a good reason to ignore a message. Future advertising, in order to ensure a relationship with the consumer, will seek to portray more and more 'real' people. This will mean showing a much greater diversity of people and breaking the WASP stereotypes.

Winston Churchill called television a 'tuppenny ha'penny Punch and Judy Show', Margaret Thatcher called it the 'most powerful medium on earth'. Today's consumer is active and knowledgeable – an expert in communication and selling techniques. She/he is a long way from the passive innocent victim of the 1950s and 1960s mass-production and mass-communication techniques. Most advertising today is produced with the implicit assumptions and beliefs about people that were formed in that era. The market place, and, indeed, the world have changed dramatically and fundamentally. In the 1990s advertising will need to change in order to compete and it must draw its assumptions about competitive and effective work from an understanding of the new experienced and expert consumer.

REFERENCES

Levitt, T. (1960) 'Marketing myopia' in *Harvard Business Review* July–August.

Peters, T. (1987) *Thriving on Chaos: Handbook for a Management Revolution*, London: Macmillan.

Peters, T. and Waterman, R. H. (1982) *In Search of Excellence*, New York: Harper & Row.

Waterman, R. H. (1987) *The Renewal Factor: How to Get and Keep the Competitive Edge*, London: Bantam Books.

Chapter 6

The limits of consumption and the post-modern 'religion' of the New Age

Paul Heelas

Traditional morality only required that the individual conform to the group; advertising 'philosophy' requires that they now conform to themselves.

(Baudrillard 1988: 13)

INTRODUCTION

Religion would appear to be the very last thing that can be consumed. After all, the great religious traditions combat the temptations of human nature, including greed and self-indulgence. Thus Judaeo-Christianity sanctions discipline (the dietary rules of Leviticus or the Protestant ethic, for example). And far from being treated as being at the beck and call of demanding consumers, God has been seen as a power able to 'consume' mortals (as in Leviticus 26:16, where God announces that 'I will even appoint over you terror . . . that shall consume the eyes and cause sorrow of heart').

According to Robert Bellah, 'one aspect of the great modern transformation [of religion] involves *the internalization of authority* and . . . this has profound consequences for religion' (1991: 223). Thinking specifically of the cultural importance which has come to be attached to 'consumers', who have 'authority', the idea is that rather than God setting limits to consumer activities, and even consuming the sinful, people are increasingly treating religion as providing commodities – acting with self-informed authority to choose those components of the religious sphere which best suit their own particular consumer requirements. Commitment to the theistic order – with all the effort which that should entail – is thereby eroded by a 'what's in it for me' attitude.

Thus Peter Berger claims that in all 'pluralistic situations', where religion 'has to be marketed', 'religious traditions become consumer commodities' (1969: 138); Reginald Bibby writes about the widespread 'movement from commitment to consumption' (1990: 169); and Bryan Wilson says of new religious movements, 'Like other leisure-time pursuits, they

are a free choice which ... are part of that consumption economy in
which men can do ... "their own thing" ' (1979: 4304). Even religious
dignitaries detect the same shift: 'religion is just another commodity to
be consumed', declares Donald Reeves, Rector of St James' Anglican
Church, Piccadilly, being regarded 'on the same level as playing golf or
washing the car or belonging to Rotary' (1986: 194).

But how can people possibly be consuming religion when this has been
historically understood as something which stands firm, over and above
the antinomian desires of consuming selves? For those who consume
religion, it might be said, the voice of external, theistic, authority has
been lost, the sacred being vandalized by its subjection to utilitarian
requirements. The apparent shift from the authority of God to the
requirements of the consumer would thus appear to entail that the
religious has lost those qualities and capacities which once made it work:
obeying an Other to obtain salvation.

To explore what happens to religion when it is subjected to consumer
requirements, I first introduce the notion of 'de-traditionalization' and
discuss the general process of authority-shift. Taking up a particular,
and arresting, aspect of this process – the development of the New Age
of the contemporary west – I then move on to examine the impact of
what has been identified as the post-modern, de-traditionalized, consumer
culture. In many regards exemplifying religion as consumer-dominated,
the New Age apparently shows that it is possible to consume religion.
However, I go on to argue that much of the New Age – when it has
been influenced by the post-modern consumer culture – has transgressed
those authoritatively imposed limits which, properly speaking, belong to
religion, thereby ceasing to be religious in any significant functional sense
of the term. This is certainly the view of Wilson who writes, in one
especially acerbic passage, that 'cults', many of which are New Age,
'represent, in the American phrase, "the religion of your choice", the
highly privatised preference that reduces religion to the significance of
pushpin, poetry, or popcorn' (1979: 96). Finally, I raise broader considerations, including the possibility that certain aspects of consumer culture
may be helpful for religion as historically conceived, rather than harmful.

DE-TRADITIONALIZATION AND THE NEW AGE

Analytically speaking, social practices based on appeals to 'the traditional'
concern 'external' loci of authority which speak with force; which make
demands; which cannot be ignored without generating feelings of sin,
guilt or fear. In contrast, 'de-traditionalization' is the process whereby
the action of authority with 'internal' voice comes into prominence: pre-
eminently, the wishes, desires, ambitions, beliefs and judgements of the
autonomous, utilitarian person.

The rise of the utilitarian consumer – the 'liberated' person exercising choice in order to obtain whatever satisfies – is closely bound up with the process whereby the locus of authority, or sovereignty, shifts from without to within. Nurtured by long-standing trajectories in western history – to do with capitalism, the liberal ethic of free individualism, and the ideology of perfection – such consumers reject anything pertaining to 'the traditional' which stands in the way of what they want (cf. Bell 1980); and otherwise use 'traditions' to satisfy their own autonomously determined ends.

Concentrating on religion, the traditional concerns the most fundamental form of inviolate, external, authority; it concerns what Durkheim meant by the term 'sacred'. This is what cannot be subjected to utilitarian demands, in the sense that if it is so subjected it ceases to exist. As Parsons summarizes Durkheim's point:

> the profane activity par excellence is economic activity. The attitude of calculation of utility is the antithesis of the respect for sacred objects. From the utilitarian point of view what is more natural than that the Australian should eat and kill his totem animal? But since it is a sacred object, this is precisely what he cannot do. . . . Thus sacred things, precisely in excluding this utilitarian relationship, are hedged about with taboos and restrictions of all sorts. Religion has to do with sacred things.
>
> (Parsons 1968: 412)

Those with theistic faith must heed the voice of sacred authority, treating the voice of self-interest as harmful temptation. The marks of tradition-defined religion thus have to do with seeking salvation from an Other, learning from this Other, struggling to aspire to this Other, and practising the disciplines which, this Other announces, are essential for those seeking to escape from the profane realm of utilitarian selfhood.

In contrast, the paradigm case of de-traditionalized 'religious' life involves the religious realm being appropriated as a means to purely personal ends. Utilitarian consumers assume that they have the right to turn religion to their own advantage, selecting desirable items from this domain. Such people fit religion into their own lives, rather than attempting to change themselves in order to conform to the divine ordinance. They refuse to be challenged by the demands of religious agency, seeking instead to be indulged or entertained. Such people can be said to 'consume' religion because it provides them with what they happen to want. In that the authority of what is required from on high is ignored, they are no longer 'believers' in the traditional sense. They have become their own 'judges'.

The New Age provides an excellent illustration of the authority shift to the self. (The question of the extent to which it is therefore consumer-dominated is taken up later.) Utilizing spiritual practices drawn from a global range of sources, the New Age first strikes one as extremely heterogeneous (from the austerities of Zen meditation to the heat of fire-walking). However, at the ('genuine') heart of New Age spirituality lies a distinctive *lingua franca*, largely bound up with 'self religiosity' (see Heelas 1991b, 1992, etc.). God – or whatever other term is used to describe Ultimacy – is located 'within', primarily within the person but also within the natural order as a whole. The God–Self is variously described as perfect, wise, energized, powerful and peaceful. The true Self is contrasted with the mere 'ego' or personality, namely that which has been imposed on our vital nature by virtue of socialization.

The logical outcome of de-traditionalization it appears – with regard to religion – is to locate God within, where spiritual agency can enhance true 'human' authority. And the New Age, if advocates are to be believed, is significantly de-traditionalized. Self-religiosity denies any value to *all* those authoritative voices which speak from beyond the in-dwelling spiritual substance, not least the pronouncements of educationalists, politicians, and theistic Christians. Ethical decision-making becomes a matter of heeding one's 'intuition' (to use the favoured term), thereby 'getting in touch with' the sole source of truth and wisdom, in-dwelling spirituality (cf. Tipton 1982, on the 'expressive ethic'; Bellah *et al.* on 'Sheilaism', a religion named after a person whose faith is 'just my own little voice', 1985: 221).

It should be emphasized here that the New Age is not a fringe curiosity. Long in the making (its roots include the Romantic tradition) and highlighting themes to do with the individualistic ideology of the contemporary west, it is now firmly entrenched as a cultural and practical resource. Economic considerations alone show that countless workshops, seminars, retreats, publications and so forth would not exist, let alone be thriving as the millennium draws to a close, were it not for the fact that demand is strong. It can safely be concluded that millions of westerners have turned to the New Age since the mid-1960s, if only on a relatively casual, 'let's try it' basis.[1]

THE NEW AGE AS A POST-MODERN 'RELIGION' OF THE CONSUMER CULTURE

Turning to the extent to which the New Age is consumer-dominated, I will now suggest that it is the 'religion' of what has been described as the post-modern consumer culture. This 'privatized and commodified' vehicle of expectation, as Zygmunt Bauman (1991: 261) describes it, is 'dominated by the postmodern values of novelty, of rapid (preferably inconsequential and episodic) change, of individual enjoyment and consumer choice' (ibid.: 278). Given that participants think of themselves as having considerable freedom and authority-cum-power, it is not surprising that those who consider religious matters assume that they have the right to bring this domain into the orbit of their self-gratificatory activities.

Looking more closely at the culture under consideration, Mike Featherstone writes that it is composed of 'a vast floating complex of fragmentary signs and images' (1991a: 3). An 'endless sign-play which destabilizes long-held symbolic meanings and cultural order' is thereby produced (ibid.). The negative effects of this de-traditionalization are – at least in measure – compensated for by the fact that 'consumer culture uses images, signs and symbolic goods which summon up dreams, desires and fantasies which suggest romantic authenticity and emotional fulfilment in narcissistically pleasing oneself' (1991b: 27). The culture is one with 'a strong emphasis... upon the sensory overload, the aesthetic immersion, dreamlike perceptions of de-centred subjects, in which people open themselves up to a wider range of sensations and emotional experiences' (ibid.: 24). It is a culture which 'has given rise to a depthless hallucinatory simulational world which has effaced the distinction between the real and the imaginary' (1991a: 4).

Featherstone notes that 'these experiences are generally held to take place within the context of consumer culture leisure' (ibid.: 11): the 'dream worlds' (as Walter Benjamin called them) of department stores and shopping arcades; theme parks, as exemplified by Disneyland; heritage sites; and so forth. Television and video machines (etc.), of course, are held to contribute significantly to the typical modes of experience of this culture. So does through-the-screen travel, John Urry (1990) arguing that tourists now typically 'consume' by way of their 'gaze'.

Little attention is paid to religion in the analysis of consumer culture.[2] However, theorists such as Featherstone (1991b: 21, 35), Daniel Bell (1980: 288–9), David Harvey (1989: 38, 63), and Fredric Jameson (1991: xvi, xx, 1, 4, *passim*) have explicitly associated post-modern developments with the '1960s', the time when counter-culturalists were rejecting the established authority structures and 'sacred' (in Durkheim's sense) features of the mainstream in order to find the freedom to express themselves. This is significant for my argument, since the New Age itself (the 'Age of Aquarius' as it was then called) came into prominence with the counter-culture.

Nevertheless, the majority of those who use New Age resources today do not themselves belong to the counter-culture as it now exists. They might have once been '1960s' people', but the majority are now what Featherstone (following Pierre Bourdieu) calls the 'new cultural intermediaries' of the post-modern consumer culture: 'the marketing, advertising, public relations, radio and television producers, presenters, magazine journalists, fashion writers, and the helping professions (social workers,

marriage guidance counsellors, sex therapists, dieticians, play leaders, etc.)'
(Featherstone 1991b: 44).[3]

Typically, these people are part-time New Agers, trying out a wide
range of appropriate goods whilst also enjoying other forms of consumer
activity (cf. Campbell 1972: 128–9). Few are seekers, moving from path
to path on a spiritual quest; even fewer are believers, engaged by specific
spiritual paths.

Favouring radically de-traditionalized, that is non-authoritative, forms
of New Age provision, these often utilitarian consumers are able to
enjoy what is on offer without being subjected to the commitments and
disciplines required by religion as historically conceived in terms of the
'traditional'. Indeed, such people do not even have to worry about having
to 'believe' in what they are doing. They are told that it is 'experience'
that matters, not 'belief', the latter being associated with the intellect,
and thus with the false, 'ego' level of life.

An excellent illustration of the 'consumer-friendly' nature of much of
the New Age, providing experiences 'beyond belief' without requiring
commitment, is provided by the following extract from *The Independent*
(18 April 1992). It concerns a workshop called 'Getting What You Want',
one participant afterwards reporting, 'I've enjoyed myself. . . . You could
spend £10 in the pub. This is more fun. It's irrelevant to me whether he
[the leader] is genuine'.

In accord with the consumeristic ideology that it is possible to buy
pretty well anything, the denizens of consumer culture pay for New Age
commodities to make their dreams come true. And they can turn to
countless New Age programmes, some promising 'spirituality' ('Instant
Enlightenment Including VAT' as author Andrew Carr puts it in the
title of his play); others promising perfection with regard to the more
psychological aspects of life ('fulfilled existence', 'energy', or
'tranquillity'); and yet others to 'transform' participants so that they
have the 'power' to obtain more secular commodities ('God is unlimited.
Shopping can be unlimited'). As Paul Vitz has noted, 'Most of the short
expressions and catch-words' in use make 'excellent advertising copy: *Do
it now! Have a new experience! Honour thyself!*' (1981: 60).

Looking more closely at what is on offer, a major area of growth
concerns what I call 'experiential holidays'. Managers go on outward
(whilst inward) bound trainings; wealthy professionals go to health resorts
epitomized by Champneys (now introducing New Age components); less
well-off professionals go to live in the tepees of 'holistic educational
camps'; others go to the Greek island of Skyros. Such contexts provide
the opportunity for people to *taste* things missing from their everyday lives
– ex-counter-culturalists, for example, participating in holistic educational
camps so that they can relive the 'Woodstock' experience. These experiential holidays, it can be noted, often use props of the kind found in

that (supposed) exemplar of post-modern consumer culture, Disneyland: tepees, 'fake' stone circles, and so on.[4]

The flavour of New Age consumption is also captured by how 'travellers', and some 'ravers', use hallucinogens: literally consumed in order to have spiritually 'significant' experiences. That they need not be especially committed to religion does not prevent them from enjoying their (paid for) 'spirituality' (see Stevens 1988). Their attitude seems to be 'what is the drug going to do for me?', the hope being that it will transport users to that enchanted 'Fantasia' where the magical is manifested. Such usage perhaps provides the best possible illustration of Featherstone's 'hallucinatory simulational world which . . . efface[s] the distinction between the real and the imaginary'.

More generally, part-time New Agers might select a workshop to experience what it is like to have mystical power (' "become" a shaman'); buy New Age music to 'take in' the experience of being peaceful; obtain a crystal to experience energy; practise rebirthing to experience 'physical immortality'; go on courses to experience their natural emotions; or do any number of other things in order to 'consume' the wealth of experiences that (supposedly) lie with the perfect realm within. (See also Fox and Jackson Lears, writing of the cultural context in which people 'even conceive of their own selves as commodities' (1983: xii).)

Cyra McFadden's ethnographic novel, *The Serial* (1978), chronicles the life of Featherstone's new cultural intermediaries. Set in Marin County (located just to the north of San Francisco), it graphically portrays how New Age components quite naturally take their place alongside all the other perfectibility items of the consumer culture of this enclave: the therapies, the affairs, the parties, the carrot cake, the hair-dressers ('Sheer Ecstasy'), the Revere Ware asparagus steamers, and so on.[5] New Age components are not marked out as being in any sense 'sacred'; they are simply there to be used – to bring about desirable states of consciousness, and, for that matter, to show you know 'where it's at':

> involved in the human-potential movement, she had like *mutated* over the years through Gurdjieff, Human Life Styling, hatha and raja yoga . . . and Feldenkrais functional integration. Currently she was commuting to Berkeley twice a week for 'polarity balancing manipulation', which, she reported through her annual mimeographed Christmas letter, produces 'good thinking'.
>
> (ibid.: 42)

Overall, much of the New Age bears the marks of post-modern consumer culture. New Age activities have been plucked out of the 'high' (and 'native') traditions to which they once belonged; have been reformulated and packaged for contemporary use; and purchased as commodities, provide as their main value *experiences* of what life can be like –

spectacles, simulations, sensations. It is surely not coincidental that Ron Hubbard (the founder of the Church of Scientology, and an important influence on the New Age) was, apparently, close to Walt Disney, both being adept at stimulating the experiential. (See Jameson's 'commodity rush', 1991: x.)

On this account, the New Age is a pepped-up aspect of the heritage industry, raiding the past to help construct all sorts of novel packages (one of my favourites is 'Zencounter', a mixture of Zen and encounter therapy) in order to cater for people who, in the words of Featherstone, are 'fascinated by identity, presentation, appearances, lifestyle, and the endless quest for new experiences' (1991b: 44; see Bauman 1991: 278; Jameson 1991: 18–19). And the potency of many New Age programmes (and, sometimes, that old standby, drugs) means that people can experience what is on offer, albeit briefly, as 'virtual reality', the distinction between the real and the imaginary being effectively erased.[6]

As for the objection that I have been over-emphasizing the utilitarian aspect of the New Age – drawing attention to provision of delights rather than demanding spiritual disciplines – it is not without significance that there is a distinct flavour of de-traditionalized consumer religiosity in settings where one might expect the spiritual quest to be taken seriously. For example, Glastonbury lies at the heart of New Age spirituality in Britain. Nevertheless, a leading New Age inhabitant is surely correct to adopt an irreverent tone, emphasizing the entertainment value of the place:

> People come to celebrate the solstices and equinoxes, to set up alternative or spiritual communities, and to make magic. There are self-styled magicians, wandering witches, weirdo warlocks, masochistic meditators and reincarnations of everything from Queen Guinevere to the latest version of the 'new Christ'. It's all good fun, a bit of a circus, and living here, especially during the summer months, has been aptly described as living in the middle of a pack of Tarot cards.
>
> (Howard-Gordon 1982)

RELIGIOUS SIGNIFICANCE

Is this kind of 'religiosity' significantly religious? The answer must be 'no'. The reason is that the religious cannot perform its historically ascribed tasks unless it has a 'sacred' (in Durkheim's sense) voice of its *own*.

Daniel Bell writes, 'The ground of religion is existential: the awareness of men in their finiteness and the inexorable limits to their powers, and the consequent effort to find a coherent answer to reconcile them to that human condition' (1977: 447). Furthermore, religion is about turning to some Other – other than how one happens to be – to find ways of transcending the limitations of the human condition, a condition which, in itself, is problematic.

To consume religion, turning to de-traditionalized forms (New Age or others, such as 'pop' Christianity) in order to satisfy the utilitarian self, is to lose sight of the sacred. This means that there is no longer any religious authority to perform what Rodney Stark calls 'the fundamental functions of faith' (1991: 202): such functions as providing firm guidelines concerning individual and group morality, alleviating existential anxieties, and providing people with the information which they require in order to save themselves from themselves.

No doubt there has always been a utility aspect to religious life, but for religion to be religion in any significant functional sense of the term there must be limits to the extent to which it panders to the consumer. It is a contradiction in terms to speak of 'consuming *religion*'; and if so, it follows that there is no such thing as post-modern *religion*. To the extent that the New Age is consumer-dominated – a form of part-time escapism, akin to 'discovering' the world as a tourist – it is not significantly religious. Thus I agree with Bell, who concludes that 'These [various New Age organizations as they can be called] are not religions' (1977: 443).

Thus far I have dwelt on the utilitarian, 'part-time' users. But there are also adherents who are 'genuine' spiritual seekers. Instead of treating what the New Age has to offer as a consuming delight, they attempt to transcend their utilitarian (or 'ego') level of functioning in order to experience the God which lies within.

In that they claim to reject external, socioculturally embedded, voices of authority, such New Agers are post-traditional. At the same time, however, they heed that *internal* voice of authority, the Self itself. Lying beyond the 'ego', this can (supposedly) function as a true *foundation*; as a salvational Other of a kind which does not belong to the post-modern condition. By exercising their 'intuition', New Agers (supposedly) acquire wisdom. 'Experience' tells them that they should try to avoid hedonistic attachments; 'experience' speaks of the importance of living in 'harmony' with nature. The God within acts in *sacred* (and thus in a sense 'tradition'-informed) fashion, it being noted that it serves to limit consumption. You do what you 'sense' is right (becoming a vegan, for example) but not what is merely enjoyable.

In short, whereas the utilitarian thrust of consumer culture has encouraged radical de-traditionalization, and thus the collapse of *religion*, 'genuine' self-religiosity is not comprehensively de-traditionalized. In other words, although the teaching encourages rejection of sociocultural voices, great importance is attached to the voice of an Other – in-dwelling spirituality – which can (supposedly) serve to regulate utilitarian nature: thereby functioning in *sacred* fashion.

CONCLUDING OBSERVATIONS

Discussing Rodney Stark and William Bainbridge's (1987) sociological-cum-psychological account of religion, John Simpson draws attention to how it relies on 'the celebration of the autonomous, pragmatic actor who both uses and adjusts to each situation' (1990: 371). When the actor cannot obtain 'rewards' by way of naturalistic means, he or she 'if only momentarily, latches onto a compensator, or indeed invents a compensator, and more or less convinces herself that for the time being things are all right' (ibid.).

Even if it is true that people always 'use' religion in the blanket sense that they are seeking 'rewards' (such as life after death), this should not be allowed to disguise significant differences in the interplay between 'users' and various forms of religious life. (See Robertson's (1992) perceptive assessment of the significance of the utility thesis.)

When I travel from the Yorkshire Dales, where I live, to do research in Glastonbury or London, I move from one religious world to another. The hill farmers of the Dales, surrounding my home, are primitive Methodists. Obeying the dictates of their God, which include strictly disciplining consumer activities, it does not make much sense to envisage them exercising their own authority, treating religion as something to be consumed. But in London, at the New Age 'Festival for Body Mind and Spirit', for example, things are very different.

As for what is happening between the extremes of primitive Methodism (etc.) and the New Age, there is little doubt that de-traditionalization (with consumerism playing an important role) has made a significant impact on the sacred. In the US, for example, the religious climate is now very different from the early Calvinistic days. A 1978 Gallup Poll found that 80 per cent of the population agree with the statement that 'An individual should arrive at his or her own religious beliefs independently of any churches or synagogues' (cited by Bellah 1983:xi). Although not many Christians would appear to 'consume' or 'play' with religion in the fashion of the post-modern New Age, there is a strong case to be made that radical individualism is now operative within the Christian context. As Wade Clark Roof and William McKinney put it,

> Of all the recent religious changes in America, few are more significant, or more subtle, than the enhanced religious individualism of our time. . . . Today choice means more than simply having an option among religious alternatives; it involves religion as an option itself and an opportunity to draw selectively off a variety of traditions in the pursuit of the self.[7]
>
> (1987:40)

However, researchers have also drawn attention to the vitality of traditional, consumer-resistant faith (cf. Davidman 1991). An interesting possibility in this regard is that the 'consumerization' of religion – that 'religious institutions should serve individuals, not vice versa', as Roof and McKinney (op. cit.: 50) put it – can serve to enhance traditional religiosity. The sociocultural pluralism of America encourages competition, and this in turn prompts religious organizations to present themselves in an appealing fashion. Participation therefore increases (see Finke and Stark 1988). Once people have been attracted – say to a church which has presented itself as providing status – they find themselves responding to the traditional theism which remains tucked away behind the packaging. Much the same argument, it can be noted, applies to some of the New Age seminars and the like, initially attracting participants by way of consumer-orientated advertising, and then employing potent 'transformational' processes to convert people to 'genuine' self-religiosity (see Heelas 1987).

Yet despite this 'consumer friendly but with an authoritative punch' scenario, it is nevertheless possible that the consumerization of religion is a self-limiting process. Granted that religion, to perform its soteriological functions, has to be in a position to do something about the deficiencies of the human condition, the more consumeristic it is the less the likelihood of it being able to cater for those seeking salvation. Consumer religion could well be self-limiting in that there will always (one assumes) be significant numbers wanting to be saved for both existential and psychological reasons, rather than simply seeking ways of indulging themselves (see Bell 1977 on 'the return of the sacred').

But this should not be taken to imply that the consumer-dominated version of the New Age amounts to a self-defeating development. So long as there is a consumer market to cater for, especially in its postmodern cultural form, spiritual Disneylands will thrive. Ignoring tradition-based limits to consumption, they cannot operate as religion. The pay-off, however, lies with what can therefore be offered – provisions for those intent on 'narcissistically pleasing themselves'.

NOTES

1 An indication of the extent to which the New Age has become established is provided by the fact that in most Waterstone-like bookshops the New Age section is as big as, if not bigger than, the Management/Business section; another is that a 1989 Gallup Poll claimed that there are an estimated 10 or 12 million New Agers in the USA. See Heelas (1991b, 1992) for more information, including material on the New Age as a whole.
2 Exceptions include Dobbelaere and Voye (1990), Featherstone (1991b: 113–22) and O'Neill (1988).
3 People working in the mainstream who are attracted to the New Age also include teachers and managers (see Heelas 1991a, 1992, on the latter).

4 A good illustration, which shows how difficult it is becoming to distinguish between pilgrims and tourists, concerns Hare Krishna (a movement with New Age affinities). It runs a recreational and spiritual retreat centre in West Virginia, which has become the second most popular tourist attraction in this state (Robbins and Bromley 1991: 194).

5 This feature – New Age items taking their place alongside other secular goods – is becoming increasingly common in Britain. For example, a recent edition of *Impression. The Magazine for the Best Things in Life* (Summer 1992) runs adverts ranging from 'French Beds' to 'Aromatherapy and Reflexology'.

6 I have not been able to do justice to the growing literature on the consumeristic aspects of the New Age. Bell (1976, 1977, 1980), Campbell (1987), Jameson (1991) and Lasch (1976, 1980, 1985) provide excellent accounts of the general cultural setting, with references to what would now be called New Age developments. Wallis (1984) explores how 'world-affirming' movements put spirituality to work to satisfy secular consumer requirements (cf. Heelas 1991a). In terms of the more popular literature, Wolfe (1990) writes of the 'Me Decade'; Ruthven (1989) portrays the New Age in California (cf. Heelas 1982, on Marin County); Snow (1991) dwells on Oxford; Greenwald (1990) and Mehta (1990) turn to the eastern homelands of the movement (cf. Smith 1992); and Storm (1991) provides an overview of the 'prosperous self'. One of the most arresting New Age documents is Ray's *How to be Chic, Fabulous and Live Forever* (1990).

7 For more material on the widespread consumerization of religion, in particular in America, see Schneider and Dornbusch on the history of movements which 'give the people what they want' (1958: 141); Bruce (1990) on 'pray TV'; Dawson (1990) on 'active conversion'; Edmondson (1988) on born-again Christians as 'consumers'; Hammond (1992) on 'personal autonomy' and the 'third disestablishment'; Iannaccone (1992) on the exercise of 'rational choice'; Luckmann (1990) on 'shrinking transcendence'; McGuire (1992) on 'privatization'; Roof and McKinney (1987) on 'the new voluntarism'; Swatos (1983) on 'pseudo-enchantment'; and Wilson (1991) on the charismatic movement.

REFERENCES

Baudrillard, J. (1988) *Selected Writings*, Cambridge: Polity.

Bauman, Z. (1991) *Modernity and Ambivalence*, Cambridge: Polity.

Bell, D. (1976) *The Cultural Contradictions of Capitalism*, London: Heinemann.

—— (1977) 'The return of the sacred? The argument on the future of religion', *British Journal of Sociology* 28 (2): 419–49.

—— (1980) *Sociological Journeys*, London: Heinemann.

Bellah, R. (1983) 'Introduction', M. Douglas and S. Tipton (eds) *Religion and America*, Boston: Beacon, i–xiii.

—— (1991) *Beyond Belief*, Oxford: University of California Press.

Bellah, R., Madsen, R., Sullivan, W., Swidler, A. and Tipton, S. (1985) *Habits of the Heart*, London: University of California Press.

Berger, P. (1969) *The Sacred Canopy*, New York: Anchor.

Bibby, R. (1990) *Fragmented Gods*, Toronto: Stoddart.

Bruce, S. (1990) *Pray TV*, London: Routledge.

Campbell, C. (1972) 'The cult, the cultic milieu and secularization' in M. Hill (ed.) *Sociological Yearbook of Religion in Britain*, London: SCM Press, 119–36.

—— (1987) *The Romantic Ethic and the Spirit of Modern Consumerism*, Oxford: Basil Blackwell.

Davidman, L. (1991) *Tradition in a Rootless World*, Oxford: University of California Press.

Dawson, L. (1990) 'Self-affirmation, freedom, and rationality: theoretically elaborating "active" conversions', *Journal for the Scientific Study of Religion* 29 (2): 141–63.

Dobbelaere, K. and Voye, L. (1990) 'From pillar to postmodernity: the changing situation of religion in Belgium', *Sociological Analysis* 51(S): 1–13.

Edmondson, B. (1988) 'Bringing in the sheaves', *American Demographics*, August, 28–32, 57–8.

Featherstone, M. (1991a) 'Postmodernism, consumer-culture and the search for fundamentals', paper delivered to UNESCO Conference on 'People in Search of Fundamentals'.

—— (1991b) *Consumer Culture and Postmodernism*, London: Sage.

Finke, R. and Stark, R. (1988) 'Religious economies and sacred canopies: religious mobilization in American cities, 1906', *American Sociological Review* 53 (Feb.): 41–9.

Fox, R. and T. Jackson Lears (ed.) (1983) 'Introduction', *The Culture of Consumption*, New York: Pantheon, ix–xvii.

Greenwald, J. (1990) *Shopping for Buddhas*, London: Harper & Row.

Hammond, P. (1992) *Religion and Personal Autonomy*, Columbia: University of South Carolina Press.

Harvey, D. (1989) *The Condition of Postmodernity*, Oxford: Basil Blackwell.

Heelas, P. (1982) 'Californian self religions and socializing the subjective', in E. Barker (ed.), *New Religious Movements*, New York: Edwin Mellen, 69–85.

—— (1987) 'Exegesis: methods and aims', in P. Clarke (ed.) *The New Evangelists*, London: Ethnographica, 17–41.

—— (1991a) 'Cults for capitalism. Self religions, magic and the empowerment of business', in P. Gee and J. Fulton (eds) *Religion and Power. Decline and Growth*, London: British Sociological Association, 27–41.

—— (1991b) 'The New Age, values and modernity', paper delivered to UNESCO Conference on 'People in Search of Fundamentals'.

—— (1992) 'The sacralization of the self and New Age capitalism', in N. Abercrombie and A. Warde (eds) *Social Change in Contemporary Britain*, Cambridge: Polity, 139–66.

Howard-Gordon, F. (1982) *Glastonbury: Maker of Myth*, Glastonbury: Gothic Image.

Iannaccone, L. (1992) 'Religious markets and the economics of religion', *Social Compass* 39 (1): 123–31.

Jameson, F. (1991) *Postmodernism*, London: Verso.

Lasch, C. (1976) 'The narcissist society', *New York Review of Books* (30 September): 5, 8, 10–13.

—— (1980) *The Culture of Narcissism*, London: Abacus.

—— (1985) *The Minimal Self*, London: Pan.

Luckmann, T. (1990) 'Shrinking transcendence, expanding religion?', *Sociological Analysis* 50 (2): 127–38.

McFadden, C. (1978) *The Serial*, London: Pan.

McGuire, M. (1992) *Religion: The Social Context*, Belmont: Wadsworth.

Mehta, G. (1990) *Karma Cola*, London: Mandarin.

O'Neill, J. (1988) 'Religion and postmodernism: the Durkheimian bond in Bell and Jameson', in *Postmodernism*, special issue of *Theory, Culture and Society* 5 (2–3): 493–508.

Parsons, T. (1968) *The Structure of Social Action*, vol. 1, London: Collier-Macmillan.

Ray, S. (1990) *How to be Chic, Fabulous and Live Forever*, Berkeley: Celestial Arts.

Reeves, D. (1986) 'Radical Christianity', in T. Moss (ed.) *In Search of Christianity*, London: Firethorn, 192–200.

Robbins, T. and Bromley, R. (1991) 'New religious movements and the sociology of religion', in Bromley, D. (ed.) *Religion and the Social Order*, vol. 1, London: JAI Press.

Robertson, R. (1992) 'The economization of religion? Reflections on the promise and limitations of the economic approach', *Social Compass* 39 (1): 147–57.

Roof, W. C. and McKinney, W. (1987) *American Mainline Religion*, London: Rutgers University Press.

Ruthven, M. (1989) *The Divine Supermarket*, London: Chatto & Windus.

Schneider, L. and Dornbusch, S. (1958) *Popular Religion*, Chicago: University of Chicago Press.

Simpson, J. (1990) 'The Stark-Bainbridge theory of religion', *Journal for the Scientific Study of Religion* 29 (3): 367–71.

Smith, D. (1992) 'The pre-modern and the post-modern – some parallels', paper delivered to 'Traditions and Identities' workshop, Centre for the Study of Cultural Values.

Snow, P. (1991) *Oxford Observed*, London: John Murray.

Stark, R. (1991) 'Modernization, secularization, and Mormon success', in R. Robbins and D. Anthony (eds) *In Gods We Trust*, New Brunswick: Transaction, 201–17.

Stark, R. and Bainbridge, W. (1987) *A Theory of Religion*, New York: Peter Lang.

Stevens, J. (1988) *Storming Heaven*, London: Paladin.

Storm, R. (1991) *In Search of Heaven on Earth*, London: Bloomsbury.

Swatos, W. (1983) 'Enchantment and disenchantment in modernity', *Sociological Analysis*, 321–37.

Tipton, S. (1982) *Getting Saved from the Sixties*, London: University of California Press.

Urry, J. (1990) *The Tourist Gaze*, London: Sage.

Vitz, P. (1981) *Psychology as Religion*, Tring: Lion.

Wallis, R. (1984) *The Elementary Forms of the New Religious Life*, London: Routledge & Kegan Paul.

Wilson, B. (1979) *Contemporary Transformations of Religion*, Oxford: Clarendon Press.

—— (1991) 'Religion and culture', *Schweiz. Z. Soziol./Rev. suisse sociol* 3: 433–49.

Wolfe, T. (1990) *Mauve Gloves and Madmen, Clutter and Vine*, London: Pan.

Part Two

Consuming culture

Chapter 7

High art and the high street

The 'commerce-and-culture' debate

Nigel Whiteley

INTRODUCTION

Traditionally, high culture was a sphere separate from consuming. A spectator was supposed to *contemplate* or *study*, say, paintings and sculptures in an art gallery in silence and, often, solitude. A serious spectator was expected to acquire the correct *type* of knowledge by studying the discipline, movement or artist, and comparing particular works. Authority resided in the authorial artwork, with meanings ascribed it by the creator and debated by professionals, such as art historians and museum curators.

How does the new, supposed authority of the *consumer* affect high culture? In an age of ideological and rhetorical 'consumer sovereignty', is the very notion of high culture anachronistic, alienating and elitist? Has the way we think of high culture been changed by the new consumer's empowerment and subsequent sense of authority? What marks out high culture as different from consuming? Is the idea of high culture something we should fight to retain?

This chapter addresses some of these issues by examining the thesis, widely adopted by critics and professionals, that commerce and culture are drawing together and becoming indistinguishable. What is the basis of the thesis? What are its values and ideology? And what are its implications?

THE COMMERCE-AND-CULTURE THESIS

'As the twentieth century ends, commerce and culture are coming closer together', declared Stephen Bayley, at the time the chief executive and driving force behind the Design Museum. 'The distinction between life and art has been eroded by fifty years of enhanced communications, ever-improving reproduction technologies and increasing wealth' (Bayley 1989: 7). Bayley's sentiments are contained in his essay in *Commerce and Culture*, the catalogue to the opening exhibition of the much vaunted Design Museum, in 1989. This exhibition, Bayley continued, 'sets the agenda for the Design Museum' (ibid.: 5). Therefore, its arguments can be taken as a serious and considered statement of its own influential position regarding culture, commerce and the consumer.

In spite of his penchant for polemical statements and newsworthy claims, Bayley's thesis was – and is – widely held: art, design, commerce and consumption are becoming irrevocably fused in the late twentieth century. We now, so the argument goes, *consume* culture whereas once we had genuflected in front of it in its austere and remote temples. And how could this new accessibility for culture be anything but democratic and anti-elitist? Here was material evidence of the power of the consumer who was demanding a changed relationship to culture and cultural institutions: evidence that the consumer triumphed not only in the market place but in the temples of the Muses.

The thesis that commerce and culture are not distinct, but positively thrive on one another is put forward by Bayley as historically normal. This was the case, he argues, before industrialization, and it has become the case in the post-industrial age:

> The stigmatisation of commerce and the consequent separation of art from industry is historically specific – a consequence of the social and technical upheavals brought about by mass production – and would have been unintelligible to artists and patrons of the past. Once, commerce and culture were all one. In the future it looks as though they will be one again.
>
> (ibid.: 5)

Modernism, it follows from this thesis, is the lacuna in the relationship between commerce and culture, and, with the death of modernism, we have the reinvigoration of the relationship.

The commerce-and-culture thesis offers different levels and types of relationship between the two parts, and these need to be separated out. First is the idea that commerce and culture are becoming harder to tell apart. Second, the view that the most creative and vital culture arises out of the conditions of commerce and competition. And third, that the traditional *role* of high art has been usurped by some of the manifestations of commerce.

The first relationship, and the one that Bayley cites as the starting point for his thesis is

> the curious observation that the gap between shops and museums is closing. Shops are becoming more 'cultural', as anybody who has been to Ralph Lauren's Madison Avenue store can testify. Here you find merchandise for sale side-by-side with a permanent exhibition about values and style, set in an environment somewhat reminiscent of the Frick.
>
> (ibid.: 5)

He compares this to the Metropolitan Museum, a few blocks away, where 'the first thing you hear when you cross the threshold is the whirr of cash-registers, evidence of a mighty commercial machine running at considerable speed' (ibid.: 5). Bayley also gives the example of Chicago's Bloomingdale's store which has each floor 'inspired by an original building by Frank Lloyd Wright' (ibid.: 51). A further example offered by Bayley is the collaboration between the Victoria and Albert Museum and Habitat: Habitat bought the right to use the Museum's textile collections as source material for a new consumer range called the 'Habitat/V&A Collection'; as part of the deal Habitat sponsored an exhibition entitled 'The Textiles of the Arts and Crafts Movement'.

In this relationship of commerce and culture, commercial opportunism is confused with cultural value. What the examples reveal is little more than the use of culture as a form of legitimization for the professional middle-class consumer – a cashing-in of cultural capital. Bloomingdale's have 'themed' their store with cultural references appropriate to the aspirations and social positioning of their clientele, whereas another store may have adopted a Disney or Civil War theme. And while design-conscious stores realize the value-added appeal of cultural references, museums have been forced to become more commercial to bolster income. Bayley does not deny this reason for change but, indeed, approves of its effect and possibilities:

> traditional museums are realising the hidden value of their collections, treating them not merely as cabinets of curios, nor even as a scholarly resource, but ever more frequently as assets which can be reproduced, merchandised and marketed. Knowledge is valuable and both shops and museums are realising it. Shops by adding quality of experience to the banal exchange of goods for money; museums by selling information and maybe, one day, even selling objects too. . . .
>
> (ibid.: 7)

The lucky consumer would not notice the seamless transition between up-market department store and museum, and so would not have to transform from being a consumer to being a spectator. The institutions would unite in offering the possibility of purchase and consumption. What is lost is a *type of engagement* that high culture offers, and a homogenization of experience – a criticism to which I shall return.

The second argument put forward to support the commerce-and-culture thesis is the belief that the best art of the twentieth century has arisen out of direct commercial circumstances. Flair, imagination and creativity have produced television, billboard and magazine commercials which, the argument goes, are more than the equal of the inaccessible and irrelevant indulgences of fine artists. From the Surrealist-inspired Benson and Hedges adverts, to the nostalgically evocative Levi jeans ads, the new creative commercials 'do not make an offer for sale, but rather seek to provide *ambience* and layers of imagery for the consumer to decode. In them texture is at least as important as message' (ibid.: 12). In line with the commerce-and-culture thesis, the 'people with real visual talent don't bother to call themselves artists; these people are too busy making potent modern art, like television commercials' (Bayley 1979b: 262).

Nor is it just commercials that rate as sophisticated and significant culture. Bayley had previously applied his thesis to industrially produced products in his book *In Good Shape* (1979). Celebrating, in the book's subtitle, 'style in industrial products from 1900 to 1960', Bayley attacked contemporary fine art for its obscurantism, arguing that 'the man who designed the Julius tomb would find that he had more in common with the methods, processes and aims that Raymond Loewy employed while recasting the Gestetner duplicator, than with someone stacking bricks in the name of "art" '. He writes of designers' 'powerful visual imaginations and persuasive intellectual skills', claiming that to 'design a vacuum cleaner which remains more or less unchanged visually and mechanically for nearly 60 years is a towering intellectual achievement' (Bayley 1979a: 10). Not only is industrial design today 'the best art we have' (ibid.: 12), but it is '*the* art of the twentieth century' (ibid.: 10). While denying neither the creativity in design, nor its contribution to visual pleasure in our daily lives, I would again argue that it cannot *replace* (although it has *displaced*) the type of engagement of high culture.

The third, related argument in the thesis is that the commercial arts and popular culture have come to play the *role* that fine art once played in our society. They are the principal outlet for imagination and the closest approximation to a shared symbolic order. This point of view can be traced back to the origins of Pop art in the mid–1950s, and were expressed clearly by the artist Richard Hamilton who, in 1961, noted

> the ability of the mass entertainment machine to protect, perhaps more pervasively than has ever before been possible, the classic themes of artistic vision, and to mark them in a poetic language which marks them with a precise cultural date stamp. It is the *Playboy* 'Playmate of the month' pull-out pin-up which provides us with the closest contemporary equivalent of the odalisque in painting. Automobile body stylists have absorbed the symbolism of the space age more successfully than any artist. Social comment is left to the comic strip and T.V. Epic has become synonymous with a certain kind of film and the heroic archetype is now buried deep in movie lore.
>
> (Hamilton 1982: 42)

However – and this is a crucial point – Hamilton did not see commerce replacing or even merging with culture, and his comments served as a warning to the artist if 'he is not to lose much of his ancient purpose' (ibid.: 42). As far as Hamilton was concerned, the answer was for the artist 'to plunder the popular arts to recover the imagery which is his rightful inheritance' (ibid.: 148). For Bayley and other proponents of the commerce-and-culture persuasion, no such recovery would be possible as the changes were historically and economically inevitable – as well as being socially and culturally desirable.

It is interesting to compare Hamilton's position about commerce and culture at the time when popular culture was impinging itself on high culture, with the present. Discussing his work in relation to advertising in 1992, Hamilton confirmed that there 'was a time when I thought advertising was much more interesting than art' (BBC 1992) because it dealt with myths, themes and ideas, and that art had to fight to reclaim its territory. But, in response to a question as to whether advertising was the best culture we now have, Hamilton asserted that 'a painter has to produce this artefact which shows his peculiar understanding of his condition of life, but also the condition of life of humanity in general'. Art and advertising – culture and commerce – were, in Hamilton's view, separate and distinct spheres, although each could trade on the other. Ultimately, however, in spite of commerce's use of culture, the more significant culture will result from the artist examining commerce: 'I think it is much more likely that, in the future, people will look at advertising through the eyes of the artist who has looked at it, and registered some thoughts about it – it won't work the other way.' Recent examples which confirm Hamilton's argument are the work of Jenny Holzer, Barbara Kruger and Cindy Sherman. The telling difference, for Hamilton and other 'critical' artists, was the way in which culture distances itself from the predominant forces in society, and offers some generalizations about society's condition.

Until the growing dominance of the commerce-and-culture approach, it would have been unnecessary to point out the broader roles that culture can play in society. But because these are now dismissed by its opponents as either elitist, marginal or anachronistic, it is important to rehearse them. Doing this will help to locate the commerce-and-culture approach ideologically and historically.

THE CASE FOR HIGH CULTURE: THE AESTHETIC REALM

The term 'high' culture can still usefully be employed if we use it in order to distinguish it as something separate from popular or commercial culture. I would argue it has two main roles, and these can be examined by reference to art. Both of them are not only significantly different from the commerce-and-culture model, but are fundamentally in opposition to it. The first is its relationship to the aesthetic. The idea that the aesthetic is a realm wholly unlike any other was fully developed in the early years

of the twentieth century and became a cornerstone of modernist belief
and ideology. It was most unambiguously expressed by the art critic and
aesthetician Clive Bell in his 1914 book *Art*. Bell distinguished between
art and life:

> the rapt philosopher, and he who contemplates a work of art, inhabit
> a world with an intense and peculiar significance of its own; that
> significance is unrelated to the significance of life. In this world the
> emotions of life find no place. It is a world with emotions of its own.
>
> (Bell 1928: 26–7)

For Bell, the aesthetic realm is an appreciation of artistic form for its
own sake, without reference to subject matter, association, or social,
political, literary, anecdotal or subjective meaning. Emphasis should be
placed on Bell's description of 'he who *contemplates* a work of art'.
Whereas, with the commerce-and-culture thesis, we *consume* culture, in
the modernist world we *contemplate* it. In so doing, the spectator inhabits
that *other* realm which is either aesthetically disinterested or quasi-spiri-
tual, studying and/or experiencing colours and shapes and their visual
relationships or artistic intensity.

This modernist discourse of the disinterested aesthetic realm reached
its apotheosis in the late 1940s and early 1950s when the American
Abstract Expressionists asserted their belief in an art divorced from the
relative banality of everyday life. Although removed from the experiences
of daily life, the art was not to be empty academic formalism or mere
decorative pattern-making but, according to the painter Barnett Newman,
a reassertion of

> man's natural desire for the exalted, for a concern with our relationship
> to the absolute emotions. We do not need the obsolete props of an
> outmoded and antiquated legend. . . . Instead of making *cathedrals* out
> of Christ, man, or 'life', we are making it out of ourselves, out of our
> own feelings. The image we produce is the self-evident one of revel-
> ation, real and concrete, that can be understood by anyone who will
> look at it without the nostalgic glasses of history.'
>
> (Newman 1948: 553)

Authority resolutely resided in the artist's mastery and his creation.
The painting was to be contemplated by the spectator, who had to learn
to study it aesthetically. The spectator had to bring to the work discrimination and sensibility: 'the faculty to enjoy rests with the observer'
(Hofmann 1948: 544), wrote another painter. Indeed, according to the
Abstract Expressionists, the spectator had a duty *actively* to appreciate
not only an aesthetic experience, but the particular aesthetic experience
created by the artist. Adolf Gottlieb and Mark Rothko asserted that 'It
is our function as artists to make the spectator see the world our way –

not his way. . . . No possible set of notes can explain our paintings. Their explanation must come out of a consummated experience between picture and onlooker' (Gottlieb and Rothko 1943: 545). That consummated experience had connotations of a religious and mystical experience, and it comes as no surprise to learn that Rothko fulfilled a commission for a series of paintings for a meditation chapel. The spectator is characterized as a person standing alone in front of a painting – often with a weighty title such as *Vir Heroicus Sublimis* (a Newman painting of 1950–1) – rapt in contemplation, and consummating the aesthetic experience.

The modernists' clear-cut distinction between art and life has – understandably – been out of favour for many years. Artists and critics rejected their exclusive definition of art and the aesthetic; they believed that you could not separate aesthetic experience from other forms of experience as comfortably as they supposed; and they found the modernists' vision of art elitist and their tone often arrogant. The modernists offered a version of high culture that was universalist, transcendent, exclusive and intolerant. It is a version which became a popular misconception of high culture, in spite of developments in the 1960s and beyond.

And yet the value of the aesthetic as an 'other' realm remained influential as a role for high art and culture. The aesthetic realm can be seen as a replacement for, but in an age of secularism, a continuation of some form of spiritual or religious realm. The crucial relationship for art until the time of the Renaissance was with religion and, as the modernist critic R. H. Wilenski pointed out, works produced in the service of religion 'constitute the great majority of works of art in the world' (Wilenski 1935: 5). Wilenski acknowledged that a very large number of works had been produced since the Renaissance which sought some criteria of justification which was not religious, but that the motivation and values were certainly not primarily justified by commerce:

> I am convinced that all the most intelligent artists of Western Europe in recent centuries have been tormented by this search for a justification of their work and a criterion of its value; and that almost all such artists have attempted to solve the problem by some consciously-held idea of art; or in other words in place of art justified by service to a religion they have sought to evolve an art justified by service to an idea of art itself.
>
> (ibid.: 6)

As a thesis, Wilenski's over-simplification is nearer the mark than the culture-and-commerce lobby's reduction of art to an integral aspect of commerce. Art has been used in western society to confer power, prestige or status and, with the development of easel painting – with its essential portability – art has frequently been commodified, but these are quite separate arguments from the one that is central to the commerce-and-culture thesis.

The spiritual and aesthetic realms of art have sometimes been seen as closely related to art's potential to effect change in society. In the nineteenth century, for example, John Ruskin's definition of art mixed religion and aesthetic experience which, together, would be combined with an ethical mission. Art would make people better – spiritually uplifted and morally more upright – members of society. In the twentieth century strident paternalism and moralism have justifiably become unacceptable, but the potentially transformative nature of art and the aesthetic experience has been upheld by critics and writers such as Peter Fuller and Herbert Marcuse. For example, in *The Aesthetic Dimension*, Marcuse attacked the orthodox Marxist view that the category of the aesthetic was entirely socially determined. He defended not only its separateness and independence as a realm, but its potential to benefit society: 'by virtue of its aesthetic form, art is largely autonomous vis à vis the given social relations. In its autonomy art both protests these relations, and at the same time transcends them. Thereby art subverts the dominant consciousness, the ordinary experience' (Marcuse 1979: ix). Since Marcuse, debate has surrounded the complex questions about the nature, role and ideology of the aesthetic, but the current commerce-and-culture thesis helps to highlight the importance of the value of the aesthetic as a realm, as something different from other modes of engagement, even if any notion of absolute disinterestedness is now untenable.

THE CASE FOR HIGH CULTURE: CRITICAL DISCOURSE

In its capacity to transcend 'ordinary experience', Marcuse hints at the other major role of high culture – art as critical discourse. Victorian narrative painting in general, and Pre-Raphaelite works in particular, often sought to present a critical point of view allied to a moral position. Modernist art also opposed commercialism and consumer values, but in the years after the second world war this critical function of art against the prevalent consumerist and capitalist values of society became a central aim and assumed role for art.

Around the same time, in the mid to late 1950s, that he was urging the artist to wrest back the initiative from popular culture and the mass media, Richard Hamilton was succinctly stating that 'an ideal culture, in my terms, is one in which awareness of its condition is universal' (Hamilton 1982: 151). The role of art in this culture was to promote critical understanding. This did not mean that the artist (as a species of intellectual) had to turn her or his back on commerce or popular culture and retreat into the rarefied environment of disinterested, universalist aesthetic experience, but it did mean that, 'although the intellectual participates in the production and consumption of popular culture he is apart from it in one important sense; he is more aware of the entire circumstances of the phenomenon as a social situation than is the normal consumer' (ibid.: 151). Whereas commerce must always ensure the furtherance of its vested interests – its fundamental *interestedness* – culture should promote a critical questioning of the wider condition, whether by reference to popular culture or, more urgently at the end of the century, to gender and race issues. However subtle, sophisticated or indirect commerce becomes in the pursuance of its interests – however artistic and 'cultural' advertising, for example, becomes – that end remains its *raison d'être*.

A development of this tendency can be traced through Hamilton and his contemporaries, to some of the more critical and questioning Pop artists in Britain, Europe and the US, and to the politicized art of the late 1960s and early 1970s. Two overlapping sub-tendencies developed in the 1960s. One was what has been called the 'de-materialization' of art in which the art object was increasingly dispensed with because of its relationship to capitalist commodification and the art market. In his book *The De-definition of Art*, the American critic Harold Rosenberg traces this stream through Minimalism, Art *Povera* and Land Art, to Conceptual Art in which socio-philosophical ideas about art, art practice or art institutions were presented instead of art objects (Rosenberg 1972: 28–38). Rosenberg refers to the 'de-aestheticization' of art, and the term is not meant to indicate art without visual quality, but works which oppose the essentialist notion of the aesthetic as a disinterested realm.

The second sub-tendency, related to the first, is the politicization of art and cultural practice. In his earlier book, *The Tradition of the New*, Rosenberg applauded the de-materialization and de-aestheticization development in art because the

> wars and revolutions of the twentieth century, including its cultural revolutions, have left no space for detached contemplation. . . . The drama of history, formerly reserved for heroes and their anxious and awestruck onlookers, has spread out to encompass the entire human race. Every watcher has interests at stake, whether he is aware of it or not. . . . Among professionals of the art world – art historians, curators, dealers – looking is a polemical act, designed to promote or to destroy.
>
> (Rosenberg 1970: 15)

Disinterestedness was no longer possible in a society of political struggles: artists had to commit themselves to a cause and oppose institutional and commercial interests. To Rosenberg and politicized artists, the idea of contemplating culture was ideologically unacceptable. But equally unpalatable was the notion of *consuming* culture.

What was developing was a dialectical approach to culture. Whereas Hamilton and some Pop artists combined criticality with an undoubted affection for the popular culture they used as source material, artists in the later 1960s and beyond saw only oppression in the dominant political and institutional forces that produced mainstream culture, and used art – high culture – as a form of opposition. For example, in his manifesto-like statement for 'Black Cultural Nationalism', Ron Karenga proclaimed that black artists must 'reflect and support the Black Revolution . . . any art that does not discuss and contribute to the revolution is invalid' (Karenga 1968: 33). If artistic freedom is subservient to and conditional on political freedom, then art has to adopt a role at the centre of political struggle. And if 'the real function of art is to make revolution' (ibid.: 34), what relevance has either a supposedly disinterested art in which the spectator contemplates culture, or an art that the spectator *consumes* as if commerce? The spectator, in viewing art and culture, should be moved to revolutionary action.

The most lasting and significant development of the tendency of art as critical discourse is feminist practices, which are themselves an integral expression of political and social developments. Reviewing feminist cultural practices in the visual arts at the end of the 1970s, the art historian Lisa Tickner reminded her readers that

> Art does not just make ideology explicit but can be used, at a particular historical juncture, to rework it. There seems to me every reason to believe that feminism, and ultimately the overthrow of patriarchal values, will transform art in just as dramatic a fashion as the bourgeois revolutions.
>
> (Tickner 1978: 247)

Tickner's comments have been taken up by artists such as Mary Kelly and Martha Rosler whose conceptual and book works, mail pieces, photographs, performances and videos deal with issues of femaleness, motherhood, domesticity, sexuality and class. Feminist practices have diversified and flourished in the 1980s and 1990s, often outside the institutional and commercial gallery systems.

The whole tendency of art as critical discourse, far from representing a conflation of commerce and culture, actively and consciously eschews commerce and the ideology of consumerism, and frequently invents strategies which oppose commodification of the object, and incorporation by mainstream institutional systems. Not to take a central account of this most vital post–1950s political, social and cultural tendency, a tendency which accepts diversity and promotes criticality – is to adopt a very partial – and superficial – view of culture and significant history. The commerce-and-culture ideology begins to come into sharper focus by contrast with legitimate and lasting alternatives to it. Moreover, when we identify the roots it has grown from, its focus becomes even sharper.

THE ORIGINS OF COMMERCE-AND-CULTURE

The direct origin of the current commerce-and-culture thesis can be located in the 1960s and is based in changes in cultural practice, critical theory, and – most importantly – socio-economic conditions that are usually associated with post-modernism. Pop Art was a central movement to the changes in cultural practice. We have seen how the first phase of Pop Art in the later 1950s, exemplified by Richard Hamilton, rejected the notion of the disinterested aesthetic, and moved art towards critical discourse. In the early 1960s a new wave of painters – fifteen to twenty years younger than Hamilton and his generation – emerged in an increasingly newsworthy and colour-supplemented art world. The term 'Pop' changed in meaning at this time from shorthand for 'popular culture' and the mass arts, to refer to, on the one hand, the type of music produced by the Beatles and, on the other, the type of art produced by the 'Young Generation' painters. In other words the new Pop Art was perceived as part of youth culture and 'swinging London' (see Whiteley 1987: 85–126).

The cultural critic Lawrence Alloway, a contemporary and friend of Hamilton with a similar outlook who was later to champion many feminist artists, attacked the new Pop painters and rejected their work. Writing about one of their number, Peter Phillips, Alloway complained of how

> He seems to use pop art literally, believing in it as teenagers believe in the 'top twenty'. In a sense, the appeal to common sources within a fine art context, one of the strongest original motives for using pop art has been lost. The new pop art painters use the mass media in the way that teenagers do, to assert, by their choice of style and goods, their difference from their elders and others.
>
> (Alloway 1962: 1087)

Alloway's fear was that art was becoming a matter of mere style, detached from its critical function. A concern with style was not at all similar to a concern with the aesthetic in Bell's or Marcuse's sense. In the hands of many younger Pop artists, Pop became a fashionable commodity of alluring surfaces. As a spectator, one would *consume* Pop Art images in a gallery rather than either contemplate or critically examine their meanings. The images were part of an expendable 'image culture' with everything judged amorally and apolitically on first impressions. Reviewing the period, *Design* magazine dismissed this type of Pop culture as 'a slide culture. Even nuclear explosions, it has been discovered, make superb photographs. It is almost as though things are not fully real until they are made into slides, or double page pictures in the colour magazines'

(*Design* 1970: 100) – or, it might be added, dazzlingly colourful images in art galleries.

The new Pop Art was an ingredient in a process which has been referred to as the 'aestheticization' of daily living. Fashion was becoming the model for daily life – at least for the affluent urban young – with the result that stylishness and fashionability, with its concomitant expendability, mattered far more than durability, good sense or 'good taste' (see Whiteley 1987: 85–126). Not only clothing, but furniture, furnishings and products were designed and presented as fashionable commodities. 'It'll be a great day', wrote one professional designer, 'when cutlery and furniture design (to name but two) swing like the Supremes' (Wolff 1965: 10). An Op Art dining room designed for Mary Quant was described as

> an exercise in pure fashion – in today, expendable tomorrow and no tears shed. There is little in the room which is intended to hold its interest for a much longer period of time than the swinging dresses worn round the table. Neither associations with the past, nor an inheritance for the future have much place here.
>
> (in Whiteley 1987: 112)

Style was everything. With the release of their 1965 single 'Anyway, Anyhow, Anywhere', the Who were billed as a 'pop art group with a pop art sound'. This, apparently, meant that their values were based on 'aesthetic rather than on ethical principles; their activities were matters of display and performance' (ibid.: 126).

This 'aestheticization of life' owed nothing to the essentialist aesthetic realm, but was really a 'stylization' of life – indeed a 'life-stylization' which formed the basis of the life-style approach to life with which we are now so familiar. The 'life-style' approach was a symptom of postmodernist values, and it began in the 1960s with the arrival of shops like Habitat which, according to one of its designers, 'Although it is a furniture company selling furniture, furnishing and decorating bits and pieces, it's actually all about a style of life' (in Hewitt 1987: 40). In a recent publication, the Henley Centre reported that, in the pre-postmodern period,

> consumers were more concerned with a product's function – efficiency, reliability, value-for-money, durability and convenience – today's customers are prepared to pay more for a stylish product as they become more affluent and visually sophisticated.... Aesthetics now play a greater part in portraying the perceived status of a particular product as functional differences between models are reduced.... The visual aspects of design have come to predominate as a means of attracting the consumer.
>
> (Henley Centre 1989: 5)

As we have moved from a society based on scarcity to one based – at least for a significant number – on abundance, so the role of design has changed. It is a change from the idea of the importance of 'primary' function – how well the product works or mechanically operates, and value for money – to 'tertiary' function – the product's perceived status and pride of possession value. Design-conscious people might prefer to pay four times the normal price for a toothbrush for one designed by Philippe Starck; or would travel to Germany to acquire a *white* Braun calculator; or own a genuine Rolex and so on. In galleries and museums, mass-produced industrial products are – literally and figuratively – placed on pedestals as if they are relics or works of art: designed objects have acquired the *status* of art. Design has become *aestheticized* with style predominantly important. It has become a social language through which consumers communicate who they are and where – in terms of life-style group – they belong.

CONSUMING MEANINGS

As Bayley rightly observes in *Commerce and Culture*, consumers now either consume meanings when they purchase a product, or think in terms of meanings when they respond to an advertisement. Interestingly and ironically, this coincides with the rise of semiological and linguistic approaches to culture. While Roland Barthes was decoding the meaning of the Citroen DS in *Mythologies*, the first generation of Pop critics was either analysing the content and meanings of the artefacts and images of popular culture, or viewing fine art as a part of visual communication. Alloway spoke of his concept of culture as

> non-hierarchic. . . . I don't believe in height and depth. I believe in a continuum – not a descending and ascending scale, and that means my interest in painting and sculpture is not incompatible with an interest in any other visual signs and symbols produced in our culture.
>
> (Alloway 1973: 62)

And the architecture and design critic, Reyner Banham wrote of the way the new cultural criticism depended

> on an analysis of content, an appreciation of superficial rather than abstract qualities, and on outward orientation that sees the history of the product as an interaction between the sources of the symbol; and the consumer's understanding of them.
>
> (Banham 1981: 7)

These approaches have developed from structuralism to post-structuralism, and from 'visual communications' to 'visual representations'. What underlies these evolving approaches is the idea of critical discourse, and the way in which the particular or individual instance highlights – in Hamilton's earlier remark – 'the condition of life of humanity in general'.

With the intention of understanding all cultural manifestations as a series of meanings, semiological approaches may have helped to de-aestheticize and de-mythologize conventionally high cultural artefacts, but they have had the reverse effect with more humble products, giving them kudos and status. Vacuum cleaners, toasters and calculators can now be discussed in terms of their sociocultural meanings with the result – given the dominant economic and social forces in society – that they become aestheticized and mythologized, acquiring an aura previously associated with fine art. For the consumer of the new culture, owning a Starck toothbrush has greater cultural capital than being able critically to engage with, for instance, a Newman painting.

But a crucial distinction remains between a tolerant and inclusive 'high cultural' approach, which is characterized by a type of engagement which is contemplative, reflective, critical and relatively disinterested, and a commerce-and-culture approach which is 'knowing' rather than critical. The mythologization of cultural commerce has resulted in consumers who have become sophisticated but it is at the level of a distracting (and often engaging) activity with little significance or generalizable criticality. Bayley praises 'beautifully crafted campaigns' that do not obviously offer a product for sale, 'but rather seek to provide *ambience* and layers of imagery for the consumer to decode' (Bayley 1989: 12). Discussing a new advertising campaign that gave a series of hints about the identity of the product, Tim Delaney, the creative director at Leagus Delaney, remarked that, rather than presenting all the information at once,

> We're using images in a much more interesting way and accepting that consumers will piece it together – work at it over a period of days to get it to fit. And when you've done it – worked out the conclusion – then there's the reward [which] . . . is to accept that the advertiser was clever enough to engage you in the first place in the content, and the 'halo effect' over the brand because they've made you get involved in the brand but enjoy the involvement.
>
> (BBC 1992)

The key stage is, of course, the purchase. The 'ambience', the 'layers of imagery', the 'texture', the 'decoding' – all of these are vested interests leading to the only rationale: a purchase. As Bayley (approvingly) puts it, 'Buy me and become me, they seem to be saying' (Bayley 1989: 12).

To be sceptical of the commerce-and-culture tendency does not imply the sceptic has a paranoia about exploitation and manipulation of the masses by a contriving cartel of advertisers and marketers. But it does mean that the sceptic would disagree with Bayley that, 'if design and art are becoming subsidiary to sales, the consumer is bright enough to realise it' (ibid.: 12). However sophisticated and 'knowing' the consumer in terms of style and fashion consciousness, there is no guarantee that s/he has an awareness of society's condition and ideology.

CULTURE, ENTERTAINMENT, AND 'LIKING THINGS'

But the greatest danger of the commerce-and-culture phenomenon is the levelling down of culture to the values of commerce – the loss of both an aesthetic realm and also critical, generalizable discourse. Bayley approves that the public demands not only superior merchandise but expects museums and galleries to provide a service which is 'not simply scholarly *de haut en bas*, but treats them more as clients in the information and entertainment business' (ibid.: 7).

Culture as a form of entertainment would seem to characterize the commerce-and-culture phenomenon. The new consumers of culture expect to be entertained and, of course, expect to be able to consume – indeed, consuming may be what it is to be entertained. Pop Art has been used in this essay to demonstrate the historical moment when the shift towards the post-modern, commerce-and-culture tendency occurred. In 1991 the Royal Academy hosted a major Pop Art exhibition. Significantly, the exhibition was entitled 'The Pop Art *Show*' (my italics), as if a cabaret or circus. The exhibition was sponsored by Mercury Communications but the preferred wording on the poster and exhibition guide was 'Mercury Communications *Presents* the Pop Art Show', again adding to its flavour as entertainment. A dedicated consumer could rush round the exhibition and head for one of the retail outlets in the Academy for serious consuming of Pop Art memorabilia. (S/he might even visit it directly without the distraction of the exhibition.) Mercury produced a 'Mercurycard Special Edition Collectors Series' of four telephone cards, each designed by a major Pop artist. Not only were these functional – the use-value orientated consumer could be satisfied – but they were limited edition artworks by famous Pop artists, so increasing the owner's cultural capital; and they might be an investment – the folder containing the cards revealed that two earlier special edition cards were now worth £250 and £75 – thus greatly increasing the consumer's economic capital.

The Royal Academy shop (which produces a full colour catalogue of its merchandise for long-distance consumers) offered not only a catalogue of the exhibition and various books on Pop Art, but Pop Art calendars, diaries, pens, biros, pencils, erasers, desk-tidies, socks, T-shirts, sweat-shirts, scarves, neckties, caps, badges, bags – and even cakes. The poster of the exhibition was for sale – to show that you had *been there*, and various inexpensive photographic prints of artworks were also available. These could be bought and taken home to be displayed as life-style cultural reference points.

The consumer may revel in her or his own sense of authority when selecting the constituent parts of the domestic life-style ensemble, but for those who feel they need some advice or information, there has been a proliferation of 'style guide' publications since the mid-1980s. Many of these are concerned with period style settings, telling the consumer how to get the 'Victorian style' or even the 'Medieval style' correct. As guidance about finishing touches for the Medieval-style environment, for example, one such book suggests that you

> hang bunches of herbs from the ceiling as decoration and to scent the air – you might also try burning incense. An open log fire is essential. . . . Apple logs smell wonderful. Religious music – perhaps plainsong, or works by Allegri or Thomas Tallis – should waft around the rafters.

The domestic environment becomes a theatre in which the consumer has the starring role. It seems a firmly established fact of consumerist society that people want – as one guide puts it – to 'create environments that express their individuality, their knowledge, their taste'.

If high culture is potent cultural capital, the art chosen for domestic display would seem to be crucial. Some authority obviously still resides in the artwork or, more accurately, the *type* of artwork – that it is by a famous artist or of a certain art movement or style, as opposed to, for example, a sentimental painting of street urchins, or a weeping pierrot. However, one of the most interesting and revealing 'style guides' – *Living With Art*, by Holly Solomon and Alexandra Anderson – deals with what art to display in your home and how to display it, and reminds the consumer that s/he has the ultimate authority. Do not be too respectful of the artwork, but make it subservient to your own life-style environment to express *your* individuality:

> You live in your home, and you can put a painting on any wall it will fit, and then assemble your furniture in a utilitarian arrangement to make the room usable. Even stacking works on the floor, something you would never see in a museum, can be a perfectly acceptable solution to limited wall space (Holly Solomon finds that 'it makes me think'). . . . It comes down to personal choice – both in the quality of the art and in its mode of display.
>
> (Solomon and Anderson 1988: 50)

That individuals have the right to determine their domestic environment is not at stake. What is significant is the question of authority. Guides like *Living With Art* demonstrate that authority is supposed to have moved away from producers, or even an awareness of the intended values of the artwork, and now appears to reside with the consumers. And so authority is little more than liking or disliking, of being *entertained*. It is less a matter of learning, experience, judgement and discrimination, and more a matter of the 'personal choice' of the consumer.

Culture and commerce become united by a denominator of this personal choice. With such seductive and populist appeal, it is hardly surprising that the commerce-and-culture phenomenon is so pervasive today. Stephen Bayley hopefully speculates that 'maybe in the future museums and shops will become the same institution, huge repositories of objects, images and information – in anticipation, they have been christened "knowledge centres" – with everything available for inspection, comparison and for sale' (Bayley 1989: 7). 'Civilisation', he continues, 'is not really under threat from these changes. On the contrary, the synthesis of commerce and culture is a unifying process, bringing together the two appetites for consumption of knowledge and of goods which were once artificially separated' (ibid.: 8). This chapter has attempted to show that today's commerce-and-culture phenomenon may be commercially astute, but that its values are spurious historically and impoverished culturally.

IN DEFENCE OF HIGH CULTURE

The idea of high culture, so much under attack in the 1980s and 1990s, needs to be defended. We must be careful to distinguish between the intrinsic worth of high culture – which I have argued is a *type of engagement* – and its popular associations of elitism. High culture does not nowadays imply a single and universal intolerant set of criteria and standards, nor a certain type of subject matter which sets it apart from popular culture, nor an exclusive social distinction which confirms the power of a particular group. The demise of modernism and the positive infusion of popular culture from the 1950s has left high culture reinvigorated and plural, a location of diverse aesthetics *and* critical positions. What those positions share is a sense of otherness from daily life and consuming – a site of opposition which promotes reflection, understanding and criticality. This is what characterizes it as a type of engagement, not a type of subject matter.

High culture may still posit authority, but it is an authority based on learning, experience and discrimination. It is no longer a singular and correct authority, but one which promotes debate and invites a critical and informed response – it is open to continual challenges and Popper-like refutations. High culture should thus not be thought of as static or staid, because it can constantly respond to new forms and challenges; it promotes learning, judgement and discrimination whereas the new consumerism, based on the model of shopping, has to make everything immediately available and accessible. A rejection of reflection, understanding and criticality is packaged as a victory over elitism, part of the process of democratization. Yet the commerce-and-culture approach homogenizes experience to a common denominator of – in the words of Andy Warhol which he uttered at the time when the shift in values was taking place – merely 'liking things' (Warhol 1963: 163).

In *The Cultural Logic of Late Capitalism*, Fredric Jameson asks why Warhol's works, which 'explicitly foreground the commodity fetishism of a transition to late capital' are not perceived as powerful and critical political statements. It leads him to 'wonder a little more seriously about the possibilities of political or critical art in the post-modern period of late capital' (Jameson 1992: 9). The popular and media success of the commerce-and-culture approach, so characteristic of aestheticization and commodity fetishism, and so much a symptom of late capitalism, must have helped to turn his doubts into fears.

REFERENCES

Alloway, Lawrence (1962) 'Pop Art since 1949', *The Listener*, 27 December, 1087.
—— (1973) James Reinish, 'An interview with Lawrence Alloway', *Studio International*, September, 62.
Banham, Reyner (1981) *Design By Choice*, London: Academy.
Bayley, Stephen (1979a) *In Good Shape: Style in Industrial Products, 1900–1960*, London: The Design Council.
—— (1979b) 'Arty art and crafty craft', *Harpers and Queen*, October, 260–6.
—— (1989) *Commerce and Culture*, London: Design Museum.
BBC (1992) 'Billboard Project', transmitted on BBC 2, 17 May.
Bell, Clive (1928) *Art*, London: Chatto & Windus.
Bourdieu, Pierre (1984) *Distinction: a Social Critique of the Judgement of Taste*, London: Routledge & Kegan Paul.
Chipp, Herschel B. (1968) *Theories of Modern Art*, Berkeley: University of California Press.
Design (1970) 'New authority, new scope and a change of purpose', January, 54.
Eagleton, Terry (1990) *The Ideology of the Aesthetic*, Oxford: Blackwell.
Featherstone, Mike (1991) *Consumer Culture and Postmodernism*, London: Sage.
Foster, Hal (ed.) (1983) *Postmodern Culture*, London: Pluto.
Fuller, Peter (1983) *Aesthetics After Modernism*, London: Writers and Readers.
Gablik, Suzi (1984) *Has Modernism Failed?* London: Thames & Hudson.
Gottlieb, Adolph, and Rothko, Mark (1943) 'Statement', reprinted in Chipp (1968), 544–5.
Hofmann, Hans (1948) 'excerpts from his teaching', reprinted in Chipp (1968), 536–44.
Hamilton, Richard (1982) *Collected Words*, London: Thames & Hudson.
Harvey, David (1989) *The Condition of Postmodernity*, Oxford: Blackwell.
Henley Centre (1989) 'Planning for Social Change' reported in *DesignWeek* 31 March 5.
Hewitt, John (1987) 'Good design and the rise of Habitat man', *The Oxford Art Journal* 10 (2): 28–42.
Jameson, Fredric (1991) *Postmodernism, or, The Cultural Logic of Late Capitalism*, London: Verso.
Karenga, Ron (1968) 'Black cultural nationalism' in Addison Gayle (1971) *The Black Aesthetic*, New York: Doubleday & Co.

Mamiya, Christin J. (1992) *Pop Art and Consumer Culture*, Austen: University of Texas.

Marcuse, Herbert (1979) *The Aesthetic Dimension*, London: Macmillan.

Newman, Barnett (1948) 'The sublime is now', reprinted in Chipp (1968), 552–3.

Rosenberg, Harold (1970) *The Tradition of the New*, London: Paladin.

—— (1972) *The De-definition of Art*, Chicago: University of Chicago Press.

Solomon, Holly, and Anderson, Alexandra (1988) *Living With Art*, London: Rizzoli.

Tickner, Lisa (1978) 'Art and the body politic: female sexuality and women artists since 1970', *Art History* 1 (2): 236–51.

Warhol, Andy (1963) 'Interview with Gene Swenson', reprinted in Michael Compton, *Pop Art*, London: Hamlyn, 163.

Whiteley, Nigel (1987) *Pop Design: Modernism to Mod*, London: The Design Council.

Wilenski, R. H. (1935) *The Modern Movement in Art*, London: Faber & Faber.

Wolff, Michael (1965) 'Life enhancing', *Society of Industrial Artists' Journal*, January, 10.

Chapter 8

Planning a culture for the people?

Celia Lury

The concern of this chapter is British cultural policy and its cultural, social and political implications. Its focus will be double-edged: on the one hand, attention will be paid to the involvement of the state, both local and national, in cultural policy and planning, while, on the other hand, the significance of cultural practices and institutions for the functioning of the state will also be explored. It will be argued that such policy is one means by which relations of governmentality, that is, relations of authority and legitimacy between the state and its citizens, are, more or less effectively, achieved. The assumption here is that cultural policy is a key sphere in which the fundamental values of modern western societies are represented; specifically, it will be suggested that the principles of cultural citizenship underlying contemporary cultural policy have mediated, interpreted and represented the modern political imperatives of participation, self-actualization and individualization for modern citizens.

As part of this analysis, it will be argued that constructs of the audience, which may include conceptions of cultural need, have been a key mechanism through which changes in such policy have been promoted, resisted and sustained. The role and significance of such constructs in cultural policy is initially presented by means of a brief review of the historical development of cultural policy and planning since the war, with particular attention paid to the sometimes tense relation between the national and the local state.[1] It is argued that, in general terms, cultural policy and planning has, since its formal inception in the immediate postwar period, been dominated by a system of state patronage (Green 1977; Greenhalgh 1989; Bianchini 1987). This patronage was initially justified on grounds similar to those invoked in relation to welfarism in general, that is, as a means of ameliorating inequality and promoting social integration; more particularly, it proposed the ideal of democratic access to the arts, both as a right of every citizen and as essential to the educated exercise of citizenship.

Cultural policy has, however, been largely dependent upon an understanding of the arts which is producer-led; that is, it makes use of an aesthetic vocabulary which privileges the artist and notions of artistic autonomy and creativity. The investment of this authority in the freedom of expression of the artist or cultural producer has, historically, been at the expense of an independent concern for the audience. Or perhaps more accurately, aesthetic value was historically defined in relation to a notion of the author as a creative, autonomous individual working in relation to an abstract, unknown audience (Lovell 1987). This historical convention of aesthetic disinterestedness has been interpreted in policy terms in such a way that concern for the audience, whether that is in terms of numbers, the composition or the quality of its members' experience, is subordinated to support for artists and an acknowledgement of the legitimacy of their work irrespective of its appeal to the audience.[2] As Simon Frith writes, this has resulted in simplistic oppositions: 'Traditionally, the Arts Councils, in subsidising artists, arts companies and arts spaces, have assumed a difference between artist and audience: the special status of the former justifying their patronage; the latter passively, contemplating the results' (1991: 9). To a large extent this assumption still continues to inform cultural policy and planning – at a national level at least – despite some changes in the kinds of activities which are included within a definition of 'arts to be subsidized'. However, a number of attempts have been made to challenge these assumptions, many of which have made use of conceptions of the audience as either an equal partner or an independent participant in the cultural field. These attempts will be reviewed here in relation to the two key principles with which such conceptions have been identified, those of democratization and decentralization. Both such principles move beyond welfarism as a form of compensation to incorporate the positive aim of representation of 'the people'. Thus the difficulty the proponents of such principles have faced has been that of forging links between cultural and political representation to create a 'popular' culture.

The latest conception of the audience to be proposed is that of the audience member as consumer, and has been associated with the so-called marketization of the arts. However, the use of the term consumer in this context is not unified, or simply a derivative of the recent resurgence of enterprise culture and the government-driven marketization of the arts, but is an unstable concept which is the site of a number of overlapping, but sometimes contradictory cultural impulses including those of democratization and decentralization as well as those making up consumerism. A key question to be addressed here in relation to each of these formulations, however, is whether, or to what extent, the adoption of these changing constructs of the audience has actually led to a greater role for its members in the creation of a popular culture.

CULTURAL POLICY AND CITIZENSHIP

The very idea of a cultural policy backed by central government grew up during the war years and emerged in 1946, with the foundation of the Arts Council of Great Britain (ACGB), a small component in a welter of social welfare legislation. Until recently there was no Ministry of Culture as such, but since 1964, under a variety of titles, there has been a Minister for the Arts who headed a small government department, the Office of Arts and Libraries. Through this department finance was made directly available to the national museums, and grants were given to the ACGB, the British Film Institute and the Crafts Council.

It was, and is, through these intermediate bodies that the state's expenditure has been funnelled and apparently disavowed by means of what is commonly termed an arm's length policy. This phrase was coined by Lord Redcliffe Maud, who described it as the method through which, by self-denying ordinance, politicians leave the Arts Council free to spend as it thinks fit. Other people, however, have noted that it is generally customary for the body to direct its arm, and suggested that what is primarily gained by the use of this term is the appearance of the removal of directly traceable control and an apparent depoliticization of the issue of arts provision. Nevertheless, the retention of such intermediary bodies allows a degree of indeterminacy of control to remain; the recent introduction of a Ministry for National Heritage threatens to remove even this limited autonomy.

A first phase in policy, dominant in the 1950s and early 1960s, consisted in little more than a series of preventative moves to preserve traditional forms of art (alternatively put, high art forms, that is opera, theatre, the visual arts, dance, and literature) from market forces which in this context meant (commercial) accountability to a known demand. This was an explicit attempt to maintain a national cultural heritage, both for its own sake and as some kind of bulwark against the rise of consumerism and what was then called mass culture. This latter phenomenon was itself often tied in with a perceived Americanization of British culture. There was little or no attempt to support or develop any forms of popular culture, or even the major new twentieth-century arts – cinema, photography, television.[3] Instead, a system of subsidy based on a notion of a funded extension of the received arts was established; such a system was wholly oriented towards support for the artist and relatively closed art-worlds and had little or no regard for mass audiences as independent arbiters of quality. In this way, then, the legitimacy of received hierarchies of taste was supported indirectly through an almost total lack of concern for the actual context of reception of art. This lack of concern with audience practices was justified by a reflex dismissal of the audience-as-market.

The second phase, emerging in the middle and late 1960s as funding in the arts began to be increased (with the election of a Labour government), has been seen as aiming at a democratization of culture. Policies were explicitly concerned with the extension of traditional art forms to wider audiences: by drawing on more contemporary themes, providing increased opportunities for access and increasing the element of participation. Educational institutions, in particular, were urged to stimulate cultural involvement. However, by continuing to channel support through individual artists, this phase of policy continued to support the subordination of audience response to the artist's artistic 'integrity'. Nevertheless, as the attempts at widening the socio-economic composition of the audience indicate, there was an acknowledgement of the view that public subsidy required popular support. This shift in the terms of cultural policy was significant in so far as it indicated that the legitimacy of the knowledge and judgements of cultural experts was coming to be dependent on their ability to gain acceptance by a political majority on the grounds of ethical and aesthetic relevance; as such, this shift represented a challenge to the internally self-regulated criteria which had previously underpinned the use of received taste as the basis for such knowledge. Simultaneously, however, it suggests that self-conscious participation in the arts was coming to be seen as a requirement of active citizenship for a greater proportion of the population.

The third phase, covering the middle and late 1970s, was dominated by the rhetoric of cultural democracy. This was introduced through wider working definitions of the arts and a stronger attempt, in which the concepts of 'community' and 'participation' were central, to involve the 'non-involved' in arts-based activities with the aim of improving their 'quality of life'. It was at this stage – through their use as a means of reaching marginal or so-called 'disadvantaged' groups – that the arts began to be associated with social problems: the problem of youth, the problem of leisure, the problem of communities. There was a widespread belief in the integrationist function of participation in arts-based activities. The development of the community arts movement, which will be discussed in more detail later, was central here.

This phase saw an uneasy redefinition of the terms of preferred audience involvement; on the one hand, there was increasing acceptance of the view that the success of many arts activities should be related, in some way or other, to the extent and nature of audience response; on the other hand, the indicators of response adopted were primarily derived from social policy, that is, they were linked to the social well-being or health of both individuals and communities. Moreover, such organicist indicators of social value tended only to be required of some arts, notably the ill-defined set of practices known as community arts, while other art forms continued to receive subsidy according to the by now well-established principles of aesthetic disinterestedness. The implementation of this double standard consolidated rather than challenged the distinction between high and popular culture.

The fourth and still current phase, emerging in the 1980s, has been characterized, at a national level, by an explicit policy of economic retrenchment and an implicit support for artistic conservatism. In the Arts Council policy document 'The Glory of the Garden', plural funding, by which national and local finance is theoretically supplemented by private patronage or commercial sponsorship, was presented as the route to any further expansion in the arts. The reduction of public subsidy for the arts forced arts bodies to develop new advocacy arguments, and in the context of an entrepreneurial culture, these soon came to include the potential contribution of the arts to economic growth. The Arts Council document, 'A Great British Success Story' (1985), written in the style of a business prospectus, marked an important shift in attitudes by making the case for the arts on economic grounds, explicitly identifying the actual and potential role of the arts in the economic regeneration of cities, in attracting tourists, and in creating employment. This case was supported by the publication of John Myerscough's report, *The Economic Importance of the Arts in Britain* in 1988. This report outlined the number of jobs, turnover, multiplier effects and overseas earnings of the arts in Britain, and produced figures showing not only that the arts were a major economic sector,[4] but also that public monies spent on the arts were a sound economic investment.

At the same time, a number of local authorities, notably the GLC,[5] put forward what has been called the cultural industries approach to cultural policy. This approach makes use of an understanding of cultural objects and services as commodities, produced, marketed and distributed by industries dependent on skills, training and investment. Rather than seeing the process of commodification as an inherently problematic process for the arts, proponents of this view suggested that the effect of the traditional separation of culture from commerce was to marginalize public policy and to make it purely reactive to processes which it blindly refused to grasp or attempt to control. They suggested that while economic dominance limits the spaces and forms available for alternative or oppositional practice, it does not preclude it.

In practical terms, the implementation of this view involved the development of new financial strategies which changed the nature of the local state's involvement with cultural production. At the GLC, for example, it led to the adoption of a strategy based on intervention, rather than response. Instead of year-by-year deficit funding, financial support was seen in terms of loans and investment to allow for a mix of commercial and subsidized work in a variety of semi-state organizations within the context of a mixed cultural economy. Initiatives ranged from setting up community recording studios, Black publishing houses and radical book distribution co-ops, to the encouragement of non-commercial video distribution in public libraries, all with the aim of strengthening the position of so-called independent producers within the culture industry as a whole. At the same time, a much broader definition of the arts than that adopted by the Arts Council was employed, and contemporary cultural forms, including photography, video, electronic music and community radio, were prioritized. Alongside this, the GLC also made a direct challenge to the conventional depoliticization of public culture through the use of its powers as a direct organizer of cultural events, in initiatives such as its festivals, where it used the arts as the medium for an explicit political message. Together with the cultural industries strategy, these projects were part of an attempt to create an alternative to the declining traditional forms of political mobilization through a kind of cultural urbanism and the construction of a new political majority out of fragmented and heterogeneous groupings.

By the 1990s, however, such arguments had been subsumed into more general strategies designed to encourage urban regeneration. Significantly, these so-called consumer-led policies redefined the audiences for the arts not simply as markets for cultural production, but also as consumers for other kinds of production. Artists and arts activities came to be seen as a way of adding value to development areas. So, for example, the section on economic value in the recent arts development policy report prepared by John Myerscough for Lancaster City Council[6] suggests that economic opportunities fall into four main areas, only the first of which is concerned with the audience for the arts in their own right (1992: 23):

1 The market for the arts and entertainment is large and expanding.
2 The arts are a strategic investment in creativity which provides a seed-bed for business through the spin-off generated in small companies and cultural industries.
3 The arts are a powerful magnet for visitors; they stimulate spending and improve the quality of consumer services in a region; they can have a catalytic effect in the regeneration process, and add value to property developments.
4 A strong cultural infrastructure plays a part in attracting commerce, industry, tourism to an area; the business community can benefit from the arts in spearheading the promotion of a place as somewhere people will want to live and work.

Furthermore, indicators of public support for investment in the arts are provided not only by measuring support for the view that 'it was "very important" that "theatres, concerts, museums, etc." were available in Lancashire for the people of Lancashire', but also for the view that the availability of the arts was 'very important' for visitors to the Lancaster district.[7] In short, the legitimacy of public subsidy for the arts has now come to be assessed in terms which derive directly from the framework which situates arts policy in the context of local and national economic development.

Such developments have been seen in terms of what has been called a marketization of the arts, one aspect of which is that audiences are viewed as consumers. This understanding of the audience is sometimes opposed to earlier views; however, this opposition ignores certain continuities between the current use of the term consumer and conceptions of the audience which underpinned previous policy phases. As the outline given above suggests, shifts in policy have generally been made in the name of processes of democratization and decentralization; however, as the outline given above also suggests, such shifts can be seen as mechanisms through which citizens are invited to realize the modern political imperatives of participation and self-actualization by taking up leisure and cultural practices requiring the adoption and display of certain kinds of taste. From this point of view, the recent move to address the audience as consumer, while certainly indicating a transformation in the kinds of practices given public support, builds on, rather than disturbs, the role of cultural policy as a device for the regulation of an increasingly pervasive culture of reflexive individualization. In other words, what such shifts reveal are not attempts to provide public support for a popular culture, but rather the changing terms through which popular support for a public culture is managed. Nevertheless, the terms which such support is required to take is obviously significant for an understanding of cultural citizenship.

ISSUES OF REPRESENTATION

Clearly, a central concern in the implementation of both democratization and decentralization as mechanisms for effecting cultural representation has been the mobilization of a social grouping, 'the people'. However, the meaning of cultural representation and its implications for cultural citizenship remain extremely hazy; this is in large part the result of a failure on the part of arts administrators and cultural producers to engage directly with the concrete activities of audiences. This failure is most evident, in the sphere of cultural policy, at the national level; however, while the regional or local level of the state and its associated agencies have come to assume a growing importance in cultural policy, especially during the most recent phases, the extent of their divergence from national policy is not great. This is partly because the process of decentralization has been differently understood by its central and local partners. The Arts Council, for example, has historically tended towards an understanding of decentralization as an administrative method for carrying out a national policy rather than as a transfer of power to independent regional bodies working out a policy suited to the specific needs of their area.[8] This understanding has helped create a situation in which regional arts policies result in a kind of mimetic isomorphism; arts centres, for example,

> are just as 'anonymous' as shopping centres – the same music programmes, film schedules and touring exhibitions in the former; the same chain-stores in the latter; the same sense of ubiquitous up-to-date taste whether one visits the Bolton Octagon or the Reading Hexagon, the Watershed in Bristol or the Riverside in Hammersmith.
> (Frith 1991: 5)

The two important institutions at the local level have been Regional Arts Associations (RAAs), recently reorganized as Regional Arts Boards (RABs),[9] and local authorities. From their point of view, decentralization might have been realized in terms of popularization in so far as it could have formed part of a deliberate attempt to lessen the dominance of a *central* culture. But obviously the success of such a project turns on what the centre and the regions mean in cultural terms. In Britain, the central culture is located in the major cities, and above all in London, while the term 'regional' cultures appears to refer to the cultures of areas literally on the periphery – Cornwall, Wales, Scotland – although it is also sometimes applied to rural characteristics in any area. In this way, it is closely connected with the distinction between metropolitan and provincial culture, and is in fact most often used to discriminate against certain areas as in some senses backward or at least limited. This, the most usual use of the term, can only hold if certain other regions – or at least one other region, namely London – are not seen in this way. In general, then, it seems as if the idea of regional cultures has little meaning or concrete lodgement in a nation whose unified spatial cultural identity has been established far longer than in many other countries. It is thus perhaps not surprising that the regional and local arts bodies have been largely unable to develop regional cultures as such, but this is exacerbated by the fact that they have often failed to move beyond a policy of response to initiatives from groups within the region, and as a result, have not intervened significantly in what are already uneven relations of cultural exchange.

Indeed, it was the notion of community or locality, rather than region, which emerged as a more effective locus for decentralization within the arts.[10] This was particularly evident in the case of the community arts movement. Its emergence in the 1970s was clearly linked to the host of complex inter-connections which surrounded the reconstitution of the term 'community' at that time: localized struggles over education, racial violence and police practice; the relocation of resources to supposedly deprived areas; the politicization of forms of voluntary action; the emergence of community action and development in response to the persistence of major social problems in the cities; and support for the recognition of the local state as having a degree of openness and accessibility to popular pressure. As the variety of these influences indicates, however, the interest in the rehabilitation of community life shifted between attempts at democratic and participatory grass-roots initiatives and moves towards more sophisticated modes of containment in social policy.

The community arts movement itself was characterized by a similarly disparate range of influences, often drawn together under a general aim of 'bringing art to the people'. Key elements of community arts practice included: an emphasis on work in groups, making use of the resources and potential of a particular place and moment; the use of notions of collective creation and a stress on the importance of collaboration and local accountability; an emphasis on the *processes* of making rather than on the finished *product*; the presence of an artist (often renamed animateur) working with a group; and a tendency to see creativity as an essential part of any radical struggle, and thus a use of the arts in the service of campaigns and issues. The adoption of such techniques was based on an understanding of cultural democracy which aimed to shift control for cultural activity into the hands of the audiences who were reconstituted as producers. However, such aims were often unrealized.

This was in part because the reliance of community arts groups on state funding led to an incorporation of some of the more radical elements of the movement into the state via social service and education departments. Owen Kelly writes:

> We were in fact constructing community arts groups in such a way that they could not exist except through revenue funding on an increasing scale. . . . The number of workers grew, the amount of equipment grew, and with them grew the dependence on state funding. . . . [We] stopped being a movement of activists and became a profession.
>
> (1984: 17)

Equally important in limiting the success of the community arts movement, however, was the vagueness in the definitions of community used; for example, it was defined 'not as an entity, nor even an abstraction, but a set of shared social meanings which are constantly mutated and created through the actions and interactions of its members and through their interaction with wider society' (ibid.: 84). This indeterminacy reflected the uncertain political and cultural basis of the notion of community.

Ironically, then, despite attempts to create dense, personally mediated networks rather than dispersed, impersonal modes of distribution and reception, the development of state provision and support for cultural initiatives at a local level tended to marginalize and suppress other existing forms of shared cultural activity. Moreover, although there was some attempt to identify particular social groups as potential partners through their relation with the gay, black or women's movements, cultural community development often struggled and failed to develop its own distinctive form of association. Instead, it came to be seen as a means of reaching marginal groups, both as a form of compensation for those without economic, social and cultural power, and as an indirect form of social control (and the use of this mechanistic term does not seem inappropriate here) as part of a programme of community and youth services. Indeed, the fact that one precondition for a wish to develop an area as a 'community' was its lack of self-generated resources suggests that the cultural development of a community is better seen as part of the general thrust of social policies to counter deprivation than as either an attack on conventional conceptions of art or part of the development of an alternative popular culture.

Indeed, recent critics of the community arts movement have questioned the very understanding of 'the popular' which it employed. In general, community arts groups drew on a sense of culture as a resource made by people for themselves, culture both as creativity and as a redeemed and unalienated everyday life. These groups thus worked with a notion of culture which was in contradistinction to those definitions which limit culture to a set of specialized practices and a definite canon of works. The community arts movement might therefore be seen to present a more inclusive model of popular cultural activity than that held by the Arts Council, especially in so far as it relies on the model of an earlier 'folk' art. However, whilst such a model was explicitly contrasted with elite culture, it was also implicitly opposed to a rival form of popular culture itself – namely, mass culture.

Within the terms of this opposition, this alternative form of popular culture is viewed as an imposed mass culture, produced and distributed by commercial apparatuses over which 'the people' have no control and which offer them no productive creative involvement. In making use of this division, the community arts movement drew on a widespread opposition to what is seen as the depersonalized and individualist ethos of modern industrialist society. In the process, a whole series of related oppositions were made use of and reinforced: production and consumption, activity and passivity, community and commodity. Thus, while the community arts movement can be seen to have challenged the traditional view of the arts as elitist in that it attempted to demonstrate that everyone is capable of acquiring those skills necessary to respond, think and act creatively, it drew, at the same time, on the remaining assumptions of the high culture tradition it was rejecting. In doing so, it not only denied the artistic validity of most popular, albeit commercially based, cultural activities, but also confirmed the existing links between the autonomous artist, traditional hierarchies of taste and the cultural rights and obligations of citizenship embedded in national cultural policy.

Surprisingly perhaps, the consumer-led policies of the fourth phase displayed some similar contradictions. While, on the one hand, the cultural industries approach appeared to embrace wholeheartedly the commercial basis of much popular culture, on the other, it still retained certain reservations: so, for example, a GLC policy document comments:

> It is important to recognize that popular culture is not always mass culture. Its newest and most dynamic forms exist precariously at the edge of the commercial world and the powerful established structures of the industry often work to exclude new voices and cultural forms.
>
> (GLC 1984: 5)

This ambiguity – the difficulty in distinguishing popular from mass culture – suggests that there were uncertainties and confusions about the role and function of the market as a means of decentralization and its relation to democratization.[11] Very often, such hesitancy resulted in the tendency to support cultural producers within the so-called independent sector rather than the major companies. Moreover, this frequently actually took the form of support for individual artists, working in an artisanal mode. However, as empirical studies of the culture industry revealed, there is no necessary reason why such a policy would work to increase the range and diversity of cultural goods and services on offer within the market; as Frith (1991: 6) notes,

> radicalism is not, in itself, a matter of marginality – independent publishing companies mostly produce mainstream culture (their independence a reflection of market specialisation rather than experimentation); 'radical' art and ideas are just as likely to emerge from the cultural bureaucracies.

Furthermore, while such policies recognized the need to differentiate between different types of markets, they did not radically disturb the nature of the relations between producers and the audience, or intervene in the conditions of reception.

In any case, local authorities faced substantial problems in translating even such truncated arguments into practice. On the one hand, the culture industry is characterized by relatively low levels of concentration, in part precisely because the major companies often prefer to work in a symbiotic rather than oppositional relation with the so-called independent sector. The disadvantages which producers within this sector face are the ones which confront small businesses in any industry – that is, lack of start-up finance, imbalance between production and marketing; and many of the resources which the GLC and other local councils provided attempted to remedy this situation. On the other hand, the so-called independent companies still had to face the commercial realities of the cultural economy, including the structuring power of major companies and multinationalism, and thus it is not surprising that intervention on a local or national level was largely ineffective, particularly at the moment of distribution.

Moreover, while the adoption of a cultural industries approach was part of a conscious attempt on the part of some local authorities to regenerate the local economy, the experience of most councils suggests that while politicizing the local economy in this way may lead to modest immediate gains and can help to crystallize issues and mobilize protest, significant intervention is, in general, not possible at a local level since only central government has the resources and power systematically to influence demand and investment. Furthermore, the growth of local authority involvement in economic development became caught up in a general conflict over spending between the central and local state. The options facing local government within the area of culture were symptomatic of the choices that it confronted more generally: either to retreat into acting as little more than a residuary body or to take on a new kind of pro-active promotional role within the locality. Many councils took on the latter, more outgoing, catalytic and entrepreneurial, role, and in the process helped to institutionalize the role of arts administrators, consultants and tourist operators as experts in the management of leisure and cultural activities as life-style.

This is clearly evident in the most recent twist in the fourth phase of cultural policy: not simply the commodification of the arts, but the commodification of their audience as part of a wider urban regeneration strategy. Tourism development strategies are prime examples here. For example, the recent Lancaster policy document recommends that the 'potential of the arts needs to be set in the framework of other policies for the future of the district'; 'in particular the arts could assist in: developing and enhancing the image and reputation of the area as a location for new investment in the major tourist centre', and 'encouraging the regeneration, modernization and diversification of the local economy' as well as 'improving the basic infrastructure and physical environment of the area' (Myerscough 1992: 46–7). Culture, and the arts in particular, are no longer to be considered merely a supplementary sector of the economy, but rather a catalyst in the economy as a whole as the complex, differentiated dynamics of taste are harnessed as an active, productive factor in the development of the citizen's consumption capacity. In short, the effectivity of culture is newly defined in economic terms through the market-driven implication of consumer demand with judgements of taste; at the same time, habitual cultural values are conceptually represented and legitimized as life-style choices and the citizenship ideals of participation and self-actualization are given a contemporary gloss.

What are the consequences of this reconceptualization of the audience for the cultural producer and the reception and evaluation of art? On the one hand, it seems as if the values of artistic integrity are being sacrificed to the market. As Frith writes, such strategies have the effect of defining 'local culture itself as the object of consumption, as a communal heritage, competing with other heritages in the leisure market, as each city rewrites its history in terms of a trademark, a sales point, a market niche' (1991: 4). It was suggested earlier that the community art focus on the local as community led to a concentration upon a traditional, pre-modern concept; it might have been thought that the use of the term 'locality' within a market perspective would preclude such nostalgia, but this has not been the case. Rather it has contributed to the reterritorialization of the regions in terms of media-driven myths of national heritage such as Catherine Cookson or James Heriot country; as Frith continues:

> The paradox here is that cultural industries policy, despite its rhetoric of seizing new technological opportunities, comes to depend for its sense of the local on the most restricted form of cultural 'tradition'; what started as a progressive move, a challenge to 'elite' culture, a determination to take popular values and tastes seriously, ends in reaction, in a sentimental story of a 'people' who never existed.
>
> (ibid.)

At the same time, however, the local is redefined in relation to the global by means of a cultural cosmopolitanism; members of the audience for events in the recent Festival of Expressionism in Manchester, visitors to Morecambe at the time of the WOMAD festival, participants at events arranged to promote Britain's presidency of the EC, are all encouraged to regard themselves 'as if' true members of multiple cultures characterized by common ideal properties of taste, habits and values ordered through a cosmopolitan life-style.

On the other hand, such strategies are often parasitic on the myth of the artist; and there are ways in which the experimentation of the avant-garde, the exoticism of the primitive, and the sanctity of official cultures are the most valuable materials for the creation of audiences as lucrative target markets. Thus it is perhaps not surprising that government funding is still largely directed towards the top twenty 'centres of excellence'; that 'participation' in the arts is still the remit of community and amateur arts alone; and that attempts are currently even being made to revive the distinction between primary and secondary cultural producers. Indeed, in a restatement of the absolute authority of the artist in contradistinction to the need to display responsibility to the audience, the recent National Arts and Media Strategy prescribes that 'Attendance should be determined by the art that is on offer' (1992: 146). In short, it seems as if strategies to realize the economic value of the arts can be combined, more or less harmoniously, with the traditional hierarchies of taste. What remains constant is the relative neglect of the audience.

What would it mean then to develop a cultural policy which acknowledges the responses of the audience? Despite, or perhaps because of their use of the techniques of market research, radical proponents of the marketization of the arts tend to ignore the cultural embeddedness of the market itself, appearing to conflate the acts of exchange and reception. Consequently they often display a surprising indifference to aesthetic questions; for example, market research is employed to extend the range of activities an audience may be encouraged to participate in alongside reception, but the nature of their specifically aesthetic experience is left unexplored. Perhaps it is assumed that any increase in the diversity of the socio-economic composition of the audience will in and of itself secure a diversity of responses. However, such an assumption collapses the space between social position and cultural formation and privileges the economic and social at the expense of the cultural. Paradoxically, it seems as if such cultural entrepreneurs fail to recognize the ways in which the culture of consumption informs the processes of consuming culture.[12]

This culture is characterized by a collapse of the conventional distance between (artistic) object and subject, a collapse which is related to both a destabilizing relativism in relation to objects induced through the abstraction of economic exchange, and the substitution of contemplation by absorption as a result of the decline of the aura of the artwork. Such modes of experience are stabilized in the life-style discourse of an individuated self-realization but are potentially available as resources for a more collective creativity. That they are left untouched is, in part, related to a wider failure to think about alternatives to the market not simply as a mechanism of distribution, but also as an apparatus of cultural representation. If, as is commonly suggested, the 'popularity' of popular culture is related to audience response, then both the cultural and social conditions, and visibility, of that response are key factors in the determination of its quality. Cultural policy should seek out alternative means by which the active engagement of the audience can feed into the process of production if it is to alter the present unequal terms of cultural citizenship. As Walter Benjamin argued, the key question to ask of any artistic work is not how it stands *vis-à-vis* the productive relations of its time, but how it stands *within* them.

The current phase of cultural policy is undoubtedly affected by both the promotion of culture by commerce and the promotion of commerce by culture. It makes use of the recognition that the arts are not only a distinct sphere for the expansion of value, but, more and more, are an integral part of the more general drive for profit; they enter directly into diverse economic processes for the realization of value. However, it has been suggested here that this most recent invocation of the audience for the arts, namely, as consumers, does not represent a shift of authority to the audience, but rather a refiguring of controlling constructs of the audience. As such, this most recent phase continues to contribute to the political project of governmentality through the creation of a public culture legitimated by reference to a phantom audience.

NOTES

1 The historical summary given here – which has four phases – draws heavily on the outline of the first three stages of this development presented by Michael Green in his paper, 'Issues and problems in the decentralising of cultural planning' (1977).

2 This support for the cultural producer has been cross-cut by other tendencies, including a prioritization of live performance and an associated reluctance to come to terms with modern cultural technologies.

3 The Arts Council, for example, did not admit jazz and photography to its canon of art worthy of public subsidy until 1967, and it only established its own Film, Video and Broadcasting Department in 1987. Broadcasting was until recently under the remit of the Home Office.

4 Myerscough's figures have since been contested; however, the case for treating the arts as an economic sector has been established.

5 Other local authorities which took up this approach included Sheffield, Birmingham, Glasgow, Wolverhampton, Liverpool and Manchester.

6 This report is used as an illustration here because it concerns my own locality; however, it is in many ways typical of current local cultural policy.

7 While 66 per cent of the adult residents in Lancaster supported the first view, even more supported the second – 73 per cent (1992: 21–2).

8 This view of decentralization is also visible in 'The Glory of the Garden' which proposed an ambiguous strategy concerning regionalism. On the one hand, the Arts Council declared its intent to encourage regionalism, notably by devolving new responsibilities for the funding of local organizations to the regional arts associations, while on the other, little practical support was offered, and there was in fact a cut in basic and flexible funding. At the same time, the Arts Council took on responsibility for the funding of 'centres of excellence' itself – major clients, or 'clients of national significance' – which, 'wherever they are located are expected to play a prominent part in the Council's policy of ensuring a more equitable distribution of arts provision in strategic areas throughout the country'. The effect of this was further to increase central control over local authority spending, since a policy of matching funding meant that regional centres of 'excellence' would only receive the extra resources if the local authorities also directed fresh funds to them. The actual result of this phase of the Arts Council's policy of regionalism was thus that central funds were directed to the prestigious regional 'flagships' of national culture, while the smaller, locally based groups bore the brunt of the shortfall in central government funding.

9 The first regional arts association, South West Arts Association, was formed in 1954. Gradually, a network of twelve regional arts associations was established, and a process of decentralization of responsibilities for the arts was begun.

10 The arts are thus one of a number of fields for which it is the locality, rather

than the regions or provinces, that provides the most important contemporary form of social organization at the level below that of the nation-state.

11 This approach drew on socialist analyses of the market, which suggested that there are theoretical grounds for believing that measures implemented through the market may be more rapid, more efficient as a means of decentralization, than myriads of planned interventions at the national or local level of the state, so many are the separate sites of decision-making in a modern economy. It is further argued that it is possible to separate the concept of the market from the capitalist mode of production, and from the special features deriving from labour as a market commodity. *If* this can be done, the market can be seen to have much to recommend it.

12 The recent national policy document, *Towards a National Arts and Media Strategy*, only goes so far as to recognize that,

> The arts are a way that people use their leisure time, as participants and consumers, alongside sport, tourism and hobbies. These activities are 'competitors', but in a broader sense they are allies: together they are a vital part of what we mean by the quality of life.
>
> (1992: 19)

REFERENCES

Benjamin, W. (1970) *Illuminations*, London: Fontana.
Bianchini, F. (1987) 'GLC R.I.P. Cultural policies in London, 1981–1986', *New Formations*, 1: 103–18.
—— (1988) 'Urban renaissance? The arts and the urban regeneration process', in B. Pimlott and S. MacGregor (eds), *Tackling the Inner Cities*, Oxford: Oxford University Press, 1991.
Frith, S. (1991) 'Popular Culture: Discussion Document', London: Arts Council.
Garnham, N. (1983) 'Concepts of culture: public policy and the cultural industries', London: GLC.
Greater London Council (1984) *Altered Images*, London: GLC.
Green, M. (1977) 'Issues and problems in the decentralisation of cultural planning', Stencilled paper, Birmingham: Centre for Contemporary Cultural Studies.
Greenhalgh, L. (1989) 'Cultural policy and the local state: Sheffield, 1960–1987', unpublished MPhil thesis, Sheffield Polytechnic.
Greenhalgh, L., Kelly, O. and Worpole, K. (1992) 'Municipal culture, arts policies and the cultural industries', in J. Bennington and M. Geddes (eds) *Restructuring the Local Economy*, Harlow: Longman.
Kelly, O. (1984) *Community Arts and the State: A Different Prescription*, London: Comedia.
Lewis, J. (1990) *Art, Culture and Enterprise*, London: Routledge.
Lovell, T. (1987) *Consuming Fiction*, London: Verso.
Myerscough, J. (1988) *The Economic Importance of the Arts in Britain*, London: Policy Studies Institute.
—— (1992) 'Towards an arts strategy for Lancaster: a policy background', Lancaster City Council.
National Arts and Media Strategy Monitoring Group (1992) *Towards a National Arts and Media Strategy*, London: Arts Council.

Chapter 9

The culture of consumption

Design museums as educators or tastemakers?

Helen Rees

INTRODUCTION

Nowadays it is a truism, among curators and critics alike, that museums are not just repositories of culture, but are powerful cultural forms in their own right. Traditionally, museums have been set apart from daily life; their high cultural credentials endorsed by the esoteric content of their collections. Conventional museums prize objects which are rare, exotic or old at the expense of those which are familiar, inexpensive and new.

Museums continue to offer a version of cultural legitimation which is rooted in an awe-inspiring distance from everyday concerns. Some objects deemed worthy of display have earned their place in the gallery by virtue of old – and often very old – age. The modern counterparts of archaeological artefacts are dismissed as banal by comparison. For example, Jack Lang, President Mitterand's former Minister of Culture and Education, was accused by both the Right and the Left for debasing French cultural values by enthusing about the work of fashion designers and pop groups. In response, Lang pointed out that the attack comes from people who would regard it as entirely proper to examine in great detail the pin fastening the robe on a Greek sculpture, simply because this fashion is 2,500 years old.

This essay argues for an integrated view of visual culture, with its implication for a synthesis of commerce and culture, and a possible meeting between producer values and consumer values. This view of visual culture acknowledges meaning and value in contemporary commercial goods, as well as in art objects and historical artefacts. This is not to deny the differences in production, circulation and use between, say, a sculpture and a kettle, but to suggest that each is worthy of distinct inquiry and understanding. Both statues and kettles have found a place in the exhibitions of an industrial age, but while art and galleries are nowadays inseparable, a paradox remains at the heart of the idea of a design museum, at least for the high-culture critics of Jack Lang.

The question asked of Monsieur Lang is why put a kettle on a plinth? The perceived absurdity of such an enterprise has as much to do with our relationship with museums, as with design. Although ostensibly open to all, public museums inspire what Pierre Bourdieu describes as a mixture of deference and hostility among all but a privileged, cultivated class. Bourdieu's thesis is reinforced by the statistics: in this country, of the 21 per cent of the population who visit museums, 41 per cent are in socio-economic category AB and 26 per cent are in category C. Bourdieu found that museums remind their visitors of a church – inhibiting the easy flow of secular communication – rather than, say, a department store.

Even museum aficionados are frequently ambivalent about the experience of looking at exhibitions. The dramatist Alan Bennett caught the mood of many a weary visitor in a piece for the *National Gallery News*:

> The art gallery, that supposed refuge and den of tranquillity, I find a troubled place. Casements on eternity, these great patient masterpieces ought to calm the mind and nourish the spirit, but seldom do, and it's rare that I emerge from the National Gallery feeling that I have really taken advantage of what's on offer. What am I supposed to think? What am I supposed to feel? ... A portion of my unease can be put down to finding so many masterpieces accumulated in one place, locked up even, the National Gallery a pictorial Parkhurst (a pic nick perhaps) where every one of the inmates is a lifer.... Get these long stay prisoners home, I feel, settle them down in normal surroundings, rehabilitate them, if you like, into the community and then I could really get to know them.
>
> (Bennett 1992)

The popular view that 'culture' is separate from daily life shapes our preconceptions of what museums are all about. As a result, the public and professional reaction to the intrusion of the commonplace into the temple of the Muses is likely to be mixed, if not confused. Curators themselves have widely divergent views about this, as was clearly shown when the *Guardian* newspaper asked a group of London exhibition organizers whether they would consider hanging a show of best-selling Athena photographic posters in their galleries. Their replies ranged from outright rejection by Helen Sloane of Camerawork ('They're an abuse of photography') to a willingness to embrace the product of the High Street. Alan Haydon of the Arts Council commented, 'Athena posters make a valuable contribution to the world of visual arts, because they raise the overall awareness of images in our society.... It's an issue of access, rather than of art.' David Chandler at the Photographers Gallery raised the thorny question of taste: 'Athena posters have to be a reflection of popular taste, so they don't shape taste, they respond to it.' Susan Copping at the Riverside Gallery admitted that social class could be a factor: 'I can't imagine us showing Athena posters ... [but] there's a vast number of people for whom these kinds of images are very powerful and relevant. They raise the whole issue of categories and hierarchies of taste, and the relationship between social class and art appreciation' (Leedham 1992).

Athena posters would need to be reinvented as art to find a place on the walls of the Institute of Contemporary Arts. Kate Bush argued: 'They're not art but they *could* be in another context. If they were shown in a gallery by someone like Jeff Koons, who re-inflected them with a sense of irony, *then* they might be called art.' Her comment implies that there is a distinct category of art, with the sole right to inhabit the gallery. This relationship is continuously reinforced as the institution and the art object are equally dependent on each other for the protection and promotion of their common objective. Each endorses the high cultural credentials of the other, which may be why so many art curators still defend their territory against the infiltration of 'non-art'.

So what happens to those museums which do admit design into their galleries? Is either the museum or the object transformed? Does the museum become a shopping mall or the designed product turn into a work of art? There is certainly a tension in a display of consumer goods in an exhibition where you can look, but not buy. Their presence in the museum tacitly acknowledges the cultural capital of the market place, but why bother to take readily available commodities out of the shops and into the gallery? One response is that the museum offers the visitor a fine filter of connoisseurship and criticism through which he or she can view the material world as a peculiarly *aesthetic* phenomenon. The price tag is replaced by the curatorial caption and, hey presto, design becomes part of the culture. Museums educate us, both for our own good and, supposedly, for our enjoyment. The slogan at the Cité des Sciences et l'Industrie at La Villette in Paris, is '*Le plaisir de comprendre*'. But the didactic has sometimes been at odds with the aesthetic in the presentation of material culture in museums, and nowhere more so than in those concerned with design for everyday life.

HENRY COLE AND AFTER

In the second half of the nineteenth century, a wave of museums of contemporary manufactures opened in the wake of the popular success of, and the critical disquiet caused by, the Great Exhibition of 1851. Many of these museums were overtly polemical, founded by men who were passionately concerned with standards of design and taste, among both producers and consumers. In 1857 Henry Cole founded the South Kensington Museum with the explicit purpose of making its collections as accessible as possible to the working population. Cole and his colleagues employed an impressive range of educational techniques designed to enable a vast number of visitors to appreciate the objects on show: long explanatory labels, illustrated catalogues, public lectures, a reference library, late-night opening and reduced admission for the poor. In Cole's own words, 'I venture to think that unless museums and galleries are made subservient to the purposes of education, they dwindle into very sleepy and useless institutions.'

Cole's aim was twofold. He believed that exhibitions of the best design from around the world would not only inspire and educate a new generation of industrial artisans, but it would also help elevate public taste and create a nation of more discerning consumers. From the outset, the South Kensington Museum was intended to provide students and the public alike with object lessons for contemplation, inspiration and emulation. Public and specialist education went hand-in-hand, stimulated by the proximity of the Normal School (now the Royal College of Art) and the use of the museum for the instruction of students.

As early as 1836 a recommendation had been made to the government to found a museum of design as part of a national defence against French luxury imports which were flooding the country in the wake of the Napoleonic Wars. Now, twenty years later, the dream was realized, giving Cole the opportunity to divert the working classes from the attractions of the gin palace, while simultaneously assisting in the revival of an ailing national economy.

One hundred and fifty years on, it is tempting to mock the confident paternalism of our Victorian forebears. Their obsession with taste as a lever in the tool bag of the social engineer, as well as an aesthetic barometer, was typical of a class which had long convinced itself that the interests of the few coincided with the welfare of the many. They genuinely believed popular choice was not always the 'best' and that public education through museums and exhibitions was an effective means of regulating consumer spending to desirable ends.

The founders of Victorian museums did not simply express a point of view; they aimed to win converts to their cause. But however persuasive their case might have been, they were essentially representatives of the embattled middle classes, preaching a message of moral and aesthetic salvation derived from the mores of their particular social group. Despite their efforts to establish trans-historical criteria of excellence, their criteria remained subjective. Good taste was what these men considered it to be, and bad taste was everything else.

The history of twentieth-century museums is the story of how the moral and social clamour of the Victorians was gradually replaced by the disinterested claims of the connoisseur. Today museums crusade by covert means, beneath a veneer of impartial scholarship. Galleries are designed to create an illusion of neutral space, and the ritual of display demands that the artefact is severed from its history of production and consumption, prior to installation in the gallery. Products designed for use are frequently presented in exactly the same way as objects created for contemplation – stripped of their functional, technological and commercial contexts. Aesthetic appreciation has gained the upper hand.

MOMA AND ITS INFLUENCE

Just as the South Kensington Museum captured the spirit of the nineteenth century, so the archetypal museum of the twentieth century is the Museum of Modern Art (MOMA) in New York. MOMA opened its Architecture and Design Department in 1932, three years after the museum was founded. In an attempt to break down the hierarchy which separated fine art from the rest of material culture, the Department treated designs for buildings and mass-produced goods in exactly the same way as one-off works of art. The modernist agenda which demanded the elimination of the boundary between fine and decorative art therefore reduced the latter to a catalogue of surface effects, just as connoisseurs had always regarded painting and sculpture. Only a single viewpoint was admitted; the non-functional, aesthetic appreciation of form.

The design gallery at MOMA was rapidly and wholly absorbed into the museum's mission to spread the glad tidings of modernism throughout America and the western world. The museum actively and effectively used its institutional authority to set a seal of approval on modernist design and architecture, as well as art. Today that original proselytizing force is long spent, so that now the museum's commitment to modernism is archival, rather than campaigning.

Two years ago MOMA reopened the debate about high versus low culture in a landmark exhibition curated by the Director of Painting and Sculpture, Kirk Varnedoe. 'High and Low' (Winter 1989/90) was an attempt to redeem the realm of commercial production by showing the extent to which banal and ephemeral objects had inspired many of the fine art masterpieces of our age. A dialogue was joined between those objects which nowadays are circulated in galleries, museums, corporate art collections and the homes of the rich, and those which are everywhere else. But by only admitting advertising, cartoons and graffiti into the gallery in order to understand its relationship with art, the exhibition failed to do justice to the constant movement backwards and forwards across the invisible bridge between art and commerce.

The two-way inspiration, derivation and reinvention which characterizes the relationship between art and advertising was illustrated more effectively in an exhibition 'Art et Pub' at the Centre Pompidou, Paris, which coincidentally ran concurrently with 'High and Low'. Here the crossovers were presented in a more open-ended and pragmatic format: sometimes the connections were surprising, often they were messy. For the first fifty years of the chronological exhibition (from 1890) advertising influenced art, while the trend went into reverse during the subsequent fifty years. And artists who worked in a range of markets criss-crossed the border many times in a single career: a poster for chocolate by Kandinsky and a perfume advertisement by Magritte indicated artists dedicated to survival, rather than 'selling out' to commercial interests.

Both exhibitions raised the possibility of two-way traffic between the museum and the street, instead of movement in a single direction. 'Art et Pub' certainly promoted an integrated, non-hierarchical view of material culture, but effectively treated everything as if it was art.

Is it the fate of design museums to swing between the opposite poles of moralizing and aestheticizing, with the result that design exhibitions are, at best, partial and, at worst, patronizing?

THE DESIGN MUSEUM AND ITS PEERS

When the South Kensington Museum divided into the Victoria & Albert Museum and the Science Museum in 1909, an unnatural division appeared in the museum world between how things work and what they look like. It seemed as though the connection between the functional and the aesthetic was lost forever somewhere in the middle of Exhibition Road, London SW7. Today many design museums and galleries share a common ambition to restore that connection and to present a holistic view of design, taking account of production, use and meaning, as well as of appearance.

None had higher hopes than the Design Museum in London, which opened in 1989 on the crest of the design wave, just months before it came crashing down as the national cash register finally closed on the Lawson Boom. Just like the South Kensington Museum and the Museum of Modern Art, the Design Museum was a child of its time, in this case a decade during which the British people borrowed and spent their way through the biggest spree ever. Low taxes and easy credit provided the perfect playing conditions for the new national sport: shopping. The old maxim of save and prosper had never offered as much satisfaction as the new hyper-eroticism of a visit to the shops. These were the years when the politics of identity finally collapsed into the consumption of life-styles, and on a grand scale. Erstwhile Marxists now debated the anthropology of aspiration, while the science of sociology resembled a shopping list. Even the most banal item of household use was vested with totemic significance, so long as it was designed by the hippest French, Italian or Catalan design superheroes.

Purchaser power was now a force to be reckoned with and the language of consumption was co-opted to describe a new style of public provision where the customer always comes first (at least in theory). By the end of the 1980s, the ethos of consumerism had redefined the contract between the individual and the public sector, including schools, hospitals, social services... and museums. Patients and visitors had been replaced by clients and customers.

During this time, bringing the museums to market exposed deep-seated tensions between curatorial and management styles. When Neil Cossons introduced admission charges to the Science Museum he said his priority was customer satisfaction: the benchmark by which the museum would either thrive or decline. Across the road, Elizabeth Esteve-Coll ruefully acknowledged that the Victoria & Albert Museum had exceeded Sir Roy Strong's ambition to become 'The Laura Ashley of the 1990s' and was already the Harrods of the museum world, part of the 'admire and acquire' syndrome which was sweeping the nation.

By contrast, the former Director of the British Museum, Sir David Wilson defended the moral high ground of public accessibility by claiming that free admission was a litmus test of the public's right to see the national collections. Similarly at the National Gallery, Neil MacGregor has castigated those museums which cater solely to international tourists with an emphasis on fast 'through-put' and high expenditure, at the expense of the local citizenry 'which is to say, the frequent visitor' (MacGregor 1992).

Commercial pressures certainly have done much to shape the fate of the Design Museum, based in a converted warehouse at Butlers Wharf, immediately adjacent to Tower Bridge on the south bank of the River Thames. The rest of the Butlers Wharf development – earmarked for shops, offices, restaurants and flats – had progressed slowly until it was finally dragged down in the property slump, with its banks appointing administrators to take over the management of the site at the end of 1990.

At the outset, the Design Museum adopted a hybrid view of design, which gave as much weight to the production, function and meaning of an object, as to its formal qualities. Didactic tools – such as an interactive computer database, film and video, audio-guides, study notes, lectures and seminars – were borrowed from museums of science and industry, and were fused with the display techniques of decorative arts museums. Other – less creative – tensions were never far away. The Design Museum was born out of struggle between respectability and iconoclasm: its quest for identity swung between the opposite poles of a place among the great museums of the world and the outright defiance of curatorial convention. Despite the pace set by its irreverent forerunner, the Boilerhouse Project at the Victoria & Albert Museum, the pull of museological gravitas, from co-operating institutions as well as from within, soon exerted a powerful force on the fledgling organization.

Controversy centred on the status and function of the Collections gallery, which began life as a rolling programme of mini-exhibitions about the history of twentieth-century design in mass-production. These were intended to provide an evolving introduction to the subject and also to the Design Museum itself, setting the exhibitions and education programmes in a broad introductory framework. The intention was neither to invent nor promote a canon of design classics, but to offer a means of investigating the development of design from a range of viewpoints. Only a small proportion of the objects on display in the Collections gallery were owned by the Design Museum. The majority were on long loan from manufacturers, designers, private collectors and other museums, with only a minimal acquisitions policy to fill the gaps where there were no lenders.

The function and success of the Collections gallery therefore depended on the balance and structure of the entire museum; it was part of a larger set of arguments, and not an end in itself. Yet the means of display in the Collections gallery were never truly adequate to reveal the complex meanings which objects acquire through their place in the lives of the people who own and use them. The language of showcases and plinths encouraged a fetishistic reading of the objects which visitors assumed had been selected according to ill-defined criteria of 'good design' or 'good taste'. It is extremely difficult to refute the view that to exhibit an object is to stamp a museum's seal of approval on it, especially when it is included in a historical survey, rather than a thematic exhibition.

The exhibitions programme at the Design Museum was therefore conceived as a counterpoint to the Collections gallery. Exhibitions lend themselves to a journalistic approach: to display the object as documentary evidence, rather than as an isolated icon. They offer the possibility of critical practice and permit commentary and provoke debate.

Initially the issues raised by the exhibitions programme were carried forward through the seminars, lectures and publications organized by the education department for both general and specialist audiences. During the first two years of its life, over eighty public seminars and lectures were held at the Design Museum, and as many films were shown. A quarterly magazine was founded and educational materials published for teachers and pupils. Together these and related activities helped establish the Design Museum as a focus for debate, as well as for display.

Within two years, however, the equilibrium of the Design Museum was threatened by a cash crisis, resulting from a dwindling grant from the Department of Trade and Industry, combined with the unpredictability of sponsorship and inadequate underpinning from its major benefactor. The inevitable decision to cut costs hit the exhibitions programme and the education programme particularly hard, because exhibitions are expensive (although they also generate income from sponsors and admissions) and education is frequently invisible (at least, to certain trustees). The Design

Museum's search for state support was particularly depressing as government responsibility for different aspects of design became a game of pass the departmental parcel around Whitehall. The difficulty was exacerbated by the fact that the main sponsor department, the Department of Trade and Industry, has a different view of the benefits of design promotion. The impact of design on the balance of payments is an appropriate concern for the DTI and its client the Design Council; it is not an appropriate preoccupation for an independent museum.

The financial crisis at the Design Museum provoked a decision to focus on the (cheaper) Collections gallery, at the expense of the exhibitions and education programmes, effectively cutting off much of the intellectual lifeblood of the institution. At the same time, the pace of change in the Collections gallery slowed down as a means of reducing costs further. (It will have been a false economy if visitor numbers drop proportionately as the museum loses its reputation for change and debate.)

This was accompanied by a simultaneous retreat back to the modernist canon, approved by the Trustees, at the expense of argument, experimentation and risk-taking. More objects were gradually acquired by, rather than loaned to, the museum. In spring 1992 Sir Terence Conran took over as Chairman, with a mission to survive rather than to explain. Inevitably, he championed a programme which reflected his own aesthetic preferences and interests. Six months later the former Director of the Victoria & Albert Museum, Sir Roy Strong, noted how the Design Museum was devoted to putting 'classics' in glass cases. He commented 'as soon as the Design Museum became a sacred temple it became in fact what Conran would have criticized the V&A for becoming' (Strong 1992).

The Design Museum is not alone for having succumbed to the compulsion to collect. The acquisitive instinct is evidently alive and well throughout the museums of the post-industrial world. In 1992, fifteen years after it opened, the Centre Pompidou in Paris mounted a massive display under the banner heading *Manifeste*, which showed the work of every department, including the Centre de Création Industrielle (CCI). The design section of *Manifeste* was particularly interesting because the CCI had only begun a systematic programme of acquisitions a couple of years earlier, and so this was its first opportunity to set out its stall for the general public. Presented warehouse-style on massed rows of plinths, the size of the collection was already impressive. Yet the objects on show rarely departed from the blend of aesthetic restraint and technological innovation which distinguishes the products of high modernism, by now familiar in every international museum collection. Now you can see Braun, Sony, Brionvega, IBM, Olivetti, Knoll and Vitra on the Rue Beaubourg, just as you can see them at Butlers Wharf and on West 53rd

Street. Design collections are increasing like duty-free shops: full of the same reassuring labels all around the world.

Londoners who enjoy looking at Charles Eames chairs and Alessi kettles are especially blessed, because now they can see the same objects twice in their own city. The Design Museum Collections gallery faces a new challenge from the Twentieth Century Gallery at the Victoria & Albert Museum. For the past decade, the twentieth century has been primarily represented in the V&A in a gallery showing 'British Design 1900–1960'. This was a frustrating affair: the cut-off point of 1960 seemed both timid and arbitrary, while the exclusively British perspective obscured the international cross-currents of modern design and manufacture. The new gallery falls into neither of these traps and concludes with a changing display of an aspect of the contemporary design scene, which will be organized by a team from outside the museum. The opening display in October 1992 featured the ubiquitous symbol of the Barcelona Olympics, the dog *Cobi* created by the Catalan designer Javier Mariscal.

The journey through the gallery from 1900 to the present is billed as 'a rich mixture of precious one-offs and mass-produced design classics' which 'provides an unrivalled opportunity to study the way we have lived and designed this century'. Inevitably, the gallery does not quite match up to the promotional hyperbole; the V&A's collection is as partial as any other, the result of the tastes and interests of curators at different times and with different budgets. While the pre-war displays emphasize aesthetic experiment of modernism and its forebears, the postwar section reflects popular taste alongside objects awarded the stamp of official approval. The difference in the public reaction to the two parts of the gallery is marked, as the confidence and delight brought by personal recognition takes over from deference to the invisible connoisseur. The woman next to me was thrilled to see her old baby bath (manufactured by Ecko in 1957) and told her daughter 'You were bathed in that, love.' As Joanna Coles commented in the *Guardian* 'There is something intensely sad about seeing what were once safe, familiar household objects now dusted down and presented on smart shelves behind glass doors' (Coles 1992).

The new gallery provides a home at last for those 'lost' objects of the modern age, such as the wireless, which did not fit into the old curatorial categories based on nineteenth-century materials (metalwork, ceramics and glass, woodwork and so on). Now radios and light-fittings have special show cases to reveal the aesthetic agility of their designers, although you still have to cross the Exhibition Road to go to the Science Museum to learn about the technology.

Whether London's residual enthusiasm for design in the 1990s can sustain two such galleries remains to be seen. There is a new mood of consumer resistance in the aftermath of the abrupt collapse of the 'caring and sharing' hyperbole with which the decade opened, as the truly awful state of the national economy becomes clear. 1980s style consumerism is no longer a viable option for individuals, households or nations. Paying to look at objects in glass cases may become a less attractive pastime as a result. Being directly dependent on visitor admissions, the Design Museum is more vulnerable than the V&A, whose purposes and sources of income are more diversified. The challenge now for both museums is to present a critical commentary on the High Street, rather than be a cosy, cultural adjunct to it.

The V&A has already begun to sharpen its analytical edge by overtly raising issues of value in contemporary design. The problem faced by the Design Museum is how to maintain a distance from commercial interests in the face of acute funding pressures. Designer- or manufacturer-led displays may be informative, but they are unlikely to speak with an independent voice. The labels 'As seen in . . .' or 'Selected for the permanent collection of . . .' add cultural prestige to an object which always acts in the interests of the manufacturer rather than the museum.

Museums should be places which enable visitors to make some sense of the world, not as passive receivers, but as critical viewers. Yet for many people the experience is constrained by the fact that they only see rare, precious or ancient artefacts in the artificial environment of the gallery. Design museums face a particular challenge and have a particular opportunity by virtue of the relationship which exists between visitors and the same, or comparable, objects outside the gallery walls. They need to develop a voice beyond the discreet label in the glass case, but will require vision and resources to do so.

The challenge is to pursue an agenda beyond the promotion of a single notion of 'good design', which frequently coincides with a particular canon of taste. To achieve this, museums must use a variety of interpretative media to dig beneath the surface of the finished product. The purpose should be not only to explain the process and technology of design, but to investigate its economic, social and cultural conditions. The model of consumer education promulgated by Henry Cole during the first industrial revolution provides a precedent, not least in his willingness to criticize as well as admire. To the extent that Cole was not interested in elevating design, but in reinforcing its centrality in a modern consumer society, his legacy remains an inspiration.

The Cooper-Hewitt Museum in New York, the National Museum of Design of the USA, recently redefined its own mission in terms of active intervention. 'The future of the environment, the quality of life, and the way in which design affects everyday living are issues of universal concern, and the Museum recognizes its responsibility as an advocate of the design process.' Henry Cole would have approved.

REFERENCES

Bennett, Alan (1992) 'Dramatist's choice', *National Gallery News*, October.

Coles, Joanna (1992) 'Fish eyes modern art at the V&A', *Guardian*, 22 October.

Leedham, Robert (1992) 'Bestsellers: the poster', *Guardian*, 12 October.

MacGregor, Neil (1992), quoted by Patricia Morison in 'An invitation to loiter with intent', *Financial Times*, 4 October.

Strong, Sir Roy (1992), quoted by Catherine Bennett in 'Monsieur le Design Pope', *Guardian*, 12 October.

Chapter 10

Framing the audience for theatre

Baz Kershaw

INTRODUCTION

This chapter aims to use theatre as a test case of the ways in which the commodification of cultural consumption may affect the distribution of authority and power in post-industrial, service-based societies. From this perspective theatre and live performance are especially rich fields for analysis; first, because much of British theatre has traditionally been subsidized in order to 'protect' it from the reign of the consumer, but in the past decade or so this protection has been reduced and theatre has been subject to increasing marketization and commodification; and second, because theatre and performance as 'discourses of power' are especially representative of a much wider range of cultural practices in society, and this is particularly the case in service-oriented economies. I wish to suggest that 'performance' may be a crucial concept for understanding how such cultures operate, and that the ways in which performance is 'theatrically framed' is indicative of widespread strategies in the struggle for authority and power in late capitalism.

My argument hinges on the notion that in almost every sphere of activity western developed countries are becoming more performance-oriented. This can be seen, for example, in the development of the heritage and tourist industries, where costume drama – whether in the form of retro-dressing or the contemporary *couture* of slick uniforms – is increasingly the norm. It can be detected as easily in the associated industries of catering and travel, where the waiter and the air-host are encouraged to add a flick of performative spice to the fare. It appears in the retail industries, where the name tag on the check-out person confers an identity which has little to do with individual character, everything to do with a quasi-personalized and dramatized conception of service. These are, I think, some of the signs of a much more pervasive 'theatricalization' of culture, through which our day-to-day encounters, our leisure activities, our politics, and much more, increasingly are framed as quasi-theatre. This appears to be producing what I shall call the 'performative society', in which human transactions are complexly structured through the growing use of performative modes and frames. If this is the case, inevitably it will have implications for our interpretations of how power circulates in contemporary society, both at the micro-level of the everyday, and at the macro-level of formations and structures.

As this volume is primarily concerned with the 'authority of the consumer' I shall approach the theatricalization of culture through the stage door, so to speak, by addressing a single question, namely: what might it mean to 'consume' a theatrical performance and how might such 'consumption' affect the authority in society of the 'consumers'? This formulation raises more general issues about the commodification of theatre and performance, and about the nature of, and relationships between, commodities, consumption and the production of culture, both in its narrow Arnoldian sense as that which provides 'sweetness and light', and in the broader culturalist sense of 'a way of life'. These last issues are dealt with elsewhere in this book, so I will confine myself to a very brief theoretical prologue here.

Marx uses the concept of commodity fetishism to explain how capitalist systems alienate people from their own labour and in the process mask the actual nature of social relations. The circulation of commodities is a phantasmagoria in which exchange-value banishes use-value and so occludes perception of the exploitative operations of capital in controlling labour for the extraction of surplus value. Thus consumption disempowers, the consumer has only a fantasy authority (Marx 1970: 71–83; Eagleton 1990: 84–8). Jameson explicates key aspects of such disempowerment in his treatise on the cultural logic of late capitalism, *Postmodernism* (Jameson 1991). Famously, he claims that one fundamental effect of post-modernism is

> the disappearance of a sense of history . . . in which our entire contemporary social system has little by little begun to lose its capacity to retain its own past, has begun to live in a perpetual present and in a perpetual change that obliterates traditions.
>
> (Foster (ed.) 1983: 125)

Other cultural critics are a little less pessimistic. For example, Susan Willis offers some interesting reflections on historical theme parks (such as the Beamish Centre near Gateshead), when she claims that the *active participation* of the visitor in a reconstruction of a culture in which use-value was not entirely effaced has the potential to 'produce a critical rupture with the present'. Such a rupture splits apart the phantasmagoria of commodification and gives access to radical empowerment beyond, as it were, the commodity form (Willis 1991: 15).

Various versions of this debate animate the work of many cultural analysts (see Fiske 1989; Frith 1983; Hebdige 1979) and it can be traced

back through the writings of Lukács, Adorno, Habermas and others of
the Frankfurt School (Thompson 1990). Walter Benjamin, though, provided its most resonant formulation for our discussion of the theatricalization of culture. In a now celebrated essay Benjamin prefigured Jameson
in arguing that:

> The technique of [mechanical] reproduction detaches the reproduced
> object from the domain of tradition. By making reproductions it substi-
> tutes a plurality of copies for a unique existence ... [and it leads to]
> the liquidation of the traditional value of the cultural heritage ...
>
> (Benjamin 1970: 223)

Such 'unique existence' Benjamin characterizes through the concepts of
'aura', 'authenticity', 'cult value' and 'ritual'; moreover, he identifies its
last (?) glimmerings in a contrast between film and stage acting.

> The aura which, on the stage, emanates from Macbeth, cannot be
> separated for the spectators from that of the actor. However, the
> singularity of the shot in the studio is that the camera is substituted
> for the public ... the aura that envelops the actor vanishes, and with
> it the aura of the figure he portrays.
>
> (Benjamin 1970: 231)

What is important here is not the problematic concept of 'aura', but the
attempt to grapple with the general meaning of the unique performance.
For in a period when consumerism seems bent on commodifying every
aspect of social interaction, including face-to-face encounters, the question
of the nature of an effective counterposing force becomes ever more
urgent.

What follows is an exploration of that question, using British theatre
as a paradigm for other productive realms, especially in the service industries. In this respect theatre and performance today offer rich pickings,
as they are areas of cultural production in which commodification is
chronically pervasive, but also where it may be kept most effectively at
bay. I shall explore the issues raised by this situation through discussion
of trends in British cultural policy in the 1980s; developments in the
operation of theatre (especially subsidized theatre) in recent years; key
aspects of theatrical theory; and ideas about the nature of performance.

COMMODIFICATION *VIA* STATE SUBSIDY IN THE 1980s

British subsidized theatre in the 1980s, in common with other cultural
institutions, was subject to massive pressures which aimed to make it
more market and consumer oriented. As we shall see, there was a fundamental shift in the ideology of the funding agencies and in the ways that
their 'clients' – in this case the national, repertory and alternative (or

fringe) theatre companies – related to the public. These developments can be described variously as a struggle between traditional and post-modernist aesthetic values; an undermining of elitism by populism; a new *rapprochement* between state subsidy and market economics; and a move from essentialist to instrumentalist views of the functions of theatre in society. As these alternative descriptions suggest, the changes were fairly complicated, but they can be summarized crudely as an attempted transfer of authority from producers to consumers.

Traditionally the Arts Council of Great Britain (ACGB) had subsidized producers, mainly through grants to theatre companies. Its policies were based on the liberal-humanist view that the artist has something special to offer to society which transcends any particular political or economic regime. Art puts people in touch with 'universal' values, so it should be protected both from market forces and state interference since, like education, health and social security, it is an essential ingredient in the satisfied citizen's life. Thus Roy Shaw, Secretary-General of the Council from 1975 to 1982, approvingly quotes Iris Murdoch's dictum that art is 'a training in the love of virtue' (Shaw 1987: 23). Such a notion derives from a very long tradition of essentialist cultural critics and art theorists which includes, for example, Ruskin, Wordsworth, Arnold, Tolstoy. Fundamentally this tradition holds that art has *inherent* redemptive, rejuvenative or recuperative qualities, and that its transformative power is somehow placed *in* the artwork by the superior productive abilities of the artist.

In the 1970s, Arts Council policy generally stuck to this line, though it was tempered by a growing commitment to arts education as a way of broadening access for more people to the 'high arts'. Its attempts to democratize an existing cultural agenda, however, attracted rising accusations of elitism from anti-authoritarian formations, such as the Council of Europe and the British community arts movement (Simpson 1976; Kelly 1984). Ironically, in the 1980s its policies met a similar challenge, but from a totally different ideological direction, as the 'reforms' of the Thatcher government demanded greater 'accountability' and 'value for money' in public institutions. The pressure shifted the Council towards a more populist stance, and simultaneously eroded the so-called 'arm's length principle', which was supposed to stop state interference in the 'freedom' of the arts (Hutchison 1982: 27–40). Thus neo-conservatism sanctioned a more interventionist role for the Council so that it could open up the subsidy system to market forces.

The rhetoric of this process is interesting for the ways in which it echoed Thatcherite doctrine. Thus the high-Tory former editor of *The Times*, William Rees-Mogg, who in 1981 had been appointed as Chairman of the Council, by mid-decade was arguing that:

The qualities required for survival in this age will be the qualities of the age itself. They include self-reliance, imagination, a sense of opportunity, range of choice, and the entrepreneurial action of small professional groups. The state should continue to help the arts but the arts should look first to themselves, and to their audiences, for their future and their growth.

(Rees-Mogg 1985: 8)

Such developments, Rees-Mogg urges, are a necessary consequence of an all-pervasive historical abandonment of 'the great twentieth century thesis . . . [of] collectivism and mass forms of production and power'. The end of communism/socialism is signalled by the emergence of a new class – the 'affluent and technically qualified . . . electronic middle class' – that will dominate the social structure. Through them the Arts Council was to become a singular force in the widespread trend to establish a new economic base for Britain in the service industries. Moreover, the yuppies and the meritocratic service class, identified in due course by sociologists and cultural critics as the social formation most in tune with postmodernism (Featherstone 1991: 35), were to be the vanguard consumers of a new arts renaissance.

Rees-Mogg had somewhat cheekily borrowed his lecture's title from Ruskin, but the name of the Arts Council pamphlet which translated his arguments into practical objectives was straight out of the Book of Thatcher. *A Great British Success Story* was offered as a 'Prospectus' spelling out the advantages of accepting 'An invitation to the nation to invest in the arts' (ACGB 1986). This glossy panegyric employs the language of big business and the stock exchange to outline the 'Dividends' which would result from a new combination of state grant-aid and private sponsorship, including: (i) low-cost job provision (at £2,070 per head per annum 'a Bargain Price'); (ii) regeneration of depressed inner-city areas; (iii) vital creative stimulus to the wider (commercial) entertainment industry; (iv) substantial tourist income; and so on. Significantly, 'pleasure' for 'millions of people' comes at the end of the list. The arts are framed generically as 'the arts industry', and their operations particularized through a metaphorical transformation into a business company, thus: 'The arts have an excellent sales record, and excellent prospects. *Customers* are growing in number, and with increased leisure one of the certainties of the future, *use* of the arts will intensify' (my emphasis). The pamphlet claims that the arts may provide a society with 'vision', but its main argument carries the clear implication that they are essentially akin to other types of consumer product.

It is important to separate out the style of discourse from what it claims for art. I am not snobbishly arguing against utilitarian notions of, say, the functions of theatre in health-care promotion; rather, I am tracing a rhetorical trend which framed the relationship between art and its

audience in a relatively new way, and which fostered new types of ideological role for both throughout the 'first world'. In Europe this was given
vigorous impetus in 1987 by John Myerscough's impressive report, *The
Economic Importance of the Arts*, which drew on extensive empirical
evidence to provide ammunition for an

> argument [that has] moved on to a higher ground, by relating the role
> of the arts to the fact that we live in an era of industrial re-structuring
> characterised by the growing importance of the service industries ...
> and of industries based on new technologies exploiting information and
> the media. The success of cities in the post-industrial era will depend
> on their ability to build on the provision of services for regional,
> national and international markets. ... The arts fit *naturally* into this
> frame.
>
> (Myerscough 1987: 2 – my emphasis)

Thus art can be used as a cultural magnet to attract 'footloose senior
executives' in search of lucrative locations for the new industries, and it
can be used to tool-up civic systems by becoming a 'catalyst for urban
renewal'. Again theatre and concert audiences, museum and gallery-goers
are transmuted into 'arts customers', but the pressure to so conceive them
is now increased by the stamp of empirical authority. Mighty statistics
promote the notion of art as a service commodity, and an especially
superior one; but not because its inherent qualities put us in touch with
supposed universal human values, rather because it can trigger off huge
transformative forces in the process of social restructuring for the post-
industrial/post-modern age.

From this position it is but a short logical step to conceive the arts
customer as the fulcrum of 'success'; for the instrumentalist vision of this
emerging policy orthodoxy shifts the location of power (and thus
authority) in art from the producer to the consumer, because, after all,
in a *service* relationship it is the latter who, at least in theory, always
calls the tune. I will return to the limitations of this model shortly. For
the moment we can neatly close the circle by two quotations from the
1987/8 Arts Council annual report, in which the Council's Secretary-
General, Luke Rittner, drew attention to 'the unique and precious com
modity that the arts represent'; while Chairman Rees-Mogg suggested that

> We are coming to value the consumer's judgement as highly as that of
> the official or expert. ... The voice of the public must ... be given due
> weight ... [and] the way in which the public discriminates is through
> its willingness to pay for its pleasures.
>
> (ACGB 1988: 2–3)

By the end of the eighties, then, British cultural policy (as represented
by the ACGB) had been refashioned by monetarist ideologies which

favoured the commodification and marketization of art; and at least at the level of rhetoric, this discursive realm relocates power and authority in the image of the consumer as sovereign queen or king.

Before we move on to consider the impact of the rhetoric on actual cultural practices it is worth noting that the new policies were implicitly contradictory, for they signalled a significant erosion of cultural boundaries that the ACGB had been, in part, set up to patrol. For example, the notion that production should follow demand implies, in post-industrial society, a pluralism which challenges the hegemony of 'high art' traditions. The arguments that located art as part of the wider cultural industries problematize its definition (Mulgan and Warpole 1986). Talking about the arts as an industry or business comparable to others in terms of productivity and efficiency suggests that there is no fundamental difference between art and other 'commodities'. Thus the new policies can be seen as part of the wider cultural swing towards de-traditionalization, de-differentiation and the abolition of hierarchies of value, commonly associated with post-modernism (Connor 1989; Featherstone 1991; Jameson 1991). Consequently, the Arts Council's position became increasingly paradoxical; for example, its frequent insistence that subsidy should only support 'excellence' in the arts highlighted the growing problem of identifying exactly what that might mean, and also evoked traces of its elitist past at the very moment of engagement in the populist, post-modernist present. Some politicians were not slow to spot the core institutional issue raised by these developments: both Labour and Liberal Democrat policies for the 1992 General Election recommended that the Council should be abolished. The Tories, apparently happy with the rhetoric, wanted it kept.

THE IMPACT ON THEATRICAL PRACTICE

Throughout the eighties, encouraged by a variety of ACGB schemes, theatres in the subsidized sector worked to improve the ways they treated their audiences, especially through advertising, at the point of sale, and in front-of-house (foyer) services. Increased spending on marketing produced promotional material that was generally better designed, slickly printed and eye-catching, while copy-writing tended towards extravagant hype (for example the English Stage Company) makes Shakespeare the hottest ticket in world theatre. Many theatres adopted quasi-corporate identities, complete with obligatory logos. Ticket buying was made easier by box-office computerization and credit-card payment, and pricing policies reflected a greater awareness of untapped markets through subscription and discounting schemes. A telling example of this general refocusing is provided by the 1992 National Strategy for the Arts, which notes:

the inspired use of the phrase 'Theatre Receptionist' for 'Box Office Assistant' at the Theatre Royal Stratford East, [which] has been shown to encourage wider staff recruitment from communities alienated by the more technical term. It has also led to more positive attitudes to *customer* care. . . .

(Barnard (ed.) 1991: 2 – my emphasis)

The general aim of these developments was to increase 'access' (a 1980s arts catchword) through what the National Strategy somewhat euphemistically calls 'audience development' (NAMSU 1992). So the notion of theatre as a cultural drop-in centre spread, as foyer areas were redesigned to make them more 'welcoming', and bar and restaurant services were developed, both to increase income and to encourage casual use by non-theatregoers. Big refurbishment schemes, such as the £6m project at Newcastle-upon-Tyne's Theatre Royal, and brand new theatres, such as the West Yorkshire Playhouse in Leeds, invariably included facilities for corporate entertainment as essential aids in attempts to woo big sponsors. Bolt-on entertainment such as foyer-cabaret, film screenings and music events became commonplace.

A cognate trend occurred in patterns of subsidized theatre programming: on the one hand there was a drift towards populism, signalled by 'a decline in the presentation of classical drama ... and a rise in musicals ... and plays by Alan Ayckbourn ...' (Cork 1985: 8); on the other hand less original work was available as fewer new plays were staged and as adaptations grew from 5 per cent of the repertoire in 1981–5 to an astonishing 20 per cent in 1985–9 (Barnard (ed.) 1991: Tables 1/2). Moreover, the distinctions between the different theatrical sectors were crumbling, as regional repertory theatres mounted co-productions with leading alternative theatre groups (the Leicester Haymarket Theatre led the way), as alternative theatre groups (such as Complicité and Tara Arts) staged shows at the national theatre, and as national theatre productions (such as David Edgar's fringe-inspired *Nicholas Nickleby*) transferred to the West End and Broadway.

As a 'customer' of the theatre, the audience member had a growing number of performance-related commodities to attend to. Whereas erstwhile the only object to take home from the show was a programme, the eighties witnessed a remarkable proliferation of theatre sales-lines: T-shirts, badges, hats, posters, pennants, playscripts, cassettes of show music, videos of the making of the show – if it could carry an image and/or title of the production, it was pressed into service. The performance itself might become a fading memory, but its traces could be registered in countless objects, the consumption of which might magically recapture the moment of gazing at the stars onstage. Thus some especially successful shows acquired their own logo – one thinks of the half-mask of the

Phantom of the Opera or the waif-face of *Les Misérables* – which by a process of semiotic condensing 'becomes' the show. Susan Willis succinctly notes that, partly because of their proliferation in contexts separate from what they signify, 'the logos become essentialised in relation to the de-essentialisation of the commodity itself' (Willis 1991: 60). We should also note that such logos may contribute to the process of de-differentiation, via which the boundaries between art and everyday life are blurred, thus opening the way to the aestheticization of the ordinary, which Lash maintains is central to post-modernism (Lash 1990: 172–98). Performance-related sales-lines might also be seen as particularly potent signifiers in relation to Baudrillard's notion of the 'hyperreality' of consumer societies, since their signifieds are simply vanished fictions (Baudrillard 1983). More mundanely, the poster-logo, together with all the other purchasable para-phernalia that theatres marketed in the eighties, signals changing patterns and types of use of theatre as a cultural 'commodity'.

In a post-industrial, pluralistic society such changes are likely to be complex and hard to describe accurately, but three developments are worth particular note for the key issues which they raise about the kinds of authority that may be constructed through cultural artefacts. First, the marketization/commodification of theatre offers growing opportunities for 'secondary consumption' of performance, in which the possession and use of spin-off artefacts may become a potent substitute for the experience itself. Thus wearing the *Phantom of the Opera* T-shirt and/or a National Theatre peaked cap may be even more culturally charged than an evening in the stalls watching the show. For, as we know from Foucault, desire can be a most powerful stimulant to the symbolic construction and con-sumption of an empirically absent universe of discourse. Second, the middle-class domination of theatre, and especially subsidized theatre, may be challenged by a growing heterogeneity of audiences. This is most marked for London, where there was sustained growth in the proportion of tourists and day visitors using the National and West End theatres, to the point where they constituted over half of the total attendances. Figures for the regions show a much smaller proportion of tickets bought by non-residents, but a much higher proportion of C2DEs than is commonly supposed by critics who claim a middle-class hegemony for theatre (Feist and Hutchison 1990: 37; Myerscough 1987: 25). Third, the trend towards heterogeneity may have been accelerated both by the collapse of the traditional aesthetic hierarchies under the pressure of populism and by the erosion of boundaries between theatre and the so-called cultural industries. The increased crossover of productions and, crucially, per-formers between theatre and film, TV, video, radio, breeds a familiarity (especially through well-known names and faces) which undermines exclusiveness. Similarly, the growth of the theatre 'package tour' – a coach trip, a meal, a show, a hotel room at an all-inclusive bargain price – turns mainstream metropolitan theatregoing into an accessible 'outing'. Thus as the cultural barriers diminish, theatre becomes the subject of a widening plurality of uses. Its place in the big business entertainment account is matched by its contributions to the heritage industry, while the once heterogeneous local audience is infiltrated by the domestic version of what Urry, following Feifer, calls 'post-tourists' (Urry 1990: 100–2): people for whom there is no correlation between *particular* cultural zones and self- or group-identity, who collect theatre experiences in order to construct the deep surfaces of the post-modern personality.

The net results of these trends for theatre, *vis-à-vis* authority, are paradoxical. On the one hand, theatre's location in the whole cultural realm is enhanced. We can identify this empirically, perhaps, in ticket sales and yield, where the total number of attendances held steady in the second half of the 1980s even though the rise in ticket prices outstripped the rate of increase of average earnings (Feist and Hutchison 1990: 4). The most likely explanation for this is that the theatre came to rely less on an established audience, and so was used by a growing number of people (who would, on average, pay less each). This suggests a rising social *status* for theatre as a symbolic commodity, an improvement which is reinforced by the more widespread growth of secondary consumption through artefacts and media reproductions. Consumers of theatre – both primary and secondary – stand to gain more authority from this enhanced general status. On the other hand, the lack of cohesion brought by the expanding heterogeneity of actual audiences, the separation of theatre from any particular social formation, suggests a dispersal of power. It becomes increasingly difficult to employ Bourdieu's concept of 'distinction' (Bourdieu 1984), or to talk, say, about the middle classes using theatre to consolidate their position in the social pecking-order. Instead, we have the spectacle of a fragmenting democratization, a growth in access which turns theatre either towards the ideological anodyne of populism or into a site of acute conflict over its use as a cultural resource by special-interest groups.

The implications of these changes for an assessment of the shifting patterns of cultural power and authority are very complex. But we can begin to address the issues by considering the ways in which power and authority may be inscribed in live theatrical performance; and this returns us to our core concern, namely, what might it mean to 'consume' live theatre and how might this affect performance as a discourse of power? We will need to theorize in more detail how commodification may affect the reception/'consumption' of theatre and performance. I shall use the rest of this chapter briefly to outline the foundations of such a theory, which will depend centrally on the distinction between 'theatre' and 'performance'. By 'theatre' I mean the institutions, buildings, modes of production that are required to stage a performance. By 'performance' I mean the live event itself. I will conclude my argument with a brief discussion of theatre-as-institution and performance-as-event in relation to notions of commodification, consumerism and consumption.

THE THEATRE AS A SERVICE INDUSTRY

The changes in the patterns of use of theatre demand that we re-evaluate the dominant explanations of its social functions. The most influential of these derive from Gramsci and Althusser in arguing that theatres are mainly used by the middle classes – or electronic, or service classes – to confirm and strengthen their power base within the social hierarchy. Thus the cultural intermediaries in charge of the subsidy system in Britain, by traditionally reinforcing the institutional dominance of the national and repertory theatres, have colluded with these (their own?) classes in the use of taxes gathered from the numerically larger subordinate groups, both to keep those groups culturally subjugated and to keep down the prices of the dominant formation's pleasures (McGrath 1981, 1990).

The paradoxical empowerment/disempowerment, brought about by the middle-class colonization of mainstream theatre has been most commonly explained through a simple duality: empowerment is achieved through the *active* occupation of the institution of theatre, while disempowerment is the result of a *passive* consumption of that theatre's performances (for example: Craig 1980: 13–14; Gooch 1984: 34–5). Now I will argue here that this account both oversimplifies and inverts the ways in which such theatre (and perhaps *any* theatre) aims to function. That is to say, we may arrive at a more accurate account if we think of the active use of the theatre institution as usually accompanied by a *passive* – or, more precisely, *implicit* – consumption of its meanings; while the apparently passive consumption of its productions may mask an *active use* of their codes.

Most theatre, and especially mainstream theatre, is a curious cultural commodity in that it requires us to pay for an acute deprivation of our freedom of movement. As with cinema, to gain access to the performance we agree to be channelled through an ever more limiting physical regime, until we are seated to focus within a narrow angle of vision, normally to remain there for a period we do not determine. Moreover, once the live actors begin their work, the audience is under a greater injunction than can ever occur in cinema. Anyone who has been impelled to leave a live performance during its course will know what constraining forces are built into the conventions created for its consumption. Viewed from this angle, the theatre consumer certainly does not call the tune; considered as a service industry, theatre offers what must be one of the most exacting producer-consumer contracts of all. But what might such an extreme contractual arrangement signify?

One way into this question is to analyse the architecture of theatre in relation to its social context, in order to understand what the performance theorist Richard Schechner calls its 'sociometric design' (1988: 161). For example, Schechner draws attention to the salient features of the nine-teenth-century proscenium theatre (see illustration: Adelphi Theatre, London), which include a hierarchy of seating/prices, with the most expensive boxes having a poor view of the stage but being splendidly placed for the display of their patrons' privilege to the rest of the audi-ence; an auditorium decorated to suggest opulence, wealth, comfort (though this diminishes with seat price); the effacement of the machinery of production by the proscenium arch and curtain; the correspondence between the open arch and a shop window. In these and other ways,

> the proscenium theatre is a model for capitalism. Today, as capitalism evolves into corporatism, new kinds of theatre arise. Cultural centres and regional theatres – art fortresses run by impresarios overseen by boards of directors – are examples of corporatism.
>
> (Schechner 1988: 164)

One might take issue with the detail of this account, but the substantive point is surely sound: in consuming theatre as a service we are more or less implicitly consuming the ideologies of the society which built it. Nor does it matter that we might have a critical attitude to those ideologies, that we might, for example, find the reconstruction of Shakespeare's Globe Theatre quaint and uncomfortable; the fact of their use is in part an animation of the values inscribed in the architecture.

Now in the post-industrial world, as Schechner points out, we are confronted by a variety of theatre architectures which model a range of ideologies. Where formerly there was a dominant form – the proscenium arch – which could be considered the 'natural' shape for theatre to take, now the logic of late capitalism has led to a plurality of sociometric models, producing the potential for the uncovering of any hegemony written into theatre viewed as a commodity form. As for other commodi-ties, this gives the illusion of choice, even of a radical escape from ideol-ogy; but the proliferation of forms is simply another version of what Ivan Illich calls 'radical monopolies'; that is to say 'the dominance of one type of product rather than one brand ... when one industrial production process exercises an exclusive control over the satisfaction of a pressing need' (Illich 1985: 52). Of course, there may still be alternatives offering a radical criticism of the radical monopoly, but generally these are pushed to the margins of the cultural system. The mechanism for achieving such marginalization is the marketization and commodification of the whole system, as described above; for the components of the contemporary pluralism of theatre are now made to signify, more or less obliquely, consumerism as a cultural practice.

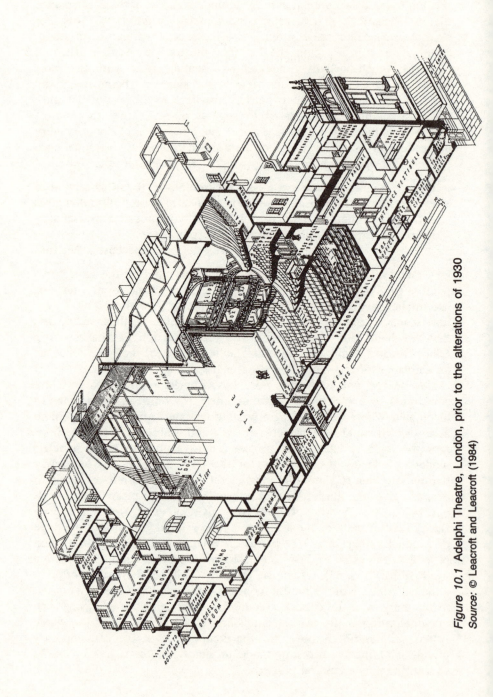

Figure 10.1 Adelphi Theatre, London, prior to the alterations of 1930
Source: © Leacroft and Leacroft (1984)

Thus theatre *may* be the site of increased access to, and a variety of uses of, what was previously a protected and privileged domain, and the dominance of the middle-class audience within and through this particular mode of cultural production may be undermined or dispersed, but the newly heterogeneous, fragmented audience is still the object of consumerism. That is to say, the contract constructed by the modified conventions of the theatre experience implicitly underwrites commodification. In a sense, the audience's bodies embody the ideology of theatre as a commodity form because by their compliance they consume its meanings. This is the case even if, as is often argued for post-modernist cultural practice, the audience entertain the theatre ironically, with a self-reflexive awareness of themselves as the consuming commodity. Such irony may produce a sense of power within the narrowing conventions; but the irony, as it were, rides on an abdication which is enforced by the growing separation of producer and consumer. Within the theatre's walls consumption of theatre is increasingly an abdication of authority. But if this is the case, and if the fragmenting audience diminishes theatre as a cultural *cachet*, why is there still an audience for performance?

PERFORMANCE AS A COMMODITY

As we have seen, the idea of the passive audience for performance has been associated usually with mainstream theatre. In the Marxist tradition the notion derives directly from Brecht's idea of *culinary* theatre, in which a gullible audience is seduced into a glazed ecstacy of sensory indulgence that is deeply conservative (Brecht 1964: 89). But the image has also been potent for other critical traditions including, perhaps surprisingly, theatre semiotics. Thus De Marinis, in an essay on the 'Dramaturgy of the Spectator', directly links 'closed' performance texts to 'the passive and standardised means of consumption found in mainstream theatre' (1987: 104). Maria Shevtsova draws attention to this tendency when she claims that some theatre semioticians cast

> spectators in the role of consumers. Thus the stage production is the product packaged on the assembly line, while the consumer is the buyer who closes the production-consumption circuit.... the buyer, who legitimates the input of labour into the commodity, is outside the productive force itself.
>
> (1991)

The image is clearly one of disempowerment; consumption conceived in terms of exchange-value, the audience excluded from the means of production. This interpretation arises because theatre semiotics is more concerned to describe the structures of theatrical sign systems than to determine the meanings which the audience may construct through its use of the signs.

In a broader framework of analysis the idea of the passive audience in some respects may also relate to the theoretical tradition initiated by Bakhtin, which has grappled with the functions of the carnivalesque in society (Bakhtin 1968). Thus the carnivalesque is a cultural practice characterized by excess, immersion, the elimination of distance between subject and object; this in turn has been related by contemporary cultural critics to the development of post-industrial consumerism, so that, for example, shopping malls, theme parks, department stores, are seen as sites of carnivalesque indulgence. Willis thus suggests that 'the amusement park is not conceived of as a site of production, but is felt instead to be a commodity itself' (Willis 1991: 16); while Featherstone draws on Baudrillard, Jameson, Feifer and Urry in arguing that consumers of such sites are aware that they are simply simulations and have the 'capacity to open up to surface sensations, spectacular imagery, liminoid experiences and intensities without ... nostalgia for the real' (Featherstone 1991: 60). I have already noted how *theatre* can take its place in this phantasmagoria of commodity fetishism; but what are the processes whereby the *live performer* is, as it were, denatured through commodification?

A common explanation in theatrical theory points to the performer's display of skill or technique. Thus the highly influential Polish director Jerzy Grotowski represents a long line of analysis when he describes what he calls the 'courtesan actor' as presenting the audience with little more than 'an accumulation of methods, artifices and tricks ... a collection of clichés' (Grotowski 1968; 34). Such a theatre of prostitution is seen as producing performances that are totally lacking in authenticity. Performance thus becomes unreal, in the sense that it is merely a simulation; and of course it is particularly prone to being perceived in this way as it is so obviously founded on artifice.

Now clearly, when the wider cultural trends of consumerism and post-modernism are encouraging all experience to be perceived as simulation, performance has increasingly less chance of escaping a hyper-real existence, in the Baudrillardian sense. Parallel lines of contemplation led the remarkable theoretician of theatre, Herbert Blau, to write:

> As we think of a new audience for a new theatre in what remains of a class society, this [the current situation] is likely to give us a sense that we come together *(de)classified*, as if the power to be an audience, for those who are one, is not the spontaneously live ideology but the fringe benefit of collective dispossession.
>
> (1990: 357)

Here, then, is the domain of the completely disempowered, where the audience is sited at what should be the cutting edge of culture, the perfect place for self-reflexive critique (as Brecht saw it), only to be robbed by their internalization of consumerism's capacity for commodifying the living body.

This is the power that Barthes assigned to the face of Garbo (Barthes 1973: 56), and, ironically, it is the nature of the power of the terrestial star (of stage or screen) which perhaps most clearly indicates how the commodification of performance can be bypassed. Anne Ubersfeld offers a singular description of the firmament in which such figures circulate when she writes:

> Theatrical pleasure is, properly speaking, the pleasure of the sign; it is the most semiotic of pleasures.... Theatre as sign of a gap being filled.... Memory and utopia, desire and remembrance, everything that summons up an absence is, in fact, fertile ground for theatrical pleasure.
>
> (Ubersfeld 1982: 129)

It follows that in the context of theatre/performance signs which summon up, as it were, immense absence with the greatest semiotic economy can generate enormous pleasure; and successful performance is made up of such signs. In parallel vein Richard Schechner (following Benjamin and others) describes how the 'presence' of a star is not dependent on a display of skill, quite the contrary. For in the star 'presence becomes an absence, a lack of anything complicated to do. In a certain way stars must practice doing very little' (Schechner 1988: 204; Benjamin 1970: 232). The impassive face of Garbo, Helen Weigel's silent scream as Mother Courage: these are the images which give you, the audience, the greatest scope to exercise your power.

PERFORMANCE BEYOND COMMODITY

It may well be that live performance is one form of cultural transaction which can, ultimately, resist commodification, and if this is the case it has profound implications for how we might theorize the theatre-consumer as having authority. This in turn may have implications for how we conceive of the authority of other types of consumer. Such a theory might begin as a parallel argument to that advanced by, for example, Fiske, when he claims that the oppressed may make subversive readings of popular/dominant culture (Fiske 1989: 191–3), but with the difference that the *very nature* of interpretation in live performance has the potential to empower an audience in ways that transcend recuperation to and incorporation in the dominant. For this effect to be produced certain conditions need to pertain, as we shall see in a moment; but first we must briefly offer a vast oversimplification of an extremely complex debate about perception and theatrical performance.

We may begin by observing that even in a commodified, post-modernist world the conventions of theatre carry the traces of older productive opportunities. As Bennett notes, the sense of occasion, the specially marked-off space, the gathering of energy and focus in ways that are unique to the live event of performance, are designed to construct a special attitude of reception which is characterized by two crucial qualities: first, to provide the potential for individuals who may not even know each other to become a collective; second, to establish a potent relationship between the actuality of theatre-as-institution and the fictionality (or the imaginariness) of the unique and unrepeatable performance (Bennett 1990: 148–50). The precise nature and outcome of this relationship as it is enacted determines the share-out of power and authority between actors and audience, and beyond theatre, as we shall see.

The potential relationship between theatre/actuality and performance/ fictionality is admirably described by States in phenomenological terms:

> The actor takes us into the world within the world itself... [and] enables us to recognise the human 'from the inside'.... I am watching Olivier *exist* as Macbeth, and through this unique ontological confusion I exist myself in a new dimension.
>
> (States 1985: 47)

Julian Hilton provides a parallel description from an entirely different standpoint:

> if the performers succeed in their task, the audience no longer feels itself to be passive, merely watching, but senses itself to be in the action, to have so fully intervened in the gaps and indeterminacies of the performance as to have broken down the distinction between the stage and the auditorium.
>
> (Hilton 1987: 133)

This 'intervention' is an exercising of the live audience's collective power; but it is also, paradoxically, a giving up of itself to the performance, for in working on the 'gaps and indeterminacies', the absences, as it were, between (and perhaps in) the sign systems constructed by the performance, the audience is accepting the valency of those systems. It is partly this which prevents a total equivalence being drawn between performance and the carnivalesque, for the immersion in the fictional world is achieved through conscious interpretations of those signs. Moreover, as Coleridge argued, this is a consciousness wrought by the fact that the audience is never 'absolutely deluded' that it is not in a theatre (Clarke (ed.) 1965: 412–13). Hence the audience at a successful performance may be not unlike the *flaneur* as characterized by Featherstone, swinging between immersion and detachment in a pleasurable oscillation (Featherstone 1991: 70–2). We may say then that while the audience consumes the performance (its signs) the reverse is also sometimes (often?) the case: the performance consumes the audience and, again paradoxically, that generates the *collective* power of the audience (Kershaw 1992: 21–35).

There are various ways in which this extraordinary state of affairs may be theorized, but theatre anthropology offers an account which is especially useful to our argument. Victor Turner characterizes art in modern societies as essentially 'liminoid', associated with leisure and play. Moreover,

> *Liminoid phenomena* tend ... to be generated by specific named individuals and in particular groups ... they ... are thought of at first as ludic offerings placed for sale on the 'free' market.... Their symbols are closer to the personal-psychological than to the 'objective-social' typological pole.
>
> (1982: 54)

Following Turner we may say, then, that it is the personal-psychological that is 'consumed' by successful performance in order to construct a collective subjectivity in the experience of a fictional world; but in theatre this is always achieved in the context of the 'objective-social' as represented by the sociometric model of theatre-as-institution. In contemporary British theatre we may then have witnessed the ironic spectacle of a middle class which enjoyed 'performance beyond commodity' as a way of producing an identity (a subjectivity) that secures social power through an institution increasingly devoted to turning performance into a commodity (*pace* Bourdieu). Marxists would no doubt identify this as an aspect of capitalism's basic contradiction; we might add that increased access for other groupings and the growth of the fragmented audience, as already noted, are likely to disperse such power by making consumption of performance as commodity the norm. Commodification does not simply take over the power of performance to create collective subjectivity; it completely undermines that most essential potential. Where performance may once have provided the site for a subversion of its own context, of society as represented in the sociometric model of the theatre, it is slowly being robbed of its power to provoke authority, radical or otherwise, in its audiences.

PERFORMANCE, THEATRE, COMMODITY, AUTHORITY

It remains briefly to draw together the strands of my argument. I have been arguing that however hard the state in a post-industrial and late capitalist society presses on to theatre the accoutrements of commodification, however much theatre actually becomes a commodity, the object of commodity fetishism, successful live performance will always transcend the effort so to contain it. In the terms of classic Marxism, this is because the unique and ephemeral qualities of performance cannot always be translated into exchange-value, as its nature, its *raison d'être*, is to give the audience access to production. This can be explained by noting that what the performer produces is, in a sense, 'pure' use-value; and it is 'pure' because it has no equivalent, even in relation to its own apparent repetition. Moreover, the signs produced by the performer invite the audience to attend to what is absent, and in so doing they become producers rather than consumers. Thus, however hard the wedge of commodification is driven between producer and consumer in theatre, performance may always have the potential to turn audiences into collective co-producers. It follows that performance-beyond-commodity is always empowering, so that even as it consumes the audience it provides grounds for enhanced authority. Audiences of performance gain power (as a basis for authority) through *not* being consumers.

However, in recent years the state in Britain, in concert with other agencies of late capitalism, has increasingly sought to turn performance into commodity. The main tools in this refashioning have been the marketization and commodification of theatre as an institution. These changes have aimed to open up the *access* to and *uses* of theatre, with a range of results, of which three are especially significant to the issue of consumer authority. First, the increasing heterogeneity of the audience has undermined the potential of performance to produce collective empowerment. Second, the shift towards a general perception of theatre as a commodity reinforces the tendency to perceive performance as a commodity. Third, consumption of theatre as a sociometric model of consumerism reinforces the naturalization, the hegemony of commodification. These trends are consonant with the wider social drift towards a post-modernism which, in the guise of giving the consumer more authority, actually disempowers her.

But, also, if we view theatre/performance as a paradigm for the more widespread service industries, it may enable us to locate the sources for a radically democratized empowerment of 'consumers'. Such empowerment is not achieved through the making of alternative or resistant 'readings' of the consumer products of popular (or any other) culture, as the tradition of analysis represented by Fiske and Hebdige would claim. Rather, empowerment arises and authority may ensue when face-to-face encounters – whether in theatre or any other cultural realm – secure the conditions needed to create performance-beyond-commodity. If we are searching for the potential of radical resistance to the commodifications of post-industrial, service-based economies, then we may find it in the billions of human interactions which are encouraged, especially, and ironically, at the point of sale of the commodity or service in the performative society.

REFERENCES

Arts Council of Great Britain (1986) *A Great British Success Story*, London: Arts Council of Great Britain.
—— (1988) *43rd Annual Report and Accounts*, London: Arts Council of Great Britain.
Bakhtin, Mikhail (1968) *Rabelais and his World*, Cambridge, Mass.: MIT Press.
Barnard, Paul (ed.) (1991) *Drama*, London: National Arts and Media Strategy Unit.
Barthes, Roland (1973) *Mythologies*, St Albans: Granada Publishing.
Baudrillard, Jean (1983) *Simulations*, New York: Semiotext(e).
Benjamin, Walter (1970) *Illuminations*, London: Fontana/Collins.
Bennett, Susan (1990) *Theatre Audiences: A Theory of Production and Reception*, London: Routledge.
Blau, Herbert (1990) *The Audience*, Baltimore: Johns Hopkins University Press.
Bourdieu, Pierre (1984) *Distinction: A Social Critique of the Judgement of Taste*, London: Routledge & Kegan Paul.
Brecht, Bertolt (1964) *Brecht on Theatre*, ed. John Willett, London: Eyre Methuen.
Clarke, Barrett H. (ed.) (1965) *European Theories of the Drama*, revised by Henry Popkin, New York: Crown Publishers.
Connor, Steven (1989) *Postmodernist Culture*, Oxford: Basil Blackwell.
Cork, Sir Kenneth (1985) *Theatre is for All*, London: Arts Council of Great Britain.
Craig, Sandy (ed.) (1980) *Dreams and Deconstructions: Alternative Theatre in Britain*, Ambergate: Amber Lane Press.
De Marinis, Marco (1987) 'Dramaturgy of the Spectator', *The Drama Review* 31 (2) (T114), Summer.
Eagleton, Terry (1990) *Ideology: An Introduction*, London: Verso.
Featherstone, Mike (1991) *Consumer Culture and Postmodernism*, London: Sage.
Feist, Andrew, and Hutchison, Robert (1990) *Cultural Trends in the Eighties*, London: Policy Studies Institute.
Fiske, John (1989) *Understanding Popular Culture*, London: Unwin Hyman.
Foster, Hal (ed.) (1983) *Postmodern Culture*, London: Pluto.
Frith, Simon (1983) *Sound Effects*, London: Constable.
Gooch, Steve (1984) *All Together Now*, London: Methuen.
Grotowski, Jerzy (1968) *Towards a Poor Theatre*, London: Simon & Schuster.
Hebdige, Dick (1979) *Subculture: the Meaning of Style*, London: Methuen.
Hilton, Julian (1987) *Performance*, London: Macmillan.
Hutchison, Robert (1982) *The Politics of the Arts Council*, London: Sinclair Brown.
Illich, Ivan (1985) *Tools for Conviviality*, London: Marion Boyers.
Jameson, Fredric (1991) *Postmodernism, or, the Cultural Logic of Late Capitalism*, London: Verso.
Kelly, Owen (1984) *Community, Art and the State: Storming the Citadels*, London: Comedia.
Kershaw, Baz (1992) *The Politics of Performance: Radical Theatre as Cultural Intervention*, London: Routledge.
Lash, Scott (1990) *Sociology of Postmodernism*, London: Routledge.

McGrath, John (1981) *A Good Night Out – Popular Theatre: Audience, Class and Form*, London: Eyre Methuen.

—— (1990) *The Bone Won't Break: On Theatre and Hope in Hard Times*, London: Methuen.

Marx, Karl (1970) *Capital*, 1, London: Lawrence & Wishart.

Mulgan, Geoff, and Warpole, Ken (1986) *Saturday Night or Sunday Morning? From Arts to Cultural Industry*, London: Comedia.

Myerscough, John (1987) *The Economic Importance of the Arts in Britain*, London: Policy Studies Institute.

NAMSU (National Arts and Media Strategy Unit) (1992) *Towards a National Arts and Media Strategy*, London: National Arts and Media Strategy Unit.

Rees-Mogg, Sir William (1985) *The Political Economy of Art*, London: Arts Council of Great Britain.

Schechner, Richard (1988) *Performance Theory*, London: Routledge.

Shaw, Roy (1987) *The Arts and the People*, London: Jonathan Cape.

Shevtsova, Maria (1991) 'Minority/dominant culture in the theatre', unpublished working paper.

Simpson, J. A. (1976) *Towards Cultural Democracy*, Strasbourg: Council of Europe.

States, Bert O. (1985) *Great Reckonings in Little Rooms: On the Phenomenology of Theatre*, Berkeley: University of California Press.

Thompson, John B. (1990) *Ideology and Modern Culture*, Cambridge: Polity Press.

Turner, Victor (1982) *From Ritual to Theatre: On the Human Seriousness of Play* New York: PAJ Publications.

Ubersfeld, Anne (1982) 'The pleasure of the spectator', *Modern Drama* 25 (1) (March).

Urry, John (1990) *The Tourist Gaze: Leisure and Travel in Contemporary Society*, London: Sage.

Willis, Susan (1991) *A Primer for Daily Life*, London: Routledge.

Part Three

Consuming public services

Chapter 11

Citizens, charters and contracts

Kieron Walsh

INTRODUCTION

The welfare state, as it developed in the postwar period, was structured by concepts of formal rationality, bureaucratic dominance, centralized authority and hierarchical control. It was assumed that, when the public realm was responsible for providing a service, it should do so by the employment of its own staff. There was an assumption of uniformity, and planning systems were developed that were intended to ensure universal access to a broadly similar range of services across the country. Premfors's description of the Swedish model captures that nature of the postwar welfare state:

> The big problems of Swedish society, as perceived by the adherents of the model, were seen to require big solutions. Big solutions meant nationwide and uniform social programmes, planned and administered in a centralised fashion by big, hierarchically organised government agencies, and financed out of all-purpose tax funds. In some services, local governments would be appropriate producers and distributors, but only following a radical process of amalgamation and centralisation.
>
> (1991: 93)

Government spending expanded rapidly, particularly in the 1960s, and the solution to social problems was seen as lying in the public realm. The result was large-scale organizations that have come to be seen, both on the left and on the right, as unresponsive, producer-dominated, inefficient, and providing services of a poor quality. From the mid-1970s criticism of the public services has mounted.

There have been two broad responses to this criticism. On the left there have gradually developed arguments for moving services closer to people, through decentralization, and for participative control of services by users, for example through tenants' co-operatives. On the right there have been arguments for the introduction of market mechanisms and private sector management approaches to the public services. In both cases the need was seen to be to move away from bureaucracy towards more participative control, though with fundamental differences about what were the appropriate forms of participation.

By the late 1980s the British government had developed a clear agenda for the wholesale change of the public service, based upon the widespread application of market principles. In the Civil Service there was to be contracting out, devolution of financial control, the establishment of arm's length agencies operating on a trading basis, and performance-based management. In the National Health Service general management was introduced in contrast to professional dominance, purchaser and provider roles were separated within an internal market, many general practitioners were given direct control of their budgets, and hospitals, and other health organizations, were able to opt for trust status. In education schools were given their own budgets, and allowed to opt out of the local education authority's control, taking grant-maintained status. In social services, as in health, purchaser-provider splits and internal markets are to be introduced, and social service departments are to be required to contract with a wider range of providers such as voluntary and private organizations. Community care is intended to be needs-, rather than service-led. In local government, competitive tendering was introduced, and internal markets established. Other parts of the public sector such as the police (Johnson 1992) and the justice system (Raine 1989) were subjected to similar reforms.

By the early 1990s the debate on the proper approach to the organization and management of the public services had been broadened into a discussion of issues of citizenship, rights and the nature of the state. The *Citizen's Charter* (Prime Minister 1991) presented an outline agenda for the future of the public services. The state was no longer to be a monolithic set of large organizations providing services directly to the public, but a body that played an 'enabling' role, ensuring that proper services were provided on a market basis, and acting as a protector of citizen rights in the market for public services, which would be provided by a wide range of public and private organizations. The agenda for the 1990s is the reform of the nature of the public services and their management in order to introduce citizen control. The aim of this chapter is to consider the debate about the nature of the public services, and their organization. I start by considering contrasting approaches to understanding the nature of citizenship. I then go on to consider the attempt to reform the public services through the introduction of charters and contracts. The second half of the chapter is concerned with the operational implications of the changes that are being introduced for the empowerment of citizens, the quality of services, and for accountability and the position of producers. I shall argue that the concept that is emerging is that of the citizen as individual consumer, contracting with the state, and that that is an inadequate basis for the effective operation of the public sector.

THE NATURE OF CITIZENSHIP

There are two basic approaches to understanding the nature of citizenship. The first is the liberal conception, emphasizing the primacy of the individual over community and state. Individuals should be free to pursue their own interests, and liberty is seen as dominating any concept of social justice, which some, notably Hayek, would see as meaningless. Interests are best pursued through the free market and the state plays a purely negative role, protecting individuals' rights and compensating for very limited market failures. The state can be seen either as being created on a contractual basis, or naturally emerging from a state of nature, as in Nozick's (1974) extreme vision. For the liberal, rights are paramount, deriving from the fundamental nature of the individual person, and justice a procedural rather than a substantive matter. Outcomes are just if they result from just procedures. In this conception citizenship is a status possessed by the individual, which the state exists to protect. The only duties which the citizen has to the state are those that are chosen and the social contract states those duties which the free citizen has volunteered to adopt through the process of contracting.

The second approach to citizenship is based upon the primacy of community rather than the individual, arguing that individual meanings are derived from group membership. Rights are not absolute but are created by the community, and duties are not chosen by individuals on a contractual basis, but incumbent upon them by virtue of community membership. Individuals take their meaning from the community, and think by means of the institutions of the community (Douglas 1987). This approach is most explicitly expressed in the somewhat austere tradition of civic republicanism (Oldfield 1990), with its emphasis upon responsibility and public obligation. The communitarian tradition tends to emphasize the importance of fraternity, seeing the need for justice, as an essentially remedial virtue, as limited in a properly functioning society, in which people recognize their responsibilities to one another. Liberty is expressed within the rules and institutions of the community, and the common good is dominant.

The liberal tradition does not deny community, and, indeed, is more realistic than many communitarians in recognizing the difficulties of conflicting community interests. A distinction can be made between moral and legal communities, and, as Galston (1991: 45) argues: 'Liberalism is an account of the manner in which moral communities can exist within a single legal community.' The liberal does not deny the common good, but sees it as following from individual conceptions of the good:

For the liberal the common good is a good precisely because it secures for individuals the capacity for free choice in conceptions of the good life, and this requirement constrains the pursuit of shared ends; whereas the common good for communitarians is precisely the pursuit of those shared ends, which constrain the freedom of individuals to choose and pursue their own life-style.

(Kymlicka 1989: 78)

The market is the natural realm of the liberal, with the state as neutral between concepts of the good, the polity that of the communitarian, forwarding a particular concept of the good. Both can adhere to democracy, though for the liberal it is typically a method of deciding between, rather than expressing, interests.

There are, clearly, difficulties in applying either concept of citizenship. Liberal theorists, such as Galston (1991) and Macedo (1990), have argued the limitations of the rigidly neutral position; communitarians have recognized the limitations of fraternalism in a complex society of strangers (Miller 1990; Ignatieff 1990). It is argued that liberalism can incorporate the communitarian critique (Caney 1992), and both liberals and communitarians are developing and rethinking their positions. Political systems will tend, inevitably, to be based on a mixture of liberal rights and communitarian responsibilities. In the postwar welfare state, the balance was clearly towards a bureaucratized paternalism, that tended to undermine the communitarian sentiments on which it needed to be based if it was to be seen as legitimate. Solidarity and fraternity were anonymized and embodied in the distant, impersonal bureaucracies of government. Bureaucracy can be seen as dividing citizens from their responsibilities. The argument from the right is that there should be a return to the market, and the recognition of individual rights. This is argued to yield more effective citizen participation; as the Omega file argues:

it must be remembered that independent providers ... are nearer to public demand than local authorities can ever be ... their perpetual search for profitability ... stimulates them to discover and produce what the consumer wants. ... In this sense the market sector is more genuinely democratic than the public sector, involving the decisions of far more individuals at far more frequent intervals.

(quoted in Levitas 1982)

On this view the market is the most effective means of enabling citizenship to be maximized, and the citizen is best seen as a customer. It is this model that is expressed in the development of charters and contracts, while the communitarian correction to bureaucracy emphasizes participation and decentralization.

Charters

The notion of charters arose out of the application of consumerism to the public services in the 1980s. Tenants' Charters had been developed for council house tenants following the Housing Act 1980, though with little impact (Malpass and Murie 1987: 16). By the early 1990s many local authorities, such as York, Lewisham, Cambridgeshire and Islington, were beginning to develop service charters, initially for relatively simple and straightforward services such as refuse collection and street-cleaning, but, increasingly, for more complex services, such as social care, education or police. The launch of the Citizen's Charter signalled the government's adoption of the principle of 'charterism' to encapsulate its proposals for the reform of the public sector. A host of charters has followed. The Citizen's Charter emphasizes the market exchange basis of the public sector:

> All public services are paid for by individual citizens, either directly or through their taxes. They are entitled to expect high quality services, responsive to their needs, provided efficiently at reasonable cost.
>
> (Prime Minister 1991: 4)

The Charter is based on four key themes: quality, choice, standards and value. The mechanisms proposed for achieving better public services are more privatization; wider competition; further contracting out; performance-related pay; published performance targets; comprehensive information on standards achieved; more effective complaints procedures; tougher and more independent inspectorates; and appropriate redress for citizens when services go wrong. The Citizen's Charter has been supplemented by specific charters for patients, parents of schoolchildren, taxpayers, rail passengers and others.

The Charter is based on the concept of the individual rights of the citizen as a consumer of public services:

> The Citizen's Charter is about giving more power to the citizen. But citizenship is also about our responsibilities – as parents, for example, or as neighbours – as well as our entitlements. The Citizen's Charter is not a recipe for more state action; it is a testament of our belief in people's right to be informed and choose for themselves.
>
> (Prime Minister 1991: 2)

Though the responsibilities of the citizen are mentioned at the beginning of the Citizen's Charter, they play little further part in the various charters, and, where they are mentioned, as in the Parent's Charter, tend to focus on the responsibility to be an effective consumer of the service involved. There is no concept of collective rights and duties and little reference to any concept of community. Citizenship is not, then, seen as creating a unified identity, but as a loose amalgam of customer roles, as parent, as patient or as passenger, in separate markets. Other Charters, such as that of the Labour Party (1991) or those of individual local authorities, do make more reference to the significance of community: 'Labour wants councils committed to providing quality services – that means reliability, variety and choice for the consumer and partnership with the local community' (Labour Party 1989: 1). But the emphasis is still predominantly on the consumer role, and the precision of individual rights tends to drive out looser concepts of commitment and mutual obligation.

Markets and contracts

The means of developing a more effective, consumer-friendly public service is seen primarily to be the use of market processes and contracts. The service is to be clearly specified in direct response to people's needs and wishes, standards are to be made explicit, and opportunities for choice created. Public servants are to have their performance measured, and be paid according to the results. Where services fail then there is to be effective redress. The individual's rights are seen as enforceable through a contractual relationship:

> Citizens must have real decision-making power. And that power must be the result of a new model of government – government by contract, with contracts giving individuals real enforceable rights. . . . We should not be afraid to hand back government power to individuals by contracting with them, in a new social contract which is built up of millions of enforceable micro-contracts for better standards of public service. This may properly be provided through private contractors where they can do it best.
>
> (Mather 1991: 5)

Similar statements can be found in the work of thinkers on the left:

> measures could include changing the contracts of service providers such as teachers, doctors or social workers so that it became part of their contractual duty to provide a service of a specific sort at a specific level which would then yield entitlements under the contract. . . .
>
> (Plant 1990: 40)

Empowerment and entitlement are central to the debate over the new public service. The empowerment of citizens involves a shift of power away from professionals, bureaucrats and elected government. It involves the establishment of user power, which will depend upon citizens possessing the resources, capacities and information that are necessary for effective participation in the market. As I shall argue, little has been done to change the practical circumstances of production, and what is emerging is a surrogate consumerism, controlled by a new consumer bureaucracy, rather than real consumer sovereignty.

The role of the state is seen as being to enable, rather than to provide. Two forms of enabling have emerged, one based upon rights, the other upon concepts of community. Nicholas Ridley (1988) argues that the enabling state will be involved with specifying, vetting and monitoring contracts. The machinery of government will be simplified, as local authorities, for example, will meet only to hand out the contracts. Politics will be asserted over administration. The other approach to the enabling state is based upon the mobilization of the totality of influences available to ensure that the community maximizes its self-development (Stewart and Clarke 1987). Markets will have a role to play in this, but will only be part of a broader regime. The primacy of government as community activity, rather than a collection of service-providing organizations, is emphasized. It is the first form of enabling that has dominated government thinking, though individual local authorities have attempted to develop the second.

The market forms that are being introduced in the public service involve only limited use of price mechanisms, and only very aggregated processes of exchange. Though radical arguments have proposed giving individuals powers to purchase goods, for example through vouchers (Le Grand 1991b; Saunders and Harris 1989), and creating a multitude of micro-contracts, large-scale bulk contracts between organizations have dominated in practice. In the National Health Service and local government the market is largely internal to the public sector organizations themselves, rather than allowing free exchange with an individual customer. Contracts operate at a number of levels, and cross-cut one another, varying in their degree of specificity and formality. The public sector becomes a network of predominantly internal contracts, the nature of which can be illustrated using the example of education. The local education authority or central government provides resources to the school to deliver the national curriculum, so that the school has a generalized contract with the authority or the Department for Education. The local education authority provides services, such as building and ground maintenance, to the school on a contract basis. The school may be seen as having a contract with the parent or pupil to provide a proper education. Teachers contract with school and the local education authority, and are rewarded according to their performance. The development of standards, performance measures, league tables and inspection involve an attempt, by central government, to ensure the completeness of contracts.

The introduction of contracting and quasi-markets (Le Grand 1991c) has had little impact on the relations of consumption in the public service as opposed to the process of production. There is little evidence that the public has been consulted by government agencies in the creation of contracts, and little public perception of difference in the way that services are provided. Large-scale public organizations still exist, with internal divisions into purchaser and provider being a cause of bureaucracy as much as its cure (Walsh 1991). There is some disaggregation, for example, through schools opting for grant-maintained status, hospitals adopting trust status, and general practitioners controlling budgets, but the user's individual power is still relatively little changed. Real customer control is only fully apparent in the sale of council houses. It may be that, in the longer term, there will be more development of individual power to purchase, raising questions about whether the sum of individual decisions will be collectively rational.

OPERATIONAL IMPLICATIONS

The empowerment of citizens to enable them to operate effectively in a market environment depends upon giving them the necessary resources, capacity and information. In practice there is little in the proposals for public sector change that acts to enhance the user's resources. The distribution of initial resources plays little part in the debate. There has been almost no attempt explicitly to empower individual citizens, through giving them direct purchasing power. Proposals, both from the right and left (Seldon 1986; Le Grand 1991b) for vouchers have been ignored. Choice will be limited the more the initial distribution of resources acts to limit the alternatives available to the individual. People must also have the capacity to make choices, which may be limited by personal disabilities, geography, or a host of other factors. Language or mental capacity may create barriers to effective choice. Much will depend upon where people live, which will limit the choices of school, hospital or doctor available to them. Personal abilities to manipulate the system may enable some people to obtain more from the public services than others. Various studies have shown the differential access to and use of services by different groups (Bramley *et al.* 1989).

The relative degree of information available to producer and consumer, and the distribution of information between consumers, will influence the efficiency with which the market will work. An asymmetric distribution of information creates problems of moral hazard and adverse selection, because people are able to behave opportunistically, misrepresenting reality to their own advantage. A significant emphasis in the Citizen's Charter is upon ensuring that information is available:

> Full, accurate information should be readily available in plain language, about what services are being provided. Targets should be published, together with full and audited information about the results achieved.

Wherever possible, information should be in comparable form so that there is pressure to emulate the best.

(Prime Minister 1991: 5)

The effective working of the market depends upon the availability of information, and if transaction costs are not to be excessively high, it must be available at a reasonable cost.

Le Grand (1991a: 100) has argued that:

equity is intimately related to the existence or otherwise of choice. If people's choices are constrained, whether because of their lack of resources, or because of preferences that are beyond their control, this is likely to create inequity.

The main emphasis of the charter movement is upon the information element in choice; there is little reference to resources or ability. Movements that are aimed precisely at empowering the disadvantaged, such as advocacy systems, have received little support (Philpot 1992). Without empowerment of the citizen, the development of citizen rights will be procedural rather than substantial.

Process and substance in rights

For the classic liberal justice is essentially a matter of proper process, but a *purely* procedural concept of justice is unlikely to be accepted as fair or acceptable in practice. The charters that have been produced are essentially guarantees of procedural rights, rather than of outcomes. The Parent's Charter reinforces the right to express a preference about the school one's child is to attend, but there is no right to a place at a particular school. You can complain and appeal, but there is no guarantee that you will get what you want. As Dowding (1992) argues, it is not so much choice that people want, as the attainment of their preferred outcome. There are statements of substantive rights in the charters, such as that in the Patient's Charter that every citizen has the right 'to receive health care on the basis of clinical need, regardless of ability to pay'. Yet as with the rights of people with needs for social care embodied in the National Health Service and Community Care Act, it is difficult to see how response can be wholly needs-led, given resource limitations. As the Audit Commission has said:

the relatively simple adjustment of putting users' and carers' needs first which then leads to the commissioning of services triggers an ever-widening series of changes, presenting a daunting challenge.

(Audit Commission 1992: 38)

It is difficult to see how essentially managerial reforms can solve needs-based problems, without a consideration of the resources available.

The danger is that the process is seen as correct – it is just that, unfortunately, it did not work for the particular individual. This issue is particularly important because the new market-based management systems themselves consume considerable time and resources, for example in promotion or the employment of additional accountants.

There is also some likelihood that the result of attempting to guarantee outcomes is bureaucratization and over-prescription, what Wise (1979), in his study of competency-based education in the United States of America, calls hyper-rationalization. The Parent's Charter asserts the 'right to a proper education', but this is still a guarantee of inputs rather than outcomes, in that it is defined in terms of the national curriculum. The testing of pupils will, theoretically, provide parents with information on whether their children's education has been successful or not. But, presuming that the information allows sensible conclusions to be drawn, it is not clear what action can be taken, especially if the failure cannot be put right after the event.

Quality and service

The charter and contract movement tends to assume that the difficulties of measuring quality and performance can be overcome by an act of will. The pursuit of quality in the public service raises difficult theoretical and practical issues. There are contrasting definitions of the meaning of quality, seeing it in terms of fitness for purpose, conformance to specification, or responsiveness. There is a potential conflict between quality and efficiency that is largely unrecognized by the proponents of charters and contracts. Quality of service is likely to be higher where the varying needs of individuals are more specifically met, but that very responsiveness to difference is likely to mean that efficiency is impaired, for example because learning by doing is reduced; as Harrison (1987: 11) puts it:

> During the past few decades, as our needs and wants have become more differentiated and unpredictable, systems have had to become more complex in the attempt to respond to consumer wants, and they have predictably become less reliable as a result.

The value of formalized bureaucratic routines is that people can become more efficient as they become more familiar with them. Continual change, in order to respond to changing need, limits continuity, and makes learning more difficult.

There is also a question about the degree to which improving quality for one person may reduce it for another when resources are limited.

Much of the reason for taking public services out of the market is that they involve fundamental conflicts of interest.

Quality of service is particularly difficult to produce because services are fundamentally different from manufactured goods. They are intangible, both in having little material character, and often being difficult to understand. Production and consumption tend to take place simultaneously, and services cannot be stored, or laboratory tested before delivery. Moreover the consumer is part of the production process, and quality failures may result from the consumer's as much as the producer's action. It is difficult to embody the control of quality in technology as can be done for manufactured goods. The difficulties are enhanced for the public service because quality may be judged on the basis of values, and the judgement of quality is not the same as the expression of preference in the market. Responding to individual preferences may conflict with collective values, for example because of externalities. Even individuals may have preferences, at a given moment, that conflict with their own deeply held values, as Hirschman (1982) argues. There is no single value base that can avoid the policy dilemmas that are confronted in making decisions in the public realm. There are, inevitably, questions of balance, for example between equity and efficiency or quantity and quality; as Nagel (1979: 128) says, dilemmas inevitably follow from the 'fragmentation of value and the singleness of decision'. The assumption in the various charters that performance measures can easily be developed ignores the long and difficult history of performance measurement (Carter *et al.* 1992).

The measurement of quality in the public service must also take account of the long time scales that are involved. As Davis and Ostrom (1991: 322) say, there will be 'uncertainty about whether particular schools generate high quality services. Only after graduation does the family of a student ascertain how well the school helped the child to increase his or her knowledge skills.' It is difficult to see how simple systems of redress would work in such circumstances. Markets do not deal easily with long time scales. The easy alternative is likely to be a focus upon short-term goals and measurable targets, but this ignores problems that follow from changing values, or the fact that preferences may not be stable over time. What I prefer now may not be what I will wish, in the future, I had preferred.

The development of formalistic quality assurance systems, modelled upon those developed in manufacturing industry, ignores the extent to which quality in the public realm is politically constructed. It may be that precisely what, for one person, is a sign of high quality, may for another, with different political values, be a sign of poor quality. Deeply held values may point in opposite directions even for the individual, for example whether children should be taken into care for their protection, or families kept together. There is no single dimension of quality even for the individual. The approach to quality will need to be much more one of judgement, of weighing and balancing contrasting and overlapping goods and bads, than one of measurement. The involvement of the user or client in the production of services creates difficulties in the judgement of service quality. The nature of what it is intended to produce is necessarily imprecise in education or social work, because the service is about the generalities of life, not the particular, about the nature of our lives, not the things we live with. These are deep questions about who it is that has the right to make judgements about service quality. In the past the producers have dominated in the evaluation of service quality, but that dominance is not now acceptable.

Trust, producers and accountability

The introduction of market mechanisms will change the role played by trust in the management of the public services. Markets assume that people know their preferences, are capable of expressing them, and can go elsewhere if they are not satisfied. It is possible for co-operation to emerge in a contractarian world, as Axelrod's (1984) work shows, but there is always a danger that individuals will revert to exploitative behaviour unless contracts and property rights are clearly specified and controlled. In the quasi-markets that characterize the public service, exit is often difficult because there are few alternatives or resources are scarce, and voice frequently ineffective because of users' difficulties in assessing services. The result has been that there is a strong reliance, in the charter and contract movement, on the role of third parties in laying down standards, and inspecting and regulating producers. The Audit Commission has been given enhanced powers to measure the performance of the National Health Service and local authorities. In social services a national inspectorate has been established, and local authorities required to establish their own inspectorates. In education, tests to assess pupil performance are laid down at national level. The emphasis is upon stated standards and measured performance, with experts doing the measuring.

The wish to develop standards and measure performance follows from the distrust of professionals, or at least of traditional professionals. The use of standards, performance targets and performance-related pay, along with competition from the private sector, may reduce the power of traditional professional producer groups such as teachers. The power of manual workers, and of their trade unions, in the public service, has been significantly reduced by compulsory competitive tendering. Trust is being transferred from traditional professions and producers to the new professional managers and to professional regulators, inspectors, auditors and accountants, who control and measure the performance of the system.

Traditional forms of accountability and trust in service professionals are giving way to dependence upon audit-based systems. The issue that then arises is how, and to whom, the auditors can be held accountable.

The danger of the quasi-market systems is that traditional forms of accountability, through the procedures of representative democracy, are no longer effective, but that mechanisms of market accountability are not effective replacements. The developments in the structure of the public sector have, so far, been largely to do with the circumstances of pro-duction. Quasi-markets have created little ability for exit, given the limited alternatives available. The vote becomes less effective as public services are insulated from politics through the spread of privatization, agencies and appointed bodies. The obvious alternative is that voice and participation should be increased to give consumers of public services more direct control. Certainly there are moves in this direction, for example through the extension of complaints procedures, and more direct involvement of users, notably on school and college governing bodies. But experience, for example in the management of housing estates and decentralization movements in local government, has shown how difficult it is to generate and maintain public involvement. The emerging quality bureaucracy may be set to replace both the politicians and the traditional professions.

CONCLUSION

The development of an effective system for the management of the public services depends upon the existence of an appropriate institutional framework of rules and expectations within which it can operate. The traditional structure of large-scale bureaucratic professional hierarchies is no longer acceptable. The system that is emerging is based upon market principles and the idea of the citizen as consumer. Competition is to replace authority as the basis upon which decisions are made, and in ensuring that there is adaptation to changing circumstances. It is necessary that the new institutional framework should deal effectively with issues of information, quality, monitoring and incentives, and that it should ensure accountability. These issues are not independent of one another, and the particular institutional framework that is needed will depend upon their interaction. Where, for example, reliable information on the quality and performance of the service that is to be delivered is easily and cheaply available to all, then it is easier to have a performance-based contracting system that pays the provider on the basis of results. But this approach will only be wholly appropriate if the outcome is fully under the control of the producer. If circumstances beyond his or her control determine the outcome, then it may be inappropriate to base payments only on results. The basis of much of the movement to charters and contracts lies in an assumed individualism that does not reflect the complexity of a world where collectivity is significant.

The debate on the future of the public service has focused on the development of markets and contracts as counterweights to bureaucratic inertia. There is a third approach which sits uncomfortably in the present debate, namely altruistic, benevolent action, of which the paradigm is the family and kinship group. Virginia Held (1990: 304) develops this approach in her contrast of mothering and contract:

> If the dynamic relationship between mothering person and child is taken as the primary social relation, then it is the model of 'economic man' that can be seen as deficient as a model for society and morality, and unsuitable for all but a special context. A domain such as law, if built on no more than contractual foundations, can then be recognised as one limited domain amongst others; law protects some moral rights when people are too immoral or weak to respect them without the force of law. But it is hardly a majestic edifice that can serve as a model for morality. Neither can the domain of politics, if built on no more than self-interest or mutual disinterest, provide us with a model with which to understand and improve society and morality. And neither, even more clearly, can the market itself.

The notion of altruistic, voluntary relationships between people is difficult to reconcile with either markets or traditional bureaucracy. In practice a great deal of work is done on an informal, caring, basis, for example in the case of social care, where state or private provision is a small proportion of the total work done.

Traditional conservatism does emphasize the role of the active citizen (Hurd 1989), which has, for example, informed much law and order policy, for example in the development of neighbourhood watch schemes. Voluntarism and altruism, though, are likely to find it difficult to live with markets, which are likely to corrode the institutions of mutual commitment (Ware 1990). An individualistic, market-based approach to altruism, emphasizing charity, takes inadequate account of the extent to which benevolence can be seen as a public good, and yielding greatest benefit when collectively organized. Voluntaristic commitment is eroded by an emphasis on commercialism and contracts, as in the introduction of contracts for care in the United States (Gutch 1992) and the Netherlands. The character of the voluntary sector is likely to change as large-scale, not-for-profit organizations emerge, displacing the smaller organizations that find it difficult to live with market mechanisms. The rigours of the decentralized market-oriented public sector may also make it difficult to involve individuals in government, for example through membership of school governing bodies, because of the increased work and responsibilities involved. There is a need to consider how voluntarism and altruism can be maintained, as well as introducing new systems.

The Citizen's Charter does not effectively recognize the communal and voluntaristic elements of citizenship, and assumes that individual rights are a sufficient base for the organization of the public service. Even within the framework of disaggregated organizations and individualism that is set to replace the large-scale bureaucracies of the past, there will inevitably be conflicts of interests. The difficulties are apparent in the conflicts in schools, such as Stratford School in London. Market mechanisms cannot resolve fundamental conflict of values. The need for governmental authority cannot wholly be replaced by market mechanisms. As intermediate institutions such as local authorities are emasculated, the decentralization to local organizations, such as schools and hospitals, and to individual producers and consumers, is likely to be paralleled by a growing centralization, as central government becomes involved in what have previously been more localized conflicts. The alternative, of shifting power to unelected bodies, such as inspectorates and regulators, is the rise of an unaccountable government by third parties.

The move to a public service that is based upon clear, objective, unambiguous standards must face up to the difficulty of the inherent indeterminacy of political objectives. Politics is necessarily concerned with balancing conflicting values and goals. Certainly the pursuit of clarity of purpose has advantages in preventing politicians and public sector employees avoiding responsibility. As Flynn *et al.* (1988: 186) argue:

> From a political point of view it is often advantageous to maintain maximum ambiguity and uncertainty about who is responsible for specific activities, when they might be expected to account for them, and what kind of outcome (if these are discussed at all) could be held to constitute success or failure. This makes it possible for politicians variously to take personal credit for beneficial actions or to blame their predecessors, their officials or circumstances beyond their control when events turn against them; it allows officials to blame politicians or finance departments; it allows all concerned at any time to choose criteria by which any activity can be judged – and in particular to identify inputs rather than outputs – and to switch between different criteria at different times. The upshot is that citizens and their representatives find it very hard, much of the time, to assess *quality* of government, that is to tell whether any policy has been a success or a failure, and to pin the responsibility on anyone in particular.

The increase of the transparency of the public services will make it clear who should be shot for failure.

Ambiguity may, though, reflect the nature of reality, particularly where fundamental values are to the fore. The positive value of ambiguity should also be recognized. Ambiguity is necessary for adaptation. Clarity and specificity, especially when embodied in contracts, may make it difficult to adapt to changing circumstances. There is already evidence that contract-based management can create inflexibility. Elements of work that are laid down in contract may not be amenable to adjustment. When faced with the need to make cuts in the face of scarcity of resources, public organizations may find themselves preserving contract-based services at the expense of other services which have a higher priority. Similarly, performance measurement may lead to an emphasis on the production of measurable outputs at the expense of the less measurable but more important.

The development of the new public service management, making extensive use of market mechanisms, draws upon a particular concept of citizenship, in the liberal, rights-based tradition. As it develops it will have to face up to issues that derive from the communitarian approach, and to difficulties within the liberal tradition itself. The debate over the nature of public service has moved from the structural and organizational concerns of the 1970s, to a more fundamental debate about the nature of citizenship and democracy. Potentially insoluble dilemmas are involved, such as the balance between individual rights and communal responsibilities, or the need for state action to ensure that markets and choice can be effective. Institutional and organizational structures need to follow, not lead, the resolution of these dilemmas.

REFERENCES

Audit Commission (1992) *Community Care: Managing the Cascade of Change*, London: HMSO.

Axelrod, R. (1984) *The Evolution of Cooperation*, New York: Basic Books.

Bramley, G., Le Grand, J. and Low, W. (1989) 'How far is the poll tax a "community charge"? The implications of service usage evidence', *Policy and Politics* 17 (3): 187–205.

Caney, S. (1992) 'Liberalism and communitarianism: a misconceived debate', *Political Studies* XL: 273–89.

Carter, N., Klein, R. and Day, P. (1992) *How Organisations Measure Success: The Use of Performance Indicators in Government*, London: Routledge.

Davis, G. and Ostrom, E. (1991) 'A public approach to education: choice and coproduction', *International Political Science Review* 12 (4): 313–35.

Douglas, M. (1987) *How Institutions Think*, London: Routledge & Kegan Paul.

Dowding, K. (1992) 'Choice: its increase and its value', *British Journal of Political Science* 22 (3): 301–14.

Flynn, A., Gray, A., Jenkins, W. I., Rutherford, B. A. and Plowden, W. (1988) 'Accountable management in British central government: some reflections on the official record', *Financial Accountability and Management* 4 (3), Autumn, 169–89.

Galston, W. A. (1991) *Liberal Purposes: Goods, Virtues and Diversity in the Liberal State*, Cambridge: Cambridge University Press.

Gutch, R. (1992) *Contracting Lessons from the US*, London: National Council of Voluntary Organisations.

Harrison, R. (1987) *Organisation Culture and Quality of Service*, London: Association for Management Education and Development.

Held, V. (1990) 'Mothering versus contract', in J. J. Mansbridge (ed.), *Beyond Self-Interest*, Chicago: Chicago University Press.

Hirschman, A. (1982) *Shifting Involvements; Private Interest and Public Action*, Oxford: Martin Robertson.

Hurd, D. (1989) 'Freedom will flourish when citizens accept responsibility', *Independent*, 13 September.

Ignatieff, M. (1990) *The Needs of Strangers*, London: The Hogarth Press.

Johnson, L. (1992) *The Rebirth of Private Policing*, London: Routledge.

Kymlicka, W. (1989) *Liberalism, Community and Culture*, Oxford: Oxford University Press.

Labour Party (1989) *Quality Street: Labour's Quality Programme for Local Government*, London: Labour Party.

—— (1991) *Citizens' Charter*, London: Labour Party.

Le Grand, J. (1991a) *Equity and Choice: An Essay in Economics and Applied Philosophy*, London: Harper Collins.

—— (1991b) 'Liberty, equality and vouchers', in D. G. Green (ed.), *Empowering the Parents: How to Break the School Monopoly*, London: Institute of Economic Affairs.

—— (1991c) 'Quasi-markets and social policy', *Economic Journal*, 101, September, 1256–67.

Levitas, R. (1982) 'Competition and compliance: the utopias of the New Right', in R. Levitas (ed.), *The Ideology of the New Right*, Cambridge: Polity Press.

Macedo, S. (1990) *Liberal Virtues: Citizenship, Virtue and Community in Liberal Constitutionalism*, Oxford: Clarendon Press.

Malpass, P. and Murie, A. (1987) *Housing Policy and Practice*, 2nd edn, London: Macmillan.

Mather, G. (1991) *Government by Contract*, London: Institute of Economic Affairs.

Miller, D. (1990) *Market, State and Community: Theoretical Foundations of Socialism*, Oxford: Clarendon Press.

Nagel, T. (1979) *Mortal Questions*, Cambridge: Cambridge University Press.

Nozick, R. (1974) *Anarchy, State and Utopia*, New York: Basic Books.

Oldfield, A. (1990) *Citizenship and Community: Civic Republicanism and the Modern World*, London: Routledge.

Philpot, T. (1992) 'Lip service that gags democracy', *Guardian*, 1 April.

Plant, R. (1990) 'Citizenship, empowerment and welfare', in B. Pimlott, A. Wright and T. Flowers (eds), *The Alternative*, London: W. H. Allen.

Premfors, R. (1991) 'The "Swedish model" and public sector reform', *West European Politics* 14 (3): 83–95.

Prime Minister (1991) *Citizen's Charter: Raising the Standard*, London: HMSO.

Raine, J. (1989) *Local Justice: Ideals and Realities*, Edinburgh: T. & T. Clark.

Ridley, N. (1988) *The Local Right: Enabling Not Providing*, London: The Centre for Policy Studies.

Saunders, P. and Harris, C. (1989) *Popular Attitudes to State Welfare Services: A Growing Demand for Alternatives*, London: Social Affairs Unit.

Seldon, A. (1986) *The Riddle of the Voucher: An Inquiry into the Obstacles to Introducing Choice and Competition in State Schools*, London: Institute of Economic Affairs.

Stewart, J. and Clarke, M. (1987) 'The public service orientation: issues and dilemmas', in *Public Administration* 69 (2): 161–77.

Walsh, K. (1991) *Competition for Local Authority Services: Initial Experiences*, London: HMSO.

Ware, A. (1990) 'Meeting needs through voluntary action: does market society corrode altruism?', in A. Ware and R. E. Goodin (eds), *Needs and Welfare*, London: Sage.

Wise, A. E. (1979) *Legislated Learning: The Bureaucratisation of the American Classroom*, Berkeley and Los Angeles, University of California Press.

Chapter 12

Consuming health and welfare

Richard Hugman

INTRODUCTION

It is part of the formal ideology of health and welfare that services, and the professionals who staff them, exist for the benefit of the wider society in general and of the individual service user specifically. This 'service ethic' has formed a key element in sociological attempts to construct a concept of professionalism (Durkheim 1957; Greenwood 1957; Carr-Saunders and Wilson 1962; Etzioni 1969). Such a picture of professionals as the servants of society has been repeatedly challenged, from the stringent attacks of Shaw (1911) through the polemics of Wootton (1959) and Illich (1971, 1976), to a corresponding reappraisal of the concept of professionalism within sociology (Freidson 1970; T. J. Johnson 1972; Wilding 1982).

More recently, the service ethic of professionalism has made a reappearance in the guise of the professional as a producer who is responsive to the authority of the service user as a consumer (Bamford 1990; N. Johnson 1990). In this form, the service ethic suggests that the patient or client exercises authority over the professional, either through market mechanisms or through administrative frameworks which duplicate the market (N. Johnson 1989; Flynn 1992). The power of the professional as producer and provider, it follows, is tempered by the capacity of the service user as consumer to exercise authority through choice. Through consumerism professionals are forced to attend to the expressed wishes of service users, rather than defining health and welfare needs in terms of professional (self-) interests. The 'conspiracy against the laity' of which Shaw (1911) wrote would be broken through a necessity for professionals to share power more openly with 'the laity', who may be seen here as service users.

However, it is the underlying contention of this paper that claims for consumerism as standing in a direct line of descent from such radical criticism is not something which can be taken at face value (as may be the case amongst some health and welfare professionals) but can be questioned both theoretically and empirically. I will briefly examine the links between the development of consumerism and the ideological position of the welfare state in industrialized societies of the late twentieth century, before exploring in more depth the related questions of the specific forms which consumerism has taken and of the responses made by professionals to consumerism. In conclusion I will consider the opportunities presented by this shift in thought and action for the future of health and welfare, particularly as this concerns the restructuring of public services in the UK around quasi-consumerist principles.

CONSUMERISM AND THE CRISIS OF WELFARE LEGITIMACY

Recent scholarship has demonstrated that the contemporary structuring of public health and welfare has been affected by two interconnected crises, the first of which is fiscal and the second of which is one of ideological legitimacy (O'Connor 1973; Mishra 1984; Cousins 1987). The economies of developed industrialized societies have been unable to sustain the growth of public welfare, a phenomenon which can be seen in the USA, Australia, Europe and Scandinavia. As a consequence policy makers have sought alternative patterns of resource for such provision (Cousins 1987; Boyce 1991). Associated with responses to this economic situation has been the rise of the political New Right, with its emphasis on individualized concepts of social relationships and a challenge to the legitimacy of the role of the state as a corporate provider of health and welfare.

An alternative challenge to welfare legitimacy can be identified in the development of service user movements which increasingly have made a mark in Europe, often drawing explicitly on the North American experience (although as a consequence of the lesser role of the state in the USA and Canada in comparison to northern Europe these movements have been more clearly focused on opposition to professional power in the former: see, for example, Brandon 1991a, 1991b). These movements have developed amongst people with physical disabilities, people with learning difficulties, children and older people, and in the UK have taken the form of groups such as NAYPIC (children in care), Survivors Speak Out (mental health patients), People First (people with learning disabilities), Grey Panthers (older people), as well as more specific patients' councils and so on (Cousins 1987; Collins and Stein 1989). Feminist and anti-racist critiques also may be seen to cross-cut these groups as well as taking an independent form in women's groups and Black groups (Phillips 1982; Dominelli and McLeod 1989). These are not challenges to the legitimacy of corporate welfare, but to the actual services which are delivered through the relationships between professionals, the state and service users.

In this historical juxtaposition of the political New Right and the service user groups there is a contradiction. Whereas the former is driven by an ideological will to dismantle the welfare state on the grounds that it interferes with the individual rights and responsibilities of the citizen, the latter exploits the weakening of the welfare state to enhance the power of the client or patient *vis à vis* professionals, while seeking to maintain or extend the services of which they are a part. In this sense the political New Right is more radical in that its goal is the complete restructuring of welfare on private market lines, while the service user groups have the goal of reforming the relationships between professionals and their clientele. They share a vocabulary of power, rights and choice, yet at the same time they are divided in relation to the goals towards which they are working. So we may even speak of (diametrically opposing) 'consumerisms', and this is reflected in the finer linguistic distinctions, between the New Right emphasis on choice *as* power and the service user groups' assertion of empowerment *in order to* exercise choice.

Common ground in the political and philosophical language of 'citizenship' appears to be occupied by these two approaches to consumerism in health and welfare, in which service users are to be seen as citizens with rights to standards of service, involvement in decision-making about their lives and control over their own use of the services (Taylor 1989; see also Walsh in this volume). However, it is in the structuring of the relationship between the service user, the professional and the state that the differences in the implicit relationship between 'citizenship' and 'consumerism' between the New Right and service user perspectives become most apparent. For the New Right the freedom of choice for the service user is exercised solely through 'purchasing power', so that professionals adapt their responses to meet the demands made on them by those who consume their services. The gauge of an appropriate service is increased demand, in a manner comparable to the models of liberal economics. The role of the state is focused on regulation. This may be regarded as 'market consumerism'. For the service user groups, in contrast, their power is to be exercised through participation in the control of the social processes which define health and welfare needs and the appropriate methods of response. Appropriateness of provision is not gauged by demand in this model, but by the active participation of the consumer in defining and controlling the supply. The role of the state becomes that of mediator and facilitator. This may be regarded as 'democratic consumerism' (Beresford 1988).

The apparent weakness of democratic consumerism is that it has developed out of the flux which is associated with the crisis of welfare state legitimacy, while at the same time it continues to assume corporate, state provision of health and welfare services. Market consumerism, arising as part of the critique of welfare state legitimacy, therefore appears at first sight as a potentially stronger influence amongst policy-makers, being based on an individual, private and contractual understanding of social relationships. However, it enters a context in which institutional and professional power also is strong, and in which there remains a high level of popular support for the idea of state welfare (Croft and Beresford 1989).

In order to illustrate the relative impact of these two perspectives, in the next section of this paper I will look at examples of how these forms of consumerism have operated in the UK, before proceeding to discuss the wider issues which emerge from these responses.

RECENT DEVELOPMENTS IN THE UK

All areas of social policy in the UK have been influenced by consumerism to some extent. However, the degree of such influence, it will be seen, relates to the extent that services are potentially universal or apply only to specific parts of the population (a point to which I will return below). The four areas of policy and practice which are discussed here have been selected to draw out these variations in the impact of consumerism. They are pensions, acute health services, community care and children's welfare. What has happened in the recent development of each of these areas?

Pensions

From the early part of the twentieth century the provision of a universal retirement pension has increasingly become one of the benchmarks of the welfare state in the UK (Macnicol and Blaikie 1989). However, by the latter part of the century it has become clear that, in common with all other industrialized countries a rising life expectancy has occurred along-side a falling birth rate (Coleman and Bond 1990). Government policy has responded to this phenomenon by characterizing it as a threat to economic stability because of anticipated high levels of demand for pensions, which are calculated on an insurance principle but in reality paid out of current revenue. Considerable encouragement has been given (for example through tax incentives) for contracting out of the State Earnings Related Pension Scheme (SERPS), and the purchasing of Private Equity Plans (PEPs), as a means to avoid a projected crisis in the next century (Groves 1987; Hill 1990). At the same time the rules for SERPS have been changed to reduce projected future costs (that is, by reducing future levels of benefit) (Groves 1987).

While it is possible to see this response also as a demographic panic (Coleman and Bond 1990), such policies are congruent with the broader social critique inherent in the views of a government established on New Right principles, of limiting the activity of the state in civil society. Moreover, consumerist ideas have been mobilized in the implementation of these changes, which are represented as ways of increasing choice and flexibility, as well as personal responsibility, in ensuring adequate income in later life. Congruence is claimed from a match between fiscal prudence and the populist idea of giving people 'greater choice' in making pension arrangements.

Health

Acute health services also have increasingly been characterized in ways which emphasize the opportunities for exercising personal choice, afforded by the private purchasing of health care (Barr *et al.* 1989). The critique of the National Health Service (NHS) has included reference to the length of waiting lists, lack of privacy, the power of professionals to determine the timing of consultations and treatment, and so on. Private arrangements, that is fee-paying at the point of service use, have been held to give the patient more control over when, where and by whom health care is provided (N. Johnson 1989).

However, most private health care is not purchased directly, but through private health insurance companies, typified by the British United Provident Association (BUPA) or the National Patients' Plan (NPP). That these operate as insurance companies defines the limits of the patient's power. The types of health care they provide are established contractually in advance, with limits set also to the amount of service which may be obtained within any given period. In this sense the power of the consumer is not unlimited, but set within boundaries that are defined by direct individual contract rather than indirect public account-ability. In this way it has been possible for private health care to marginal-ize the largest areas of demand, namely that amongst elderly people or those with long term ('chronic') health needs, either by charging higher premiums or by refusing cover altogether (Barr *et al.* 1989). In such circumstances choice can be exercised only by those who have the neces-sary private resources, thus excluding high proportions of specific groups (such as elderly people).

Market consumerism has also influenced the internal organization of the NHS, so that where choice cannot be created directly through market relationships these are simulated in the administrative structures of state provision (Cousins 1987). Budget-holding general medical practitioners (GPs) are being encouraged to direct patients to hospital services they judge to be the best to meet the patient's needs. Hospitals are encouraged to become independent trusts, so that they are free to compete to supply health care. Sensitivity to demand is thus built into the corporate organiz-ation, replicating market consumerism, although the individual is not paying at the point of service use (Barr *et al.* 1989; N. Johnson 1990; Flynn 1992).

Community care

In contrast, the services for people with chronic health problems, or long-term disabilities, have been seen as less easy to recast in the mould of the free market. There are two reasons for this. First, there is little possibility of people who require such services being able to make the financial contributions needed within a private insurance model. If able to obtain employment at all, people with long-term needs are more likely to be low income earners. Second, these needs are met also by the personal social services, which in the UK (as in some other countries) have been directed to those who are regarded as least able to provide for themselves and who may be judged as 'deserving' on other criteria (such as a willingness to co-operate with professional definitions of need) (Parry and Parry 1979; Hugman 1991).

In these areas, which include services for people with physical disabilities, people with learning difficulties, people with mental health problems and elderly people, debates about consumerism have been more clearly between the participation of service users in defining and managing services on the one hand and the privatization of services on the other. Examples of the former would include disabled people's groups, while a key example of the latter is the mushrooming of private residential care for elderly people on the guarantee of state funding for those residents who cannot otherwise afford to pay (Henwood 1986). The former are instances of democratic consumerism, while the latter are fashioned on the market model while being underpinned by state intervention.

Both these elements have been incorporated into the recent National Health Service and Community Care Act (1990), in which the budget-holding GP is paralleled by the 'case manager', who may be a nurse, an occupational therapist or a social worker (Renshaw 1988; *Caring for People* 1989; Challis 1990). In brief, case management is a system in which:

1 specific budgets are allocated to service users, in the form of units of service;
2 a named professional is designated case manager, with responsibility for the use of the budget;
3 service goals are agreed between the service user and case manager;
4 the budget is used to purchase services to meet the agreed goals.

In this way the individual's needs and wishes are integral to the utilization of public funds. However, while the expression of preference by the service user is central to this approach, budgetary responsibility and control rests with the professional.

Children's welfare

In most of the area of children's welfare there appears to be even less scope for a straightforward market consumerism to operate. This is because many of these services are imposed on children and families on behalf of the state, either as a means of controlling children and young people ('juvenile justice') or as a means of controlling their carers ('child protection'). In this context welfare has a social policing dimension (NISW 1982). In what ways is it possible to think about consumerism in relation to these services?

First, recent UK legislation in this area, notably the Children Act (1989), has incorporated the concept of the rights of children and young people to privacy and participation when they are in the care of the state (Allen 1990; Fox Harding 1991). In this way certain consumerist elements are built into the legislation, placing an obligation on professionals to provide the service in ways which 'take account of' the needs and wishes of the child or young person. There is a degree of equivalence between this aspect of the law and consumer protection legislation (for example, the Consumer Protection Act, 1971), which similarly sets out standards to which reference can be made in disputes between a customer and supplier of goods.

Second, there is a stress on the separation of the needs and rights of children from those of their parents within the Children Act (1989), and there is a parallel emphasis on the rights of parents in relation to professionals (in particular social workers) (Allen 1990). This is matched also by changes in the educational sphere which are claimed as the basis for reshaping parents' wishes against those of teachers (Every 1992). Even where there is a statutory basis for professionals to intervene in a family to protect the child, possibly from the actions of a parent, there is at the same time a limit set on the professionals in the form of legally defined rights for parents.

The idea of civil rights underpins contemporary child welfare (Fox Harding 1991). Yet in both the aspects which have been discussed this principle may be seen to have become interwoven with consumerist concepts, so that the boundary between civil rights and standards of service is blurred in such a way that 'liberty' may come to be fused with 'quality' (possibly even confused). In this curious mixture the power of professionals (as producers over consumers) and of service users (as consumers over producers) is held in check by the state which, through the institution of the courts, controls interventions in families. The rights of the market consumerist citizen, idealized as freedom from 'interference' by the state, in practice come to be established in relation to managerial controls over professionals and the development of quality assurance systems (cf. Dalley 1992). Such controls also buttress the power of professionals as agencies of the state in issues of social control and so serve to limit the extent to which market consumerism can realize civil rights.

TOWARDS CONSUMERISM?

What common themes can be identified here? First, there is the broad background political concern to increase individual social responsibility. This may take the form of emphasizing parents' rights and obligations with regard to their children, or of attempts to reduce the level of welfare expenditure against demographic expectations, shifting the cost away from society as a whole towards the individual wherever possible. This latter manifestation can be seen most clearly in the changes concerning pensions and some acute health services. Second, following from this, there is the view that state provision should be directed towards those who for specific reasons cannot make provision for themselves ('targeted'). This includes people with long-term disabilities or health needs, and some children. Third, the targeting of public resources is based on the belief that access to services which are provided by the state, directly or indirectly, should be negotiated by individuals through professionals who exercise discretion within clearly defined limits.

In summary there are three component principles to the impact of consumerism in health and welfare in the UK:

1 wherever possible individuals should take responsibility for their own health and welfare, and make provision to meet their own needs;
2 corporate state provision should be residual, for those who are unable (and not simply unwilling) to make their own provision;
3 that access to corporate services should be mediated by professionals, working within clearly defined limits.

Therefore, the forms of consumerism which can be identified in these UK policy developments may be seen as 'mixed', containing elements of market and democratic consumerisms. So it is possible to detect an emerging orthodoxy: that services are provided more effectively if the service user is involved *in some way* and *to some degree* in decisions about content and style of delivery (although the balance of involvement varies between the different policy areas).

Focusing specifically on community care, this is succinctly expressed in the report by Griffiths on the provision of community care services, in his recommendation that assessments of needs should reflect the personal preferences of service users, and take 'account of the views and wishes of the person to be cared for, and any informal carers, [to] decide what packages of care would be best suited to the needs' (1988: 6). Service users (including informal carers) are to be taken account of, rather than participate in the control of health and welfare services, just as the supermarket is able to provide cheap but good quality produce because it satisfies sufficiently the wishes of a large enough number of customers. This is consumer demand interpreted by marketing exercises and sales figures rather than by customer participation in the planning and managing of product delivery, and power to make the final decision remains with the service provider. It is market research rather than democracy (Beresford 1988). So, is it this model which has been introduced to health and welfare services through budget-holding GPs and community care case managers?

Professionals and consumerism

As I have noted above, the professional model here is that of occupational authority and power, derived from the state through the professionals' role as intermediaries between the state and individual citizens. T. J. Johnson (1972) typified this model as that which was most evident in nursing, social work and similar 'semi-professions'. This 'mediative' model is compared by Johnson with 'collegial' professionalism (in which the ends and means of the profession are established within the occupation) and 'patronage' professionalism (in which the ends and means of the profession are negotiated between occupational members and their clientele). Market consumerism in health and welfare can be seen as the attempt to promote the patronage model of professionalism, and, where the conditions do not otherwise occur, to create them through administrative arrangements. On an individualist understanding of social relationships and responsibility this must be the appropriate goal, as the choice expressed by the patron is the formalization of power possessed in relation to professionals.

However, it must be recognized that the mediative model is the weakest type of professionalism, and as such we may expect to see it resisted by those occupations which can lay claim to a stronger form. The most likely candidates for this response would seem to be doctors (*Lancet* 1988), although social workers also have expressed some disquiet about the way budget holding and case management have been introduced (British Association of Social Workers 1990). This latter response is based partly on the democratic consumerist perspective, but also derives from an early enthusiasm for case management as a means of enhancing social work with less valued service users, particularly elderly people (Challis and Davies 1986). Moreover, budget-holding doctors and case-managing nurses, occupational therapists or social workers are in a different position from the supermarket grocer in that they can, indeed must, develop an understanding of the needs and wishes of each individual service user (Challis 1990), with the implication that demand-led sensitivity in service provision should go beyond marketing or sales.

Nevertheless, the government policies which have led to the introduction of these developments are concerned not directly with extending the power of service users over professionals, but to reshape the welfare state and to reduce the fiscal obligation of the state in health and welfare provision. For this reason there may be a congruence between the interests of the New Right and service users in limiting the power of collegial professionalism, but a conflict in the extent to which a move to patronage relationships should be state funded. So the mediative model is a compromise which enables such changes to be supported ideologically while maintaining the dominance of the interests of the state over and above those of the civil society. The interests of professionals can be partly satisfied with the maintenance, or even enhancement, of their technical autonomy in the methods of their professional practices (the chance to do 'real medicine/nursing/occupational therapy/social work' within budget holding or case management, although this may be contested by critical professionals, as noted above) (cf. Derber 1982).

Dividing purchasers and providers

The central mechanism in the consumerist restructuring of the welfare state has been the internal division of agencies into service-providing elements and those which act on behalf of patients or clients as the purchaser of services (Vass 1990; Flynn 1992). The underlying principle is to create the possibility of choice for service users through the delegation of discretion to the budget holder or case manager about the source of a specific provision. In theory this may include the independent sector (whether not-for-profit or profit-making), although in practice the degree of discretion may be limited by the extent to which budgets are notional or actual. In other words, the idea of the purchaser-provider split may be more concerned with creating cost centres and devolving discretion than in breaking up bureaucracies.

So, does the purchaser-provider split give any assurance to service users about the recognition of their wishes and needs? In order to address this, a system of inspection and complaints procedures also have been established through the legislation (*Children Act* 1989 and *National Health Service and Community Care Act* 1990), which are intended to make public agencies accountable both to the state and to individual service users. Whereas the former (inspection) relates only to the providers of services, the latter (complaints procedures) covers both purchasers and providers. (Budget-holding GPs are to be covered by the Audit Commission.) In this way it is intended that the consumerist safeguards which apply to the customer of the supermarket will be available also to the user of health and welfare services.

However, no matter how carefully the mechanisms may be planned and managed, exercising consumerist power in a complaint about health or social care is of a much greater order than asking for a refund on tinned fruit which is not of merchantable quality. The emotional and psychological demands faced by a vulnerable individual in such a situation are enormous. One is dependent, to some extent, for health and well-being on the person about whom the complaint is being made. At the time of writing the new structures and procedures have yet to be tested. Nor is it clear whether the purchaser (budget holder or case manager) will be expected to play a part in complaints against service providers, or whether the considerable vestiges of collegial professionalism will consti-tute a barrier to this process.

CONSUMERISM: OBSTACLES AND OPPORTUNITIES?

From the earlier part of the discussion, which looked at the broader context of developing consumerism, the focus has narrowed to its impact in specific aspects of health and welfare in the UK. I want now to widen the discussion again, to consider the prospect for a continuing consumerist influence in this area, and for the opportunities provided by the current situation for varying outcomes, in which market consumerism may be moderated or challenged to different degrees by forms of democratic consumerism.

A major distinction between the areas of social policy identified above which affects the extent to which market consumerism and privatization have been possible within them is the proportion of the population able to take individual financial responsibility (that is, to purchase alterna-tives to the state directly). In this sense the order of topics in the dis-cussion above (pensions, acute health, community care and children) reflects an ordering of areas in which it is possible for people to be consumers on a free market basis and those areas in which such a model is less appropriate.

Are we to conclude, therefore, that the advantages of consumerism, power and choice, are to be available only to those with sufficient personal resources (even if this does in some aspects include a majority of people in the UK)? Or is it feasible to extend these social benefits to those who may be otherwise discriminated against because of disability, illness or age, or even because of race and culture, gender or sexuality? Claims to a greater possibility of participation made in the consumer rhetoric of recent welfare state developments in the UK are challenged by other models for change which also draw on a combination of market and democratic consumerisms (Brandon 1991b). The first of these I want to consider is the Canadian model of 'service brokerage', and the second is the possibility of using service user groups as a vehicle for enabling user participation.

Brokerage, in some senses, takes case management to its logical conclusion in consumer oriented community care. It does not devolve the budget for public service provision to a professional (even though that person may have close regular contact with the service user) but gives it directly to that service user (Brandon 1991a, 1991b). The service user then is able to spend the money on the purchase of services from whomever she or he judges is most appropriate, or else employs someone to act as a broker to locate and employ caring services. In this way, although the resources come from the state, they are managed in such a way as to duplicate the spending power of the individual private citizen.

There are some potential difficulties with this approach. The first is that it may leave the unwaged recipient of long-term community care services in a direct client relationship to the state. The Canadian system of income maintenance and disablement benefits is both clearer than that in the UK and founded on a more well established concept of rights to such benefits. Without such a basis the service user is still subject to the control of professionals, acting on behalf of the state, in determining eligibility (Hugman 1991).

There is also the question of how service users with particular types of disability (such as severe learning difficulties or Alzheimer's Disease) are able to express choice. Here there is a clearer solution, in the form of the 'advocacy' movement, in which either the person is helped to learn to express choice (self-advocacy) or else communicates through another person who is not a professional with other interests in the situation, such as control over the care resources (citizen advocacy) (Williams and Shoultz 1982; Rhoades 1986; Lawson 1991). In this approach the individual does not stand alone, nor is dependent on professionals for the expression of wishes and choice, but is supported collectively to some degree. The advocacy approach is not tied to brokerage (indeed, it predates that development) and can be applied to other service relationships. Advocacy has a place in more 'traditional' welfare state structures and practices because it is a way of empowering service users to speak about their own needs and wishes, and is not related only to one pattern of service delivery (Williams and Shoultz 1982; Gould 1986). It does, however, force professionals and policy-makers to pay more attention to service users.

This leads to the second broad opportunity for democratic consumerism, namely the service user group movement. As I noted earlier in this paper, these may be focused around specific health or welfare issues (for example, children in care, or mental hospital patients), or they may reflect other shared perspectives (such as women's groups, or Black people's groups). Such groups may be involved not only in the advocacy of individual needs and wishes, but also in the formulation and expression of consumer views about health and welfare from groups of service users (Croft and Beresford 1989; Hugman 1991). Such a potential shifts the focus from attention to services at the point of consumption to their formulation in policy and planning. This is collective consumerism, as opposed to the individualism of the market model. Such groups have successfully made an impact on services, in the UK as elsewhere, although there are areas also where they have to struggle to be heard (Collins and Stein 1989; Croft and Beresford 1989).

As democratic forms of consumerism, these developments address the inequalities of social power which are much more evident in some parts of the welfare state than others (whether access is discretionary or of right), and which are structured chiefly by the ability of the citizen to pay for an alternative even when public services are being used. (Factors such as gender, race and other aspects of class also play a part in this.) Power is addressed more clearly precisely because such groups are collective. They provide a basis for the voice of service users who otherwise lack social power to be expressed in a context where the other actors, the state and the professions, also are collectivities and are not private fee-charging service providers (Hugman 1991).

CONSUMERISM IN THE FUTURE?

As we have seen, the influence of consumerism on the provision of health and welfare in the UK has two main strands, that based on individual, private free-market relationships, and that based on a collective, democratic approach to identifying and expressing the needs and wishes of service users. The balance between these competing influences varies in relation to the possibility of citizens making alternative arrangements, either by payment of fee at the point of service delivery or through the prior purchase of insurance. At the same time, it has been noted that the increased concern with consumerist ideas has been closely bound up with crises in the welfare state, both fiscal and ideological, which have set the stage for the way in which the detail has been played out.

So, how substantial are the promises offered by consumerism? There does appear to be some solidity to innovations based on consumerism, precisely because the social power of those who can pay has been used as a lever to exert a change of direction on very well established institutions, either directly or as a model for organizational change. There is an appeal in these developments for those who must rely on the welfare state, as evidenced by brokerage and advocacy. Nevertheless, even the mixed model of consumerism as it has been incorporated in health and welfare does make assumptions which empirically remain questionable:

1 that the interests of professionals and service users can be harmonized, and that both are able equally to articulate their interests;
2 that the range of services available is sufficient and appropriate, or that market-style forces will lead to the development of such services.

The first of these assumptions may or may not be true in individual instances (I have argued elsewhere that generally it is not the case – Hugman 1991); but to ensure a consistency across society requires strong state control which overtly is at variance with other parts of the New Right agenda (Gamble 1986). Furthermore, the New Right have used public disquiet about the power of professionals, as well as left-wing critiques of professionalism, as part of their strategy for change (Mishra 1984, 1986). The resulting contradiction weakens the force of this assumption as a general principle. The second assumption as yet requires concrete evidence. As a hypothesis it may be plausible, although the counter-argument that corporate state welfare emerged as a means of solving social problems which had developed under liberal capitalism is equally robust (Thane 1982).

So, while consumerism can be said to have played a part in the reshaping of relationships between professionals and service users in the welfare state, it must be seen only as a part of the changes which have taken place in the last decade. Moreover, it is one which has been mobilized in contradictory ways by competing social groups. As such, conclusions about the possible contribution of consumerism to the structures and practices of health and welfare depend on the perspective of the observer. While the market model has been used to reinforce the advantages of those who can pay directly for health and welfare, these contradictions mean that scope remains for a more democratic consumerism in the form of service user groups. This is an optimistic possibility for otherwise disadvantaged consumers of health and welfare.

REFERENCES

Allen, N. (1990) *Making Sense of the Children Act 1989*, London: Longman.
Bamford, T. (1990) *The Future of Social Work*, London: Macmillan.
Barr, N., Glennerster, H. and le Grand, J. (1989) 'Working for patients? The right approach?' in *Social Policy and Administration* 23 (2): 117–27.
Beresford, P. (1988) 'Consumer views: data collection or democracy?' in I. Allen (ed.) *Hearing the Voice of the Consumer*, London: Policy Studies Institute.
Boyce, R. (1991) 'Hospital restructuring – the implications for allied health professionals', in *Australian Health Review* 14 (2): 147–54.
Brandon, D. (1991a) *Innovation Without Change*, London: Macmillan.
—— (1991b) 'Implications of normalisation work for professional skills', in S. Ramon (ed.) *Beyond Community Care*, London: Macmillan.
British Association of Social Workers (BASW) (1990) *Community Care: Whose Choice?*, Birmingham: BASW.

Caring for People, Cm. 849 (1989), London: HMSO.

Carr-Saunders, A. M. and Wilson, P. A. (1962) *The Professions*, London: Oxford University Press.

Challis, D. (1990) 'Case management: problems and possibilities' in I. Allen (ed.) *Care Managers and Care Management*, London: Policy Studies Institute.

Challis, D. and Davies, B. (1986) *Case Management in Community Care*, Aldershot: Gower.

Children Act (1989), London: HMSO.

Coleman, P. and Bond, J. (1990) 'Ageing in the twentieth century', in J. Bond and P. Coleman (eds) *Ageing in Society*, London: Sage.

Collins, S. and Stein, M. (1989) 'Users fight back: collectives in social work', in C. Rojek, G. Peacock and S. Collins (eds) *The Haunt of Misery*, London: Routledge.

Consumer Protection Act (1971), London: HMSO.

Cousins, C. (1987) *Controlling Social Welfare*, Brighton: Wheatsheaf.

Croft, S. and Beresford, P. (1989) 'User involvement, citizenship and social policy', in *Critical Social Policy* 26: 5–18.

Dalley, G. (1992) 'Quality management: lessons from the NHS', in I. Allen, (ed.) *Drawing the Line: Purchasing and Providing Social Services in the 1990s*, London: Policy Studies Institute.

Derber, C. (1982) 'Managing professionals: ideological proletarianization and mental labor', in C. Derber (ed.) *Professionals as Workers: Mental Labor in Advanced Capitalism*, Boston: G. K. Hall.

Dominelli, L. and McLeod, E. (1989) *Feminist Social Work*, London: Macmillan.

Durkheim, E. (1957) (trans. C. Brookfield) *Professional Ethics and Civil Morals*, London: Routledge & Kegan Paul.

Etzioni, A. (ed.) (1969) *The Semi-Professions and Their Organization*, New York: The Free Press.

Every, J. van (1992) 'Who is the family? The assumptions of British social policy', in *Critical Social Policy* 33: 62–75.

Flynn, R. (1992) *Structures of Control in Health Management*, London: Routledge.

Fox Harding, L. (1991) *Perspectives in Child Care Policy*, London: Longman.

Freidson, E. (1970) *The Profession of Medicine*, New York: Dodd Mead.

Gamble, A. (1986) 'The political economy of freedom', in R. Levitas (ed.) *The Ideology of the New Right*, Cambridge: Polity Press.

Gould, M. (1986) 'Self-advocacy: consumer leadership for the transition years', in *Journal of Rehabilitation* 52 (4): 39–42.

Greenwood, E. (1957) 'The attributes of a profession', in *Social Work* 2 (3): 44–55.

Groves, D. (1987) 'Women and occupational pension provision: past and future', in S. di Gregorio, *Social Gerontology: New Directions*, London: Croom Helm.

Henwood, M. (1986) 'Community care: policy, practice and prognosis', in M. Brenton and C. Ungerson (eds) *The Yearbook of Social Policy in Britain 1985–6*, London: Routledge & Kegan Paul.

Hill, M. (1990) *Social Security Policy in Britain*, Aldershot: Edward Elgar.

Hugman, R. (1991) *Power in Caring Professions*, London: Macmillan.

Illich, I. (1971) *Celebration of Awareness*, London: Calder & Boyars.

—— (1976) *Medical Nemesis: the Expropriation of Health*, London: Marion Boyars.

Johnson, N. (1989) 'The privatisation of welfare', in *Social Policy and Administration* 23 (1): 17–30.

—— (1990) *Reconstructing the Welfare State*, Hemel Hempstead: Harvester/Wheatsheaf.

Johnson, T. J. (1972) *Professions and Power*, London: Macmillan.

Lancet (1988) 'Curtains up on NHS review' (editorial), ii (1320): 247–9.

Lawson, M. (1991) 'A recipient's view', in S. Ramon (ed.) *Beyond Community Care*, London: Macmillan.

Macnicol, J. and Blaikie, A. (1989) 'The politics of retirement, 1908–1948', in M. Jeffereys (ed.) *Growing Old in the Twentieth Century*, London: Routledge.

Mishra, R. (1984) *The Welfare State in Crisis*, Brighton: Wheatsheaf.

—— (1986) 'The left and the welfare state: a critical analysis', in *Critical Social Policy* 15: 4–19.

National Health Service and Community Care Act (1990), London: HMSO.

National Institute for Social Work (NISW) (1982) *Social Workers, Their Role and Tasks (The Barclay Report)*, London: Bedford Square Press.

O'Connor, J. (1973) *The Fiscal Crisis of the State*, New York: St Martin's Press.

Parry, N. and Parry, J. (1979) 'Social work, professionalism and the state', in M. Rustin, N. Parry and C. Satyamurti (eds) *Social Work, Welfare and the State*, London: Edward Arnold.

Phillips, M. (1982) 'Separatism or black control?' in A. Ohri, B. Manning and P. Curno (eds) *Community Work and Racism*, London: Routledge & Kegan Paul.

Renshaw, J. (1988) 'Care in the community: individual care planning and case management', in *British Journal of Social Work* 18 (supplement): 79–105.

Rhoades, C. (1986) 'Different organizational models for self help groups that serve people with developmental disabilities', in *Journal of Rehabilitation* 52 (4): 43–7.

Shaw, G. B. (1911) *The Doctor's Dilemma*, London: Constable & Co.

Taylor, D. (1989) 'Citizenship and social power', in *Critical Social Policy* 26: 19–31.

Thane, P. (1982) *Foundations of the Welfare State*, London: Longman.

Vass, P. (1990) 'Principles and practices of devolved budgets', in I. Allen (ed.) *Care Managers and Care Management*, London: Policy Studies Institute.

Wilding, P. (1982) *Professional Power and Social Welfare*, London: Routledge & Kegan Paul.

Williams, P. and Shoultz, B. (1982) *We Can Speak For Ourselves*, London: Souvenir Press.

Wootton, B. (1959) *Social Science and Social Pathology*, London: George Allen & Unwin.

Working for Patients, Cm. 555 (1989), London: HMSO.

Chapter 13

Consuming education

Oliver Fulton

INTRODUCTION

Something is certainly going on in education. At the policy level, recent changes in primary and secondary education include the introduction of a national curriculum, the virtual abolition of the long established structures of local democratic control and independent national inspection, and the quasi-privatization of schools; while in higher education the number of autonomous universities has been nearly doubled, the established mechanisms of academic planning and control have been downgraded or replaced, and student demand has become one of the main vehicles for differential funding of institutions. At the same time, the education system's outputs are changing dramatically: both qualification levels (as proportions of the relevant population cohorts) and the demand for non-compulsory education are rising at rates that, as recently as five years ago, were regarded by policy-makers and analysts as possibly desirable but certainly unattainable.

How do we explain these changes, and how central to the explanation are the 'consumers' of education? The present government would claim that the voice of the consumer is now, or will shortly be, sovereign – indeed, in logic it ought to give most of the credit for the proclaimed success of its policies to consumers themselves, achieving the fulfilment of their long-unmet needs via the hidden hand of the market: its own role being merely that of the modest enabler of long suppressed market forces. Its critics would retort that the alleged market is largely a fake, designed to conceal the true intentions and the authorship of politically motivated policy changes; and that like all markets it selectively benefits a limited number of favoured 'consumers'.

In this paper I shall try to unpack some of the processes that seem to be going on, and shall argue (predictably, no doubt) that the truth is more complicated than rhetoric allows – though the rhetoric itself needs examining. I believe that we need to think much more clearly about cause and effect: is it really plausible that changed control mechanisms such as the (limited) shift from planning to markets, even if accompanied by determined efforts to change the surrounding political discourse, have led to such dramatic changes in education's output? Is it not more likely, instead, that changes in the demand for education and in its social and economic functions have prompted both political intervention and also cultural shifts in attitudes to and expectations of educational institutions and their workers?

RHETORIC AND REALITY: THE BACKGROUND TO CURRENT POLICIES

The rhetoric

The attempt to introduce market 'discipline' into schools and universities is often described as part of the Thatcherite crusade against an alleged grand conspiracy of professionals – especially those employed in the public sector. The indictment has several parts, but its central claim draws on the language of market economics to label professionals and their associations as self-serving monopolies of producers, one of whose key functions is to act in restraint of trade. Examples are the lack of 'customer' choice which is imposed by assigning pupils to schools on the basis of geography and administrative convenience; or the tendentious way in which members of the 'educational establishment' (a term which begs a few questions) describe themselves as 'providers' of a public service at public expense rather than 'producers' of a good whose true price can obviously only be determined in the market place. There are, government economists wearily point out, no satisfactory criteria intrinsic to education which would indicate the appropriate level of government expenditure (which they refer to as 'public subsidy').

The implications of this free market rhetoric have been partly worked out in some of the major Conservative educational reforms of the 1980s. These have included the gradual demolition of local education authorities' (LEAs) control of school budgets in favour of 'local' (that is school-based) management, by strengthened governing bodies, of resources which are allocated by per capita funding formulas; or in higher education the replacement of the University *Grants* Committee (UGC) by two successive '*funding* councils' with substantially non-academic membership, mandated to distribute funds in ways that will reward popular institutions; and in both sectors repeated efforts to relate employees' salaries both to individuals' 'performance' and to their labour market situation. The preferred model, therefore, is one of private enterprise: converting public agencies into 'firms' exposed to all the disciplines of the market that can be applied to them.

So much for the rhetoric. However, there are alternative views which treat it with total scepticism, arguing that the policy agenda has little or nothing to do with the abstract pursuit of better services through the operation of autonomous markets, and everything to do with another set of Conservative agendas, dominated by the business of satisfying or placating a series of special interest groups – among whom education professionals do not rank high.

The wider policy agenda

There is a strong case for saying that the more significant 'market' mechanisms so far imposed on education are designed much more to cut costs than to empower the public. Although policies to cut public expenditure may be given the ideological twist that the public services rig the market and are inherently inefficient, the truth is that Conservative governments have hunted throughout the 1980s for politically acceptable ways to reduce public spending, egged on by industry and by their traditional wealthy supporters, and have very successfully claimed the credit at the ballot box for safeguarding 'the taxpayer's' interests. And there are several reasons aside from ideology why education should have been a prime target. They include changing demography – the huge decline in pupil numbers which rippled through the compulsory sector from the mid–1970s onwards; the size of the national education budget; and education's exceptional political vulnerability, compared with other large national or local expenditure areas (see pp. 228–30).

There are two ways to reduce government expenditure. One is to cut unit costs and the other is to find someone else to pay. There has been plenty of the first of these, but in education there is little attempt to disguise the aim of shifting costs from the taxpayer to anyone else who can be induced to pay them: pupils and students and/or their parents; members of the community (but as 'voluntary' contributors, not as local taxpayers); private industry, whether as philanthropic donor or as the beneficiary of education's services. There is certainly a supporting rhetoric of market responsiveness, the suggestion that, in the best Friedmanite tradition, those who buy the lunch will choose the menu. But it is pretty clear that the main thing, from government's point of view, is that somebody else should pay for it: specific beneficiaries – individual graduates, industrial clients for research or teaching and so on – can be identified and therefore should not have a free lunch at the taxpayer's expense.

There are other Conservative policy imperatives. Among them at present are:

- a determined hostility to any local government agencies with substantial executive or spending power – with LEAs as the paradigm case;
- indifference to the needs of the less well off and the disadvantaged;

- a commitment to the 'traditional', high-culture curriculum, even in defiance of the expressed views of employers' organizations;
- the need for a scapegoat for the economic and social disasters of late capitalism, as currently practised in the UK.

Add to this a range of sharp conflicts among stakeholders in education:

- between government ministries for the political credit for dealing with education (or avoidance of blame for its failures);
- between HM Inspectorate representing a 'professional' viewpoint and the executive arm of the Civil Service;
- between sectional trade unions and associations;
- between 1991's universities and the former polytechnics for status and resources;
- between voluntary bodies (mainly Church-related) and the representatives of wholly-maintained schools and colleges; and so on.

There is no space here even to begin to spell out all the interactions in this thoroughly murky brew (see Ball 1990 or Chitty 1989 for recent attempts from somewhat different theoretical perspectives). But what should be clear from this list is that any notion of the market as the overriding philosophical principle is likely to be overdone. Certain aspects of marketization may fit more or less neatly with certain other Conservative policy goals, but that is a very different matter. However much the fundamentalists may hanker after a privatized, marketized, enterprised society, they come up against insuperable contradictions – like the weak state/strong state dilemma of Conservatism discussed by Marquand (1992) – and tensions between the demands of the different interest groups to whom the Conservative party must respond.

CONSUMERS AND PRODUCERS

Despite these pressures, I differ from some analysts (for example Ball 1990, Fairclough 1991) who see consumerism in education as a consequence of governments simply *imposing* market mechanisms or greater degrees of consumer responsiveness either for intrinsic reasons or for ulterior purposes. Not only is the government agenda more complicated, but there is also evidence of consumer disquiet and producer weakness which has not all been got up by the press, by the radical free-marketeers with their 'discourse of derision' (Ball 1990) or by the state.[1]

'Consumer' demand and consumer interests

Education is one of the great growth industries worldwide, and the UK in the postwar period is no exception. The proportion of young people achieving given levels of education has risen sharply, though not evenly. Put very crudely, sharp rises in the indicators in the 1950s and 1960s were followed by a plateau in the 1970s and early 1980s, and this in turn by further very sharp increases in the last few years.

Economists point out that increased participation can be interpreted both as consumption and as investment in human capital. The debate on the balance between the two is esoteric, but it is obvious that there has been an element of each. The investment motive has always been important for post-compulsory education. The Robbins Report (1963: 6) quoted Confucius ('it [is] not easy to find a man who [has] studied for three years without aiming at pay'), and plenty of research evidence shows that students staying on after 16 and choosing to enter higher education have definite if not precise ideas about the likely financial and career advantages. Changing rates of demand both for higher education as a whole and for specific subjects within it are certainly related to perceived rates of return.

What seems to have changed over the last twenty years is the spread of this concern with 'investment'. As the proportion of young people achieving qualifications has increased, so too has the salience of educational achievement for life chances. The UK, like other western European societies, has quite recently become a fully fledged 'credential society' in which employment prospects and all their consequences are dependent on educational success, certified by qualifications: witness the growth of new qualifications, as well as the growing proportions achieving each.[2] But as certification expands its reach, its effects alter: instead of simply rewarding success, the labour market makes educational 'failure' more consequential as it becomes less common. No wonder, with youth unemployment rates rising since the 1970s and now chronically high, that school pupils as well as students, and their parents, are anxious: and their anxiety has provided the foundation for governments, the press and other opinion-formers to manipulate the discourse of 'falling standards'; and hence to suggest that consumers, if suitably empowered, will take steps to protect their investment by demanding better results.

The evidence that education is viewed as a consumption good is less clear cut. From an economist's point of view it may be enough to say that participation in education has increased, worldwide, broadly in line with increasing prosperity: the consumption of education does seem to have grown along with other products of the culture industries, if that is what education is. But how would we know if being a student is really a form of cultural consumption? In the post-compulsory sector being a student is certainly supposed to be enjoyable: it allows you to pursue strong academic interests if you have them (and many higher education entrants still say they do), and if you are a young full-time student it gives you independence from home, the prospect of an exciting social life (if you can afford it) and postpones the prospect of work for another few years (Roberts and Higgins 1992). What's more, you should emerge from some higher education institutions and some courses (but how many?) with your general culture-consuming capacity and your cultural status considerably enhanced.

But does this make higher education students 'active' or 'enterprising' consumers, likely to flex their collective muscles as their numbers grow, or to make good use of any new financial levers they are given? And what about pupils or students in other sectors? Do any of them feel they have the right to demand that either school or higher education should always be pleasurable experiences? The truth is that from primary school to doctoral research, the experience of education (both learning itself and the whole experience of being a pupil/student) is traditionally a peculiar mixture of excitement and boredom – probably much more of the latter – with a fair amount of humiliation thrown in. Could democratization, changing consumption patterns, or the imposition of market mechanisms really alter that balance?

Producer authority

School teachers' status and their collective authority have never been equal to those of the older professions. Possibly – and market enthusiasts would presumably argue this – the profession's weakness has something to do with employment in the public salariat (without the benefits of European civil service status) rather than in private enterprise.[3] But the two key components are social origins and expertise. First, school teaching, especially in primary schools, was traditionally a legitimate aspiration for groups excluded from more discriminatory professions, notably for women and for able working-class people of both genders. Inevitably this has worked to the disadvantage of the profession at least as much as to the advantage of those who have joined it, damning teaching by implication as the resort of marginalized groups who deserved no better, and reducing primary teaching especially to a role which is feminized – and hence undervalued – by recruitment as well as by content. The more recent democratization of other occupations has not helped: their higher status and rewards have relegated teaching to the bottom of the list for able or ambitious people who would previously have been glad to join it.[4] The point is underlined by the admissions market in which some of the lowest entry grades are asked for teacher education courses, especially those in specialist colleges.

The question of expertise is at least as crucial. The classic account of the professions is that protection from the market is granted in return for the provision of expert services – of which the consumer cannot be an adequate judge. Here the school-teaching profession is weakest.

Historically the actual practice of teaching has never carried much conviction as requiring high-level or esoteric skills – originally it was a craft learned by apprenticeship and example rather than through the study of written texts. Indeed, the higher levels of teaching asserted their relative status not by claiming more advanced techniques but by emphasizing the importance of subject knowledge, and the irrelevance of formal training for classroom practice. During the 1960s and 1970s there was a determined attempt by the school-teaching profession to establish technical expertise in the practice of education itself. Teaching qualifications were extended and upgraded; and specialisms such as the psychology and sociology of education became part of the compulsory training curriculum. However, it is now clear that the attempt comprehensively failed. An extended counter-attack has included systematic derision of the status of teachers' supposedly expert knowledge. Even areas such as the teaching of reading, where it seems virtually self-evident that both research and daily experience might have something to add to lay opinion, have been fair game. The latest outcome is that government reform proposals in 1992 involve the virtual elimination of anything but subject knowledge from the formal teacher training curriculum: everything else is to be reduced to a list of 'competences' which are to be acquired in the classroom alongside experienced teachers.

But why did the attempt fail? One could rehearse the same arguments as before, seeing (as many do) the derision of teachers' skills by government and others as deliberate ideological or discursive manipulation. But there are also the social changes referred to earlier, notably the greater salience of education for life chances, giving parents and consumers good grounds for concern with the effectiveness of esoteric techniques; as well as the effect of rising levels of education, which gives lay publics the confidence to question previously accepted bases of authority. Finally, though, one has to add that peculiar feature of education, alone among all the professions, that lay people have spent an immense amount of their earlier lives (15,000 hours by the standard calculation) observing (and enduring) this particular professional practice in action. As a result they have a sharp eye for these particular emperors' clothes, and in most cases a few grudges as well: for teachers do have power even if they lack authority.

In higher education even more than in secondary schools, subject knowledge or, to be more precise, involvement in research and scholarship have been the basis for claims of expertise. Public esteem for the profession is said to have reached a peak after each of the world wars, when in Britain as elsewhere university 'boffins' were said to have made an invaluable contribution to the war effort. But as the system has grown, time, space and resources for research have become impossible to provide for every academic. Meanwhile the profession has been ambivalent about the job of teaching: despite the consistent findings of surveys that the majority of British academics value their teaching activities as much as or more than their research, it is only in the last fifteen to twenty years that attention to the skills of teaching has become in any way fashionable – and even so, very few academics are systematically trained for their most time-consuming role. The recently growing emphasis on teaching quality in the older university sector seems imposed rather than organic, mainly out of government concern for better 'value for money' paid to idle and inept professionals. Whether imposed or adopted, it does not help much with the profession's status: it emphasizes both a public lack of confidence in teaching and the loss of research from the defining features of the modern university.

The social origin point is less persuasive: entry to the higher education profession has never been as democratic as to school-teaching. Women, especially, have been a small minority with markedly lower representation at higher grades and in permanent jobs. It seems more likely that the sheer expansion of the profession has taken the shine off whatever glamour it may once have possessed – aided, no doubt, by Posy Simmonds' definitive scrutiny of the archetypical polytechnic lecturer. In any event, one result is clear-cut. Halsey's calculations show that the average academic salary has slipped steadily from a value of 3.7 times average earnings in 1928 to 1.5 times in 1989 (Halsey 1992: 131).

EDUCATIONAL MARKETS, PRESENT AND FUTURE

There are in fact multiple markets in education, with different arrays of consumers and producers in each. The main market to which the present government claims to attach importance is that in which educators and their organizations are the producers and the pupils/students and/or their families are the consumers. However, in reality, the single most important quasi-market relationship is that between the state and the education providers. As the major or sole purchaser of most of education's output, government enjoys monopsony power, and uses it to drive down the price of services. In principle this was true of earlier governments; but price competition was not part of their weaponry. The DES seems to have stumbled in the early 1980s on the discovery that institutions could be forced into competition. The National Advisory Body (NAB), given a fixed budget to distribute to polytechnics and colleges, chose to allocate most of it on a student per capita basis. Although government policy was that student numbers should not rise, and the NAB had therefore fixed in advance the maximum student numbers it was prepared to pay for in each institution, almost every polytechnic and college regularly over-recruited, to be sure that its proportional allocation the following year would not be adjusted downwards. Thus real per capita costs fell year after year, despite the NAB's serious reservations about the effects on the quality of education. The NAB's successor, the Polytechnics and Colleges Funding Council (PCFC) also adopted this method of funding increased numbers, and so in due course did the UFC.[5] The fact that both PCFC and UFC, and later their combined successor, have agreed on a system in which lower prices ('greater efficiency') appear to be the end and competition merely the means is scarcely disputable.

In the case of schools, the invention of local management and per capita funding was designed in part to shift the responsibility for identifying, and in effect closing down, schools made redundant by the declining population of children, from reluctant LEAs to a contrived consumer market. However, the simultaneous policy shift (not yet fully implemented) from local funding to direct central funding via the 'grant maintained' system (GMS or 'opting out') will result – provided that large numbers of schools in fact opt out or are forced to do so – in far greater purchasing power shifting to the Department for Education as sole purchaser, giving it in future the opportunity to reduce prices well below those paid by the more generous LEAs.[6] It will also expose schools to influence over their academic policies: deviations from the national curriculum will be much easier to control via a single direct funding system. Thus central government has deliberately strengthened both its commanding market position and its managerial powers *vis-à-vis* schools and higher education suppliers.

I turn now to what government chooses to refer to as the market, that of students or their families as consumers and educational institutions as producers.[7] Here we need to look both at choices at entry – the original purchase, so to speak – and further choices by pupils/students once within an institution. We also need to distinguish analytically between the exercise of pure consumer power, to buy or not to buy, and that of consumer pressure. Hirschman's Exit and Voice distinction provides a helpful analogy, as long as we realize that the two are not totally distinct: behind attempts to influence through internal mechanisms lies the implicit threat of purchasing power. Government policy is ambiguous in its view of the relative weight to be placed on consumer pressure and consumer choice, and this ambiguity has led to apparently inconsistent policies.

Parental choice of schools

In the case of schools, the pure market version seems to dictate a clear set of principles. Since the 1988 Act, schools have been funded by formulae which require LEAs to distribute virtually all basic recurrent funding on a per capita basis. Each parent's or child's choice of school brings fixed resources with it: hence popular schools will prosper and unpopular schools will fade away, or improve their response to the market place. Parents are to be aided in their choice by information on school performance: government is now collecting and publishing comparative (though crude) figures on examination passes, will shortly add indicators such as truancy rates, and will require schools and LEAs to distribute them. The hope is that informed market decisions will set up a general structure of incentives and rapid rewards for improvement.

However, there are flaws in the argument. First, there is a very limited number of choice points for parents and children: entry to primary and to secondary school, and in some cases further transfers to middle schools and to a range of choices at 16 plus. Thus the decision to 'purchase' education is not repeated as it is with most consumer goods. Theoretically there is the exit as well as the entrance option, but parents are extremely reluctant to remove children from schools, for good and obvious reasons. Thus the market is likely to operate with considerable time-lags after new information appears. The quality of this information is also subject to challenge. Statisticians have discovered that many standardized 'performance indicators' are quite volatile from year to year – which raises serious doubts not so much about their reliability (data for the simpler measures is expensive but not difficult to collect and process accurately) as about their meaningfulness.

Others again have argued that the information necessary to make a well-informed choice of school is too complex and subtle for the average parent to understand. Here they refer mainly to the technicalities of 'value added' comparisons: these are based on the claim that, given the variability of intake between one school and another, effectiveness is best measured not by raw scores but by scores adjusted for intake. There are two difficulties with this line of attack. One, which the right has no trouble in articulating, is that it is patronizing to parents to suggest that they cannot weigh up complex evidence perfectly sensibly. There is some truth in this – schools and LEAs have been guilty of exactly this kind of patronizing assumption in the past – but there is no reason to suppose that access to information, and the ability to use it, are more equitably distributed in relation to education than they are in relation to other products where clever marketing is perfectly capable of deceiving customers. The other objection, about which at present there seems to be a conspiracy of silence, is that parents may very well prefer to look at raw, unadjusted scores. These may not measure teaching effectiveness, but they are not a bad proxy for respectability – something about which parents may care just as much. Ask parents to choose between a school in a deprived area whose pupils' rates of delinquency, though high, are commendably lower than the national average for such schools, and another school whose rate, though very low, is rather higher than predicted, and there is not much doubt about which they will prefer. The same logic is probably applied to schools' academic achievements.

But the final objection is the most crucial one, and that is the extent to which parents will engage in market-optimizing behaviour. It is quite clear that while academic (and social) standards are important, parents' willingness and even ability to respond to them, particularly in primary education, are severely dampened by other factors, including religious affiliation and, especially, physical proximity. Neighbourhood schools are extremely popular, both for convenience and also for their relationship to the local community (even if this only means that children like going to school with their friends and neighbours). Economists would presumably claim that marginal shifts are all that is necessary to achieve effective market responsiveness, and that really bad and really good schools will certainly be appropriately punished or rewarded. However, limited experiments or simulations with education 'vouchers' have suggested that one of two extreme outcomes is likely – either there will be virtually no change, or there may be such a flood of applications to a very popular school that its character is completely transformed from what parents believed they were getting.

Finally, even if the introduction of per capita funding were to lead to substantial shifts of school populations, this is a market which, even more than most, is likely to amplify social and educational inequalities in access to its products. There may be dispute about whether middle-class parents are better equipped to assess the available evidence on which to select a school, but they are certainly better equipped to put their choices into practice. Greater wealth (and the habit of consumer choice in other areas) provides the means to collect evidence beyond the glossy brochures on which secondary, and some primary, schools are now spending their scarce funds; to transport children further from home if need be; and of course to collect and contribute extra resources to help their chosen school. Standard funding levels are so low in many parts of the country that parents' contributions are needed not just to embellish schools but to renew basic requirements like libraries and essential equipment. The effect of market-based funding could well mean that schools which cannot appeal to more affluent parents are tipped down a spiral of declining resources, from which they have no hope of escaping – whereas under the older funding regime LEAs might sensibly have chosen to give extra resources to schools in difficulty. There are certainly those who believe that the present government is not so much indifferent to the prospect of growing class-based inequalities as determined on perpetuating and amplifying them.

Parental influence on schools

However, government policy is ambiguous. While the pure market prin-ciple is supposed to work through the allocation of funds, its limitations are recognized in the alternative principle of empowering parents to exert voice rather than exit pressure. Governing bodies have been steadily reformed over the past ten years to increase the membership of parents (and of other lay people such as local employers), and their powers and formal responsibilities have been sharply expanded. In addition, schools have been required to provide more detailed information on their performance to all their current parents, in the hope, presumably, that they will come under much greater pressure to improve.

Research on governing bodies by Deem and Brehony (for example Deem 1993) shows that in essential features relationships have not greatly changed. While a small number of governors have been actively drawn into one major new area, helping headteachers with their new financial and staffing responsibilities, the tendency is still to leave the academic areas to the professionals. (Their research also shows very clearly the gap between governors and those they are elected to represent: lay governors as a whole, and active ones in particular, are disproportionately drawn from predictable social groups – not least from older age groups than the average parent.)

As to more direct channels of influence, individual parents are probably little better off than in the past. There is the sheer improbability of exit referred to above: beyond the vague implication that dissatisfaction will do schools no good, there is little parents can do to insist on their wishes being taken seriously. Even if schools have taken to marketing themselves, there is much less sign of changing habits of accountability, beyond satisfying the new legal requirements. (But there is not much evidence to suggest that, having made their entry choices, parents are enormously interested in the aggregate performance of their school as opposed to its service to their own children.) And then there is the contrast referred to above between the low authority possessed by the teaching profession as a whole and the much higher authority and power that teachers can exert as we move from the national scale to LEAs (while they still exist), to schools, and then to individual teacher–parent and teacher–pupil exchanges. It is the professionals who control the informal agenda in LEA and school settings; and especially when parents meet teachers to discuss their children's progress, the combination of generalized professional authority and very specific power over the child's present happiness and future success is enough to intimidate all but the most well-informed and determined parents.

Thus if the potential power of exit is quite limited in practice, so even more is that of voice. Schools cultivate parents for general support, and increasingly for their potential for fund-raising, but are much less likely to attend to their wishes on areas that fall within the professional arena – and if we accept that there is such a thing as professional expertise, perhaps rightly so. Nevertheless, it may be that it is exactly this inattention which fuels more generalized public discontent.

But if this turns out to be a failure in government policy it has been compounded by further inconsistencies. The National Curriculum was justified by its proponents as clarifying parents' (or rather pupils'/ students') entitlements, and ensuring consistency of information on educational quality to enable good consumer choice. But as its detractors constantly point out, it also marks a dramatic shift towards centralized control, and a refusal to trust the market. Logically, after all, free-marketeers should have no objection to allowing a school's curriculum to evolve in response to local consumer preferences (and a few of them have said as much). In fact, the idea of the National Curriculum seems to have developed out of other constraints – the bureaucratic imperative for the DES/DFE to demonstrate effective management of resources (a constant and much-criticized weakness in the previous DES/LEA 'partnership'); and the ideological pressure of that section of Conservative thought, not especially sympathetic to markets, which Ball (1990) calls the 'cultural restorationists'. At the same time, the simple idea that markets would help weak schools to a quick end has been undermined by the opportunity of 'opting out' of LEA control: government has been so anxious to finish off the LEAs that it has been prepared not just to tolerate but to encourage grant-maintained status for schools condemned by LEAs to closure, even on good market-based grounds.

Higher education

There are now immense financial pressures on higher education institutions (HEIs) to maximize their intakes, and in many of them internal resource models transfer the same pressures down to department level. The new dispensation at the end of the 1980s created a semi-market system. On the 'producer' side block grants were replaced by a combination of fees and per capita grants (and by fees alone after a certain threshold);[8] while the student/consumer's previous entitlement to free tuition plus a (means-tested) grant for living expenses has been replaced by combining a grant which is steadily declining in real terms with a repayable loan. There is now talk of a home tuition fee, also to be covered by loan finance. It is the clear expectation that these changes will replace a professional–client relationship between the two sides with a set of more commercial expectations.

Again we need to distinguish consumer choice of institutions and degree courses from consumer influence within institutions. Much the same reservations apply, *ceteris paribus*, to choice at 18 plus as at earlier choice points: limited information (feedback to schools and colleges is not very efficient and other sources like student guides are not particularly reliable), once-for-all choice (still applicable to most students despite the growth of credit transfer) and restrictions on freedom of choice (living costs, proximity, etc.); and the fact that for the more selective subjects and institutions university admissions are a seller's market. Moreover, the primacy of research over teaching as a determinant of prestige applies to institutions and courses as well as to the profession as a whole. Many departments take great care to avoid damaging their research capacity or reputation by making themselves, as they see it, too accessible: maintaining a reputation for selectivity is believed to be one of the best ways of sustaining an elite niche in both the admissions and the research markets (Fulton and Ellwood 1989). Thus even severe financial pressures have not necessarily given much extra leverage to the potential buyers,[9] who seem in any case to be almost as interested in elements outside the institution's control (for example its location) as they are in course content and structure (Roberts and Higgins 1992), let alone the more esoteric features such as the effectiveness of teaching.

But consumer power may be more effective within higher education. There is a growing number of HEIs where departments also receive per capita funding, and where modularized curricula allow students wide freedom of choice within their overall degree programme. The combination certainly heightens staff's attention both to students' expressed wishes and to the results of student evaluations; however, it is also liable to introduce new levels of unpredictability which can damage departments' capacity to sustain other activities, such as research or postgraduate teaching, and to promote outright competition between departments and individuals which may have a corrosive effect on established patterns of interaction.[10]

But many of the other reservations about consumer choice at entry do not apply within HEIs. Information is much more easily come by, and in modular structures with free and frequent choices it is easy for students to act on it without drastic changes in their life plans. There is little of the time-lag involved in the choice of whole institutions and programmes. Whether students act wisely on the basis of their information is another matter; but at least they can act effectively.

But what about the voice of consumer pressure? In principle this can be exerted both at the individual level and in the aggregate. Individual students, by virtue of their greater maturity and the more informal hierarchies of higher education, are not without authority when it comes to direct negotiations with tutors, whether over a choice of special subject or a disputed mark. Indeed, there are those in the USA and possibly in this country as well, who would attribute the undoubted phenomenon of rising grades not to improved standards of learning or teaching but precisely to the growing importunity of students and the declining authority of staff. It is impossible to be sure whether this is fair comment – though the apparatus of double marking and external examining ought to provide some structured protection for uneasy British tutors which is not available to their American counterparts.

But the aggregate level may anyway be more significant. There is an important difference between schools and higher education. Growing educational participation means that the parents of schoolchildren are gradually becoming more educated and hence presumably a little better equipped to argue the toss with professionals, even if the odds are still heavily against them. For students, however, the most important effect of educational growth is simply that there are more of them. The power of the critical mass, which startled both universities and national governments in the 1960s, quickly led in most countries to students' partial incorporation into the governing structures of their institutions, and gave them far greater authority and even power than their parents could ever wield at a school parents' evening, while their mass organizing potential outweighs anything that parent–teacher associations can aspire to. It is clear that while the present government may favour individualized consumer pressure, it dislikes and even fears the potential of collective student movements. But although student activism has been closely entangled with larger political movements, the 1960s eruptions had their origins in the internal problems of the universities – problems induced by the last period of rapid growth – and had nothing to do with explicit consumer movements or policies for marketization. In a recent article on markets in higher education, Neave (1991) contrasts what he describes as the ideologically driven commitment to marketization of the British government with a wider European movement which sees market-based policies simply as a way of increasing efficiency and galvanizing long-established institutions and practices. He contends in fact that the idea of the market now seems to be evoked by governments of almost every political disposition as a lever for change of any kind. But he goes on to say that in practice, at least in France and Germany, the voice of students has become the voice of the status quo, 'more of a brake upon government policy than an accelerator' (Neave 1991: 30).

This leads to one final question: what do the consumers, that is both students and government, really want from a semi-marketized higher education system? For students the full answer will not be simple. It will depend on the balance between consumption and investment – pleasure and utility, means and ends; and it will need disaggregating by type of course, by academic discipline, and by the kind of student. One of the defining features of 'mass' higher education is that students are no longer a homogeneous group: even within selective institutions their interests may conflict. For the present government, too, there is ambivalence, masking internal conflicts. The Conservative Party is united in its distaste for students' unions, but not much else. The 'cultural restorationists' regard students' collective action as a symbol of the betrayal of elite higher education; but they also fear the market which has led to accelerating expansion – and dilution. Free marketeers also dislike students' collective voice, like that of any organized interest group. But if students would only act as the isolated economic individuals of economists' dreams, the radicals would probably welcome expansion, which will help to erode traditional authority structures. As for the producers, there is still some life in the more traditional structures of power and authority. But that is another story.

NOTES

1 Connoisseurs of government language will have enjoyed the DFE's response to complaints that ministers have overdone their attacks on teachers. In the 1992 White Paper *Choice and Diversity* a word-processor appears to have been used to search out each use of the word 'teachers' and insert in front of it the words 'our mostly excellent'.

2 GCSEs, for example, are deliberately designed to be obtainable by virtually the whole ability range – though not with the approval of a large section of the Conservative party.

3 But I doubt if, apart from a few well-known public school heads, independent school teachers are accorded noticeably higher status or authority than their state-employed counterparts.

4 There was a time (from the late nineteenth century even up to the 1950s) when the extraordinarily limited career choices even for single women made secondary teaching an enviable occupation (Summerfield 1987); but that is no longer the case.

5 Ironically, the UFC only came to it after a short-lived flirtation with direct, but complex, price competition: it invited universities to bid for student numbers at both core and marginal prices. However, neither side could handle the system: universities played safe (and possibly conspired to fix prices), while the UFC found it could not manipulate the results to retain the planning controls which it was still unwilling to give up.

6 There are plenty of complaints at present about the 'bribes' on offer to schools which opt out, in the form of extra grants for capital spending. Civil servants of a government which so obviously dislikes spending public money have surely assured the Treasury that the long-run gains will outweigh the short-run outlays.

7 There is some ambiguity here. By conventional criteria, it is students themselves who are the consumers, but in compulsory education, where students or pupils are below the age of legal majority, it is reasonable that parents should act as their proxies. But this raises obvious questions about the extent to which school pupils' or students' perceptions of their needs and interests coincide with their parents' views. First, the two parties are likely to weigh up investment and consumption considerations to different effect. And second, there is a generational issue: parents are often accused by teachers, in a restatement of the lay-professional conflict referred to earlier, of judging the quality of their children's education by the outdated standards of their own schooling many years earlier.

8 This is a relatively recent development for 'home' students. But it had been piloted: in 1981 the DES determined that overseas students should pay the

estimated full cost of their courses, and that HEIs could retain their full earnings from this source. It was widely remarked that the incentive persuaded HEIs to develop very effective recruitment and marketing methods at unprecedented speed. (But not to the same students as previously: there was a marked shift in overseas student recruitment from less to more affluent countries.)

9 This is not to say that buyers are powerless. At the height of a recent accommodation crisis, student unions in one or two institutions discovered that a threat to buy national advertising space to warn potential applicants off their university or college concentrated the authorities' minds quite impressively.

10 In the US, with long experience of modular curricula, universities do a great deal to insulate themselves from the market by insisting on core curricula which demand a wide breadth of study and so help to spread student loads away from popular departments or fashionable subjects. After the first enthusiasm for unrestricted modular systems we might expect to see similar protectionist moves in this country.

REFERENCES

Ball, S. J. (1990) *Politics and Policy Making in Education*, London: Routledge.

Chitty, C. (1989) *Towards a New Education System: the Victory of the New Right?* London: Falmer.

Deem, R. (1993) 'Education reform and school governing bodies in England; old dogs, new tricks or new dogs, new tricks?' in M. Preedy and R. Glatter (eds) *Managing Schools*, London: Paul Chapman.

Fairclough, N. (1991) 'What might we mean by "Enterprise Discourse?"' in R. Keat and N. Abercrombie (eds) *Enterprise Culture*, London: Routledge.

Fulton, O. (1993) 'Paradox or professional closure? Criteria and procedures for recruitment to the academic profession', *Higher Education Management* 5 (forthcoming).

Fulton, O. and Ellwood, S. (1989) 'Admissions, access and institutional change', in O. Fulton (ed.) *Access and Institutional Change*, Milton Keynes: Open University Press.

Halsey, A. (1992) *Decline of Donnish Dominion: The British Academic Professions in the Twentieth Century*, Oxford: Clarendon Press.

Marquand, D. (1992) 'The enterprise culture: new wine in old bottles?' in P. Heelas and P. Morris (eds) *The Values of the Enterprise Culture*, London: Routledge.

Neave, G. (1991) 'On visions of the market place', *Higher Education Quarterly* 45 (1).

Robbins Report (1963) *Higher Education: Report of the Committee appointed by the Prime Minister under the Chairmanship of Lord Robbins 1961–63*, Cmnd. 2154, London: HMSO.

Roberts, D. and Higgins, T. (1992) *Higher Education: the Student Experience*, Leeds: HEIST.

Summerfield, P. (1987) 'Women and the professional labour market 1900–1950: the case of the secondary schoolmistress', in P. Summerfield (ed.) *Women, Education and the Professions*, Leicester: History of Education Society (Occasional Publication no. 8).

Chapter 14

Retailing the police
Corporate identity and the Met.

Tony Heward

In August 1988, Wolff Olins presented a report to the Policy Committee of the Metropolitan Police which contained proposals for changes to the corporate identity of the force. Wolff Olins is one of the best known corporate identity consultancies in Britain; its managing director is Wally Olins, the 'high priest of the cult of corporate identity' (BBC Radio 4 1991), whose recent projects include the DTI, the Prudential and the controversial British Telecom identity. The proposals caused a great deal of comment in the press, including the tabloids; none the less the force proceeded to implement the scheme which has cost a large amount of time, effort and money. A corporate identity for a police force raises a good many questions related to the theme, the 'authority of the consumer'. Who consumes the services of the police? How does a corporate identity 'empower' consumers? What kind of 'authority' can consumers exercise over a body which represents the *power* of the state? What problems can corporate identity solve for the police? Before addressing some of these questions it will be useful to examine the modern discipline of corporate identity.

THE RISE OF CORPORATE DESIGNERS

Since the 1960s corporate identity has become a significant sector of the design industry and a part of the 'communications mix' of a modern corporation, together with advertising and public relations. However, practitioners would argue that corporate identity serves longer-term goals than advertising or public relations and arises from almost anything a corporation does:

> corporate identity is the process of explicit management of some or all of the ways by which the organisation is perceived. In business organisations ... identity emerges through three areas of design: – products or services, i.e. what you make or sell – environments, i.e.

where you make or sell it – communications, i.e. how you present what
you do, and how you do it.

(Olins 1988b: 55)

Corporate designers usually separate the discipline into three components:
'corporate image', 'corporate personality' and 'visual identity'. 'Corporate
image' refers to how the corporation is perceived both by internal and
external 'audiences'. 'Corporate personality' is the essential or true nature
of the corporation, which may be different from its corporate image.
'Visual identity' is the component most familiar to the general public and
consists of a myriad of items including, for example, the logo or symbol,
sign systems and stationery. Corporate designers maintain that these three
components are interdependent, and that a change in visual identity alone
is purely cosmetic and useless in the long run. In order to achieve anything
significant, a change in visual identity must be the expression of a change
in corporate personality. For this reason some consultants include not
only design services but also the related disciplines of management con-
sultancy and marketing. Thus they would deny the accusation that their
work is superficial or manipulative – the '£2,000,000 just for a logo' school
of criticism. Visual identity may play only a small part.

Corporate identity schemes have various objectives. They may be
implemented in order to communicate that strategic changes have already
taken place and in order to promote further changes, such as the British
Telecom identity of 1991. This was intended first to proclaim that the
company was no longer a bureaucratic public service which treated callers
as nuisances, and second to further the transformation of BT into an
efficient customer-orientated business. Ian Vallance, chairman of British
Telecom, said '[the intention is] to get away totally from the public utility
background from which BT springs' (quoted in Hancock 1991: 16). Other
schemes have been introduced with the intention of *initiating* change, like
that of Network South East of 1986 which was intended to shift the focus
of the service from commuters to leisure travel during off-peak hours.

Schemes also need to carry a variety of 'messages' and one of the tasks
for corporate designers is to identify 'audiences' and the impressions to
be conveyed to them; there are both internal and external groups to be
considered. For a private sector business, the main external audiences are
institutional consumers – national and local government, the City, the
media, the unions and other companies. There are also audiences of
individual consumers – customers, potential employees and the wider
public. Internal audiences are mainly the employees of the company but
shareholders and pensioners may be included in this group. A company
may want to present itself as dynamic and profitable to the City, depend-
able to an employee and helpful to a telephone inquirer. For internal
audiences, identity programmes may be intended to promote loyalty, pride

and self-confidence, as well as to promote standards of behaviour. This last aim was particularly important for the Metropolitan Police: '[corporate identity] is to do with getting people inside the organisation to develop a clear instinct, intuition, or feel for what is and what is not appropriate for the organisation' (Olins 1984: 39). This instinctive sense of 'our way of doing things' may start as a vision on the part of the senior management but will be transmitted to the rest of the organization by training programmes and by policies for promotions and sanctions. The organization will reward those who do things 'our way', and penalize those who do not.

Corporate identity consists of a range of management disciplines and design services which enable companies to *control* how they are perceived and, therefore, how they perform in the market place. This may mean drastically changing a company, with staff training programmes, changes in working practices or extensive redundancies – in other words making strategic changes to the corporate personality. These changes may be directed towards 'empowering' the individual consumer. Changes in visual identity might encourage consumers to perceive a corporation as approachable and responsive. However, visual identity must be underpinned by changes in working practices in order to ensure that the corporation really is approachable and responsive. This would be brought about by establishing mechanisms for consumer feedback via questionnaires and market research, and by ensuring that staff who have direct contact with consumers are trained to be courteous, attentive and unflappable. Companies such as British Gas which were previously bureaucratic, remote and more likely to treat the public as nuisances, now subject consumers to a 'charm offensive'. It is on this level that consumers of a police force will be 'empowered'. Before considering who these consumers are, it will be helpful to discuss some of the strategic problems faced by the Metropolitan Police.

POLICING LONDON IN THE 1980s

During the 1980s the British police were caught between conflicting demands from a variety of quarters. The government required public sector bodies to be more accountable and responsive to the needs of the public, while controlling public expenditure very tightly. Opinion polls and other publications revealed the public's anxiety about the ability of the police to contain the 'crime wave', while the media were quick to draw attention to any failings in the police – racism, corruption, fabricated evidence and false confessions, not to mention accidental shootings and brutality against striking workers. The 1980s provided a long catalogue of events in which the British police appeared to be oppressive, politically motivated and thuggish. Police officers began to feel besieged – doing an impossible job, unappreciated by the public, unsupported by politicians, reviled by the media and, increasingly, the victims of violence themselves.

Not surprisingly, policing London brought these problems into sharp focus and they were analysed in a series of studies and reports published during the 1980s. The decade started badly for the Metropolitan Police with the Brixton riots which prompted the first report, by Lord Justice Scarman. It investigated the causes of the riots, the handling of them by the police and the aftermath of them. The belief that the police had victimized the black community was widespread, and Scarman acknowledged the 'ill-considered, immature, and racially prejudiced actions of some officers in their dealings on the streets with young black people' (Scarman Report 1981: 64).

In 1983 an exhaustive study by the Policy Studies Institute revealed that officers routinely used racist language among themselves, and that some officers were rude and bullying towards members of the public. The PSI study also suggested that most Londoners were favourable towards the police until they actually came into contact with them:

> There is a strong tendency for those who have been stopped by police and for those who have been arrested to be critical, but other kinds of contact, where the person is not being treated as offender or suspect, are also associated with critical views.
>
> (Smith 1983b: 326)

Three years later *The Islington Crime Survey* was published and expressed concern about the level of distrust of the force, among young people and the black community:

> a considerable number of people in Islington believe the police do act illegally and unfairly towards certain groups. If this were just a *belief* it would by itself be unfortunate in its consequences, but it is all the more so in that it is backed up by *directly experienced evidence* of interviewees and their friends [original italics]
>
> (Jones *et al*. 1986: 205)

These studies made various recommendations about recruitment, training and policies on policing, some of which were put into practice, such as those on community policing, and organizational structures, but the problems were persistent. To an alarming extent the force was losing public confidence, without which it simply could not operate, and so decided to try a different solution. It asked a number of corporate design consultancies and advertising agencies to submit ideas, and in the course of time Wolff Olins was commissioned to analyse the existing corporate identity of the force and to recommend how it could improve the performance of its public duties and, therefore, the public's perceptions of the force.

A FORCE FOR CHANGE

The Metropolitan Police project followed the usual procedure adopted by Wolff Olins. After background research Wolff Olins' staff conducted more than 250 formal interviews with 'opinion formers', both from inside and outside the force and sat in on daily police activities. They carried out a 'visual audit' – an examination of a wide range of printed literature, stationery, sign systems, uniforms, vehicles and existing logos. The investigations took six months and resulted in the report *A Force for Change*. Not surprisingly it revealed similar problems to those made known by Scarman and others.

The report spoke of a deeply divided organization, with little common sense of purpose, and few shared assumptions about the nature of policing. Divisions existed between police officers and civilian staff and between the uniformed and plain clothes branches. There was a clear sense of hierarchy which gave little status to 'front line' officers policing the streets. The job was becoming more and more difficult; public expectations were rising, the media were more and more critical and assaults on the police were increasing. Police officers tended to live lives with very little contact with the public outside policing duties and this had led to a 'siege' mentality; as the report put it, 'many policemen and women feel beleaguered and misunderstood.' (Olins 1988a: 11).

Recruitment and retention of staff was a problem. With a poor corporate image the Metropolitan Police was an unattractive employer. Experienced officers were leaving in significant numbers, to take up other jobs or to transfer to other forces. Further problems were identified concerning the internal communications system, as well as external communications – relations with the press and television. The premises of the force had 'an atmosphere of shabby confusion' and gave an impression of caring neither for the public nor for employees: 'This atmosphere is bad for the Force, it contributes to an uncared for feeling, it is also bad for relations with the public' (ibid.: 14).

The report argued that the cumulative effect of these problems was serious, especially the lack of public confidence in the police and their ability to combat crime. Police forces in western liberal democracies cannot operate without broad public consent or co-operation. If crimes are solved they are done so predominantly with the help of the public, not by the police just happening to be there. This point had been made in other analyses of policing, including *The Islington Crime Survey*: 'successful policing is dependent on the public to a degree which is not conventionally realised. A full 95% of crime known to the police in Islington is made known to them by the public; direct police apprehension of offenders involves only 3.8% of offenders' (Jones *et al.* 1986: 203).

A Force for Change concluded by making a number of recommendations. In order to clarify the objectives of policing, the force should adopt a new 'mission statement' and publicize it both internally and externally. They should then work towards far-reaching changes in the culture of the organization in order to realize the ideals expressed by the new mission statement:

> the types of change we have identified fall into three categories: management and attitudes, communications, [and] visual identity. . . . There must be demonstrable progress in changing the reality, that is the management and attitudes component, before we begin to project a new visual identity.
>
> (Olins 1988a: 18)

Changes in visual identity were not given a high priority and it was made clear that cultural change should precede and inform any change in visual identity. As Olins points out elsewhere. 'A police force is perhaps the ultimate service activity . . . each contact that we have with a police force largely depends on the behaviour of each police officer' (Olins 1989: 34). Behaviour depends on attitudes, and the attitudes to be changed were those of Metropolitan Police officers towards the public, and towards each other. Emphasis was to be given to greater cohesion, courtesy and sensitivity – in short a 'service ethos' which had parallels with the likes of Marks and Spencer.

RESPONSE OF THE MET.

The senior management of the force spent several months digesting the recommendations of the report. Their deliberations resulted in a long-term programme of reforms which began in April 1989 with the publication of a new mission statement, the 'Statement of our Common Purpose and Values'. This replaced the original one of 1829 and was intended to set new standards of corporate behaviour, with more importance attached to responsiveness to the public. It defined the manner in which Metropolitan Police officers should carry out their duties: 'compassionate, courteous, and patient . . . professional, calm and restrained in the face of violence' (Metropolitan Police 'Statement').* The final paragraph provides the key to understanding the new corporate strategy: 'We must strive to reduce the fears of the public and, so far as we can, to reflect their priorities in the action we take. We must respond to well-founded criticism with a willingness to change' (ibid.).

These changes obviously needed more than good intentions on the part of senior management. Consequently they launched a complex programme of training, reorganization and restructuring; this began in

* The author gratefully acknowledges the assistance of the 'Plus' team of the Metropolitan Police in providing material necessary for the writing of this chapter.

September 1990, and was called the 'Plus' programme. The purpose was to ensure that the attitudes of Metropolitan Police officers lived up to the ideals of the mission statement. Robin Goodfellow, head of public relations of the Metropolitan Police, spoke of the need to 'bring about a change in the ethos and the culture of the police force itself and to turn it from a police *force* into a police *service*' (my emphasis) (quoted in BBC Radio 4 1991).

The 'Plus' programme was divided into nine components, which were intended to bring about the necessary changes in attitude. There were components dealing with management and command structures at all levels, while others concentrated on rewards for good performance and sanctions against poor performance. Further components were concerned with the communication of information, both within the force and to the media, as well as with the simplification of record-keeping and information processing systems.

Three other components are more relevant to this study and will be discussed at length. These include the first – 'Adopting the Statement of Common Purpose and Values', the aim of which was 'Ensuring every member of the Metropolitan Police service understands and practises the organisational values' (Metropolitan Police, 'Plus Briefing: Why Embark on Plus?'). This provided an over-arching goal to which all other parts of 'Plus' were directed. Component eight is the most visible and deals with the 'Appearance of the Force', by 'working towards a coherent, consistent and instantly recognisable identity' (ibid.). The ninth component was concerned with 'performance indicators' and related to the need for responsiveness to the public.

To satisfy the requirements of component one, all 44,000 employees were to undergo a day-long training seminar called 'Working together for a better service'. The seminars started with a videotaped address from Sir Peter Imbert, the Metropolitan Police Commissioner, and discussions followed which were led by two professional 'facilitators'. Twenty police personnel, from all levels, made up each seminar, and were encouraged to identify honestly what they did well but also where they had been rude or unhelpful either to other police personnel or to the public, and where they had given a bad impression of the force. The seminar was followed by a debriefing by an immediate superior to reinforce what the individual employee had learnt about his or her own behaviour and attitudes. The next stage was to set goals for changing and improving the individual's performance, to be included in the process of appraisal.

The eighth component of 'Plus' was the visual identity of the force. The intention was to create 'pride and confidence in the eyes of police, civil staff and the public by demonstrating a professional, consistent, caring and efficient image' (Metropolitan Police 1990). A special internal team was established and it concentrated its efforts on five areas: the new

logo, stationery, premises, vehicles and uniforms. The team made forty-
five recommendations intended to be implemented over a number of
years. A new crest was introduced at an early stage and was to be applied
to a wide range of stationery to establish some consistency in a chaotic
variety of designs. Vehicle livery was to be standardized as white with
the new crest in blue. Uniforms were to be modified: blue pullovers and
anoraks would be accepted for certain duties. Women police officers
would no longer carry handbags and would wear trousers as standard:
the title 'WPC' would be replaced by 'PC'. The helmet badge would be
retained but numerals would be removed from shoulders and replaced
by numbered badges. A recommendation to include officers' names was
rejected on the grounds of individual safety. Filofaxes would be worn on
belts in order to do away with the 'bulging pocket look'. Senior officers
from 'uniforms' would actually wear uniforms; saluting was encouraged
and calling cards were to be provided for officers on home beat and
crime prevention duties as well as for community policemen. Chief super-
intendents and higher ranks were to have personalized Christmas cards.
The premises of the force would be improved so as to end the unwelcom-
ing, institutional feel of many police stations; the familiar blue light would
be retained but signs would be made more visible.

The force was to develop a clear sense of 'customer care', the foundations for which may be seen in the ninth component: 'performance
indicators'. It was described as: 'Promoting an effective customer
survey. . . . Establishing simple, effective indicators, linked to personal
performance, rewards and sanctions' (Metropolitan Police, 'Plus Briefing:
Why Embark on Plus?'). This meant that the force was actively to seek
'feedback' from the general public about contacts with police officers; the
data produced would be taken into account in appraising the record of
individual officers. An internal team implementing this component sought
the advice of outside management consultants who made a comparative
study of 'performance indicators' in public bodies as well as in private
sector companies such as the AA, and the Midland Bank.

The results of the first customer survey ever conducted by a British
police force, were reported in *The Times* in February 1990. Over 800 visits
to 40 police stations were monitored. Out of 600 victims and witnesses of
burglary, auto-crime, and assault, 75 per cent said that they were satisfied
with the police; 80 per cent found staff 'friendly, helpful and smart'; 25
per cent said that on first contact police officers showed little interest,
but that subsequent contact was better. The survey revealed 'general
satisfaction' among 'customers', as well as suggestions of a 'sense of
intimidation at visiting stations' (Tendler 1990: 4).

The corporate identity scheme was intended to communicate that
changes had taken place, partly to external audiences – the public, the
government and the media – but mainly to employees of the force. It

would be more accurate to regard 'Plus' as a large-scale *internal* marketing programme; employees were the primary targets but the general public was intended to be the ultimate beneficiary. The overriding intention was to realize the senior managers' vision of new corporate values. These would be transmitted initially by the training seminars, but would be reinforced by the components dealing with 'rewards and sanctions' and 'performance indicators'. Once the programme was under way the public would receive a better standard of police service. Officers were intended to become more courteous and genuinely concerned with the public, whether as victims of crime or witnesses. Police procedures and the layout of premises would facilitate this. Officers who actually came into contact with the public – 'front-line personnel' – would be given greater status.

The new corporate values will come up against a formidable barrier in the form of the existing corporate values, with all the shortcomings reported by Scarman and others. These are values which have developed over many generations and they provide a mirror image of society at large, for instance the impulses which lead police officers to lie, cheat and bully are the same ones which lead members of the public to do likewise. The question is: can a mere corporate identity programme really take on societal forces? The force clearly recognizes how important it is for the scheme to succeed. John Newing, Deputy Assistant Commissioner wrote of 'Plus': 'The need to carry the public with us is a fundamental tenet of policing theory, not just in Britain but worldwide. The alternative is an army of occupation' (Newing 1989: 1270).

The Wolff Olins report confirmed what the force already knew – that it had an unfavourable corporate image in the eyes of its consumers and needed to develop a sense of 'customer care'. The corporate identity project is an attempt by the force to take control of its identity and change it in such a way as to re-establish a climate of 'policing by consent' in London. 'Plus' may be seen as a means of winning back the support of staple customers – the mass of law-abiding Londoners.

THE POLICE AND THE CONSUMER

Many aspects of the 'Plus' programme show a police force determined to bring about significant cultural change and much time and effort have been devoted to this. The reforms bring a sense of openness to some routine police activities which must be welcomed and this reflects well on the response of the management of the force to the Wolff Olins proposals. These proposals have led to something far more than a superficial styling job, in spite of lukewarm reactions in the ranks. If the scheme manages to improve relations between the Metropolitan Police and its consumers, then it will have been a worthwhile exercise. However, the reforms have taken place in a wider context of changes in other public services since 1980. In this wider context a number of inherent contradictions begin to emerge, together with a confusion of the roles of the citizen and the consumer – a point further explored in Walsh's chapter.

The introduction of 'customer care' into policing the capital was influenced not only by the Wolff Olins report but also by government policy on the public services. Thatcher governments in the 1980s required public bodies to be more responsive to the needs of their clients, privatization being the extreme expression of this policy – but where this was inappropriate the government established pseudo- or internal markets. Privatization was part of a wider policy of introducing the discipline of the market place to the public sector which, according to the government, had become remote, bureaucratic and unresponsive to the public. The spirit of the Thatcher reforms has been given clear expression in the recent 'Citizens' Charter':

> citizens, or consumers of state services, shall be equipped with rights which seek to provide substitutes for the rights which they would have in a private market. The Citizens' Charter, if it is to be effective, must imitate in some sense the rights which people have as customers in a competitive market.

> (Pirie 1991)

The Citizens' Charter has encouraged a number of imitations dealing with health care, education and others; collectively they set out what consumers of public services may expect – for example, a choice of school for a child, prompt repairs to council homes, or trains running on time. The Wolff Olins proposals pre-dated the charter, but the principle of 'customer care' or 'empowerment' is similar. Even before the publication of the charter, clients, users, and customers were encouraged by the government and by advertising campaigns to feel that they had some power in the provider–user relationship. 'Plus' may be seen as a response to the climate of 'consumer authority' which was created during the 1980s and has, therefore, similarities with other public service reforms.

For some providers of services 'consumer authority' represents a challenge to the integrity of their expertise, with a shift of authority away from themselves and towards the recipients of their services. However, this model has only limited relevance to police forces, whose duty places them in a contradictory relation to the public. It is the job of the police to maintain law and order as well as to protect citizens and their property from crime. The police, together with the armed forces, *are* the power of the state and therefore exercise authority over those who consume their services. For this reason police officers are invested with powers to detain, question and arrest. These powers are denied to ordinary citizens, and inevitably bring the police into conflict with certain groups in society such as criminals or suspected criminals, who are equally members of the public. Sir John Woodcock, Her Majesty's Chief Inspector of Constabulary said: 'The abusing husband, the foul drunk, the lager lout and the belligerent squatter are customers.... Different but equally as much customers as the victims of crime, the frightened child, the tourist asking the time' (Campbell 1992: 1).

It is this paradox which prevents the police from devolving, or even appearing to devolve, any substantial authority to their consumers. This is an example of the contradictory authority relation mentioned in Fairclough's paper in connection with the promotion of financial services. The police face a similar dilemma: how to regulate and control the public, while at the same time selling the idea that they are 'customer orientated'.

The public has been encouraged by the government to feel 'empowered' in relation to the public services, but this is as individual consumers; it is a vision of individuals asserting individual rights in order to do the best for themselves and for their families. Thatcher's pronouncement, 'There is no such thing as society. There are only individual men and women, and there are families' (quoted in Riddell 1989: 171), finds an echo in many of the reforms in the public services. This view sees the individual as paramount, and the collective or the communal as a distraction, fiction or danger. If the recipients of the services of the Metropolitan Police are enjoying 'empowerment' this shifts them towards a position as *consumers* of services supplied personally to them, no longer as *citizens* receiving services supplied for the common good. This helps to establish a climate which encourages consumers to regard their own needs as taking precedence over communal needs.

In common with some of the other public service reforms those of the Metropolitan Police emphasize procedural change over change in substance, or even disguise change in substance. The reforms avoid some of the larger issues concerning the police and society. An exercise in meaningful 'empowerment' would need to raise some of the broader questions of civil liberties – protecting the rights of the individual in relation to the powers of the state as vested in the police. It is difficult to see how any genuine 'empowerment' can take place against the creeping centralization of power that has taken place in Britain since the beginning of the 1980s when a good many powers started to seep away from local government to central government. Police forces were not immune to this shift in power and although they remain based in the counties and urban centres which they serve, there were occasions in the 1980s, such as the miners' strike of 1984, when they began to operate as an unofficial national force and when their political impartiality was widely questioned, even by police officers themselves. As one Police Constable remarked: 'I think we are in serious danger of being used as a tool. Like we were during the miners' strike. No question, we were "Maggie's boys". I hated that' (Graef 1990: 74). These developments, together with recent proposals for further centralization of some police activities and changes in legislation such as a strengthened Official Secrets Act, do not bode well for civil liberties in Britain. This is despite the Police and Criminal Evidence Act and the Police Complaints Authority which, with all their imperfections, are meant to safeguard the rights of the citizen in relation to the powers of the police. Operations such as 'Plus' may reassure the *consumer* being dealt with by a police receptionist who is courteous, efficient and concerned, while the *citizen* may be alarmed at some of the changes taking place behind the scenes.

REFERENCES

BBC Radio 4 (1991) 'Profile', 13 March.

Blake, Avril (1986) *Milner Gray*, London: Design Council.

Buddensieg, Tilmann (1984) *Industriekultur*, Cambridge, Massachusetts: MIT Press.

Campbell, Duncan (1992) 'Police chief admits public faith shaken', *Guardian*, 18 June.

Deakin, Nicholas and Wright, Anthony (1990) *Consuming Public Services*, London: Routledge.

Gorb, Peter and Schneider, Eric (1988) *Design Talks!*, London: Design Council.

Graef, Roger (1990) *Talking Blues: The Police in their Own Words*, London: Fontana.

Hancock (1991) 'Volume control: BT turns it up', in *Design* (June) 510.

Jones, Trevor, MacLean, Brian and Young, Jock (1986) *The Islington Crime Survey: Crime, Victimisation and Policing in Inner-city London*, Aldershot: Gower.

Keen, Clive and Warner, David (eds) (1989) *Visual and Corporate Identity: A Study of Identity Programmes in the College, Polytechnic, and University Environment*, Banbury: Heist.

Metropolitan Police (n.d.) 'Statement of our Common Purpose and Values' (internal document, unpaged, undated).

—— (n.d.) 'Plus Briefing: Why Embark on Plus?' (internal document, unpaged, undated).

—— (1990) 'Plus Briefing: the Plus Programme, a Synopsis' (November, internal document, unpaged).

Newing, John (1989) 'Plus points of the Met's initiative', *Police Review*, part 97, 23 June.

Olins, Wally (1978) *The Corporate Personality: An Inquiry into the Nature of Corporate Indentity*, London: Design Council.

—— (1984) *The Wolff Olins Guide to Corporate Indentity*, London: Wolff Olins.

—— (1988a) *A Force for Change*, London: Metropolitan Police.

—— (1988b) 'Identity – the corporation's hidden resource', in Gorb and Schneider.

—— (1989) *Corporate Identity: Making Business Strategy Visible through Design*, London: Thames & Hudson.

Pirie, Madsen (1991) *The Citizen's Charter*, London: Adam Smith Institute.

Pevsner, Nikolaus (1960) *Pioneers of Modern Design: From William Morris to Walter Gropius*, London: Pelican (1st edn 1936).

Reiner, Robert (1985) *The Politics of the Police*, Brighton: Harvester.

Riddell, Peter (1989) *The Thatcher Years*, Oxford: Blackwell.

Scarman Report (1981) *The Brixton Disorders 10–12 April 1981: Report of an Inquiry by the Rt. Hon. The Lord Scarman OBE*, London: HMSO.

Smith, David J. (1983a) *Police and People in London: Volume I. A Survey of Londoners*, London: Policy Studies Institute, no. 618 (November).

—— (1983b) *Police and People in London: Volume IV. The Police in Action*, London, Policy Studies Institute, no. 621 (November).

Tendler, Stuart (1990) 'London's survey of policing presents a positive picture', *The Times,* 13 February, 4.

Chapter 15

Conversationalization of public discourse and the authority of the consumer[1]

Norman Fairclough

This chapter will discuss linguistic and discursive aspects of commodification (the reconstruction of, for instance, public services on the analogy of commodity markets) and consumerization (the reconstruction of their publics or clients as consumers). I assume that consumerization is a dimension of commodification, and I mainly use the latter more general term below, referring specifically to consumerization where necessary. I shall discuss first the commodification of public[2] discourse, a process which involves the generalization of the communicative function of promotion (of goods, services, institutions or people). I shall then discuss a partially independent but overlapping process affecting public discourse, its 'conversationalization' – the modelling of public discourse upon the discursive practices of ordinary life, 'conversational' practices in a broad sense. Commodified public discourse tends also to be conversationalized. The final section of the chapter links it to the theme of 'the authority of the consumer' through a discussion of whether the conversationalization of public discourse is part of a shift in authority in favour of 'the public', including a shift from producers[3] to consumers. I suggest that the cultural value and significance of conversationalization is more ambivalent, and that the evidence of conversationalization indicates caution about such claims.

COMMODIFICATION OF PUBLIC DISCOURSE

I want to suggest that commodification is to a significant extent a linguistic and discursive process. We can think of it in terms of the weakening of boundaries between 'orders of discourse' (Fairclough 1992): between on the one hand the discursive practices of the market in the more traditional sense, and on the other hand the discursive practices of politics, public services like health and education, government and other forms of public information, and even the arts. In part, this is a matter of the colonization of these domains by market *discourses* – I use the term *discourse* as a count noun (that is with a plural) for a particular way of signifying and constructing, roughly, a 'subject matter' (for example, there are patriarchal as well as feminist discourses of sexuality). The following extract is an example:

> The vocational preparation product is usually a programme. Its design and implementation are therefore central parts of the marketing process, and should start from the needs of potential customers and clients and the benefits for which they are looking.
>
> (Further Education Unit 1987)

This comes from a pamphlet produced by the Further Education Unit, and the extract is actually referring to pre-vocational education courses: a course becomes a 'product' which is 'designed' and 'implemented' to meet the 'needs' of 'customers' and 'clients'.

Commodification also involves the *genres* of the market colonizing new domains. I understand a genre to be the language associated with a particular socially ratified type of activity, such as a job interview or a scientific paper (*and* conventional ways of producing, interpreting and using texts within that activity type). Politics, public services and the professions in Britain are nowadays manifestly colonized by *advertising genre*. A relatively early stage of the colonizing process was the spread of advertising from manufactured commodities to economic services such as banking and insurance. The second extract is part of a 1984 brochure advertising Barclaycard (see Fairclough 1988):

USING IT'S SIMPLE
YOU DON'T EVEN HAVE TO
SPEAK THE LANGUAGE

Wherever you see a Visa sign you can present your Barclaycard when you wish to pay [1]. The sales assistant will put your Card and sales voucher through an imprinter to record your name and account number [2]. He will then complete the voucher and after ensuring that the details are correct, you just sign it [3]. You'll receive a copy of the voucher, which you should keep for checking against your statement, and the goods are yours [4]. That's all there is to it [5]. You may use your Barclaycard as much as you wish, provided your payments are up to date and you keep within your available credit limit (this is printed on the folder containing your Barclaycard) [6]. Occasionally the shop may have to make a telephone call to Barclaycard to obtain our authorisation for a transaction [7]. This is a routine requirement of our procedure, and we just make sure that everything is in order before giving the go ahead [8]. In an effort to deal more quickly with these calls, Barclaycard is introducing a new automated system [9]. This will save time for you, but *please note that any transaction which could take a Barclaycard account over its credit limit could well be declined* [10]. *It is important to ensure that your credit limit is sufficient to cover all your purchases and Cash Advances* [11]. When you wish to take advantage of a mail order offer it's so much easier to give your Barclaycard number rather than sending cheques or postal orders [12]. Just write your card number in the space provided on the order form, sign it and send it off [13]. Or if you want to book theatre tickets, make travel reservations or even make a purchase by telephone, just quote your card number and the cost can be charged to your Barclay-card account [14]. You'll find your Barclaycard can make life a whole lot easier [15].

Actually, in the original the text occupies only 40 per cent of the page, and the other 60 per cent carries a photograph of a smiling Japanese receptionist in a hotel offering a pen (together with a flower) to a customer. Dependence upon visual image is itself of course an advertising feature which has been widely influential. And the presence of a headline (typical in being mildly humorous) and a final signature line gives the extract something of the generic structure of standard commodity advertisements. Another advertising feature is direct address – readers are addressed *individually* with *you* – as well as the use of *we* to personalize Barclaycard in terms of collective identity.

Colonization by advertising genre does not just produce advertisements in all sorts of surprising places. Rather, it produces hybrid generic forms which fuse advertising with other genres. There are many such hybrids around, certainly in contemporary Britain. Look in this case at meanings which have to do with *requirements* of or obligations upon the Barclaycard user. Notice for instance sentence 3, especially the word *just (you just sign it* – used also in sentences 13–14 and elsewhere). It is a common word in advertising, communicating the core advertising meaning of simplicity – 'it's easy'. Here it minimizes what is required of the customer. In financial regulations, you would expect a lot of requirements of the user to be expressed, and I count ten in this text. Yet only one has explicit obligational modality (with a 'modal' verb) – *you should keep* in sentence 4 – and even there the meaning is advisability rather than obligation. The italicized part of the text, sentences 10–11, is the most clearly regulatory, yet even here requirements are toned down: notice that *it is important to ensure* is an impersonal 'objective' modality in Halliday's terms (Halliday 1985), without the face-threatening force of a 'subjective' modality like *you must ensure*.

The Barclaycard text hybridizes financial regulations and advertizing. This places the advertiser in a contradictory position and a dilemma, which links to the issue of consumer authority. In traditional banking, the bank has authority over the customer – money is lent on the bank's terms. In advertising, the customer, as they say, 'is king' (or queen), or at least is portrayed as such: the advertiser is trying to 'sell' to the 'consumer'. These are contradictory authority relations, and this is the advertiser's dilemma: to regulate the lending of money, yet sell its services. The effect textually is a compromise which is manifested in the forms of realization of requirements: they *are* expressed, but in an indirect and mitigated form. Hybridization, then, affects this extract in a double way: it is a *heterogeneous* text which mixes features of two genres, and it contains compromises between contradictory authority relations.

Commodity advertising is just the most salient of a number of *promotional genres* which are colonizing other orders of discourse. Look at the reproduction of the front page of a 1991 pamphlet about the Citizen's Charter, a British government initiative to improve public services, on the following page. There is a visible divide between the top half of the page, which uses the visual semiotics and language of official information – the royal crest, the definite nominal group *The Citizen's Charter* – and the bottom half of the page which uses the visual semiotics and language of promotion. This is the type of promotion you find for organizations such as political parties and (these days) universities – the 'logo', and the slogan *Raising the Standard*, both of which are used on a wide range of government publications dealing with the Citizen's Charter. There is also a contrast in typography and colour between the top and bottom: the coat of arms and *The Citizen's Charter* are in fact white, *Raising the Standard* and *A Guide* are yellow, the logo is blue and white, while the rest of the page is cerise (deep pink). The promotional genre 'invades the space' of the official information genre through the subtitle, *A Guide*, which belongs typographically as well as in colour with the promotional genre. And also through an embossed logo covering the whole of the right side of the page (unfortunately not visible on the reproduction).

In other cases, the forms and meanings of promotional genres may not be so evident, but the injection of a promotional communicative function or goal – to 'sell' goods, services, organizations or people – nevertheless generates significant transformations of genre. The next extract is an example. It is a page from the 1990 undergraduate prospectus of Lancaster University. One change in university prospectuses over the past few years is greater reliance on visual imagery, as in advertising. Another is rather less obvious. This extract is similar to the Barclaycard extract in the contradiction between the traditional laying down of conditions and regulations, and the new imperative of 'selling' the University to prospective students. Again, the contradiction shows up in the treatment of *requirements* imposed on applicants and students. In this case, most of the requirements are located in the graphics section on the right. This avoids

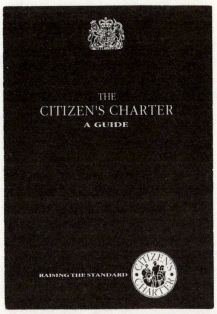

Figure 15.1 Front cover of a 1991 guide to the Citizen's Charter
Source: Crown copyright. Reproduced with permission of the Central Office of Information

having to explicitly 'word' obligational meanings: as in the case of the Barclaycard text, the meanings are there, but backgrounded. Where there is explicit wording (notice *YOU WILL NEED*), the University's authority is again backgrounded – compare *you must have* or *we require*. Actually, the new technical resources of graphic design project a number of cultural values (up-to-date, good management, student-oriented) as well as helping to resolve contradictions and dilemmas arising from pressure to promote the institution. The overall result is a significantly transformed genre.

The increasing salience and generality of promotion as a communicative function consequent upon commodification is having pervasive and I believe profound effects upon public orders of discourse. In Fairclough (1989), I introduced the concept of *synthetic personalization* for the manipulation of 'interpersonal' meanings and forms for strategic and instrumental purposes – for instance, the personalization of advertiser and audience (for example *you* and *we* in the Barclaycard text) which is so widespread in advertising and now in domains colonized by advertising. Actually, 'ideational'[4] meanings and forms are *also* subordinated to the overriding purpose to promote: it is becoming increasingly difficult to differentiate 'informative' discourse from 'persuasive' discourse (or, 'telling' from 'selling'), since information is so widely covert promotion. From the point of view of text users and consumers, there is I think

AMERICAN STUDIES

Enquiries to: Director of Admissions
Teaching staff: members of appropriate departments

Lancaster students have always shown lively interest in American subjects, whether in the English, History, Politics or other departments. Now it is possible to take a specialised degree in American Studies. This degree combines different disciplinary approaches to the study of the United States and offers options covering American history, literature, and politics from the earliest colonial settlements to the present day.

In addition, American Studies majors will spend their second year at an American university, such as the University of Massachusetts at Amherst or another selected American university. Lancaster's close American connections make it possible to integrate the year abroad into the degree, so that, unusually in British universities, the American Studies degree can be completed in *three* years. Special counselling will ensure close integration between the year abroad and the two years at Lancaster.

Degree studies at Lancaster call on specialists in a number of departments,

and, as with most Lancaster degrees, students will gain valuable experience in more than one discipline. But a substantial degree of flexibility is maintained, and it is possible for students to concentrate substantially on either history or literature or politics if they so choose.

The first year is largely devoted to providing a disciplinary grounding, and students pursue the normal first year courses in the History, English, and Politics departments, taking American options where they exist. Thereafter the course of study is almost exclusively devoted to American topics, and may include the writing of a dissertation on an American theme.

American Studies graduates pursue careers normally associated with a humanities or social science education: education, business, journalism, publishing, librarianship, and social service, with the wider opportunities which may come from students' transatlantic experience and perspective.

Figure 15.2 Details of the American Studies course at Lancaster University from the 1990 prospectus

a generalization of distrust: we don't read documents like university prospectuses as we used to, we are too 'knowing' about their promotional designs upon us. But the effect on people as the subjects of public discourse is not just what one might regard as a healthy cynicism: it is difficult not to be involved in the business of promotion and self-promotion as a text producer, and difficult not to be faced with problems of sincerity and authenticity. Hochschild (1983) has graphically described such problems as they affect air hostesses. Moreover, the impact of promotion is not only upon those discursive practices which overtly sell organizations like universities to the 'public'. The elevation of promotion in the hierarchy of institutional practices tends to mean that *all* the practices of an organization (even for instance the 'internal' discursive practices of teaching and so forth in universities) come to be constructed with a view to their *promotability* (Wernick 1991).

B A Hons **American Studies** *Q400*

First Year

History (American options)
English
Politics

Second Year

Four or five courses in American subjects taken at a United States university, including at least one interdisciplinary course.

Third Year

Four or five courses, normally from:
History:
The History of the United States of America

Religion in America from Jamestown to Appomatox, 1607—1865
From Puritan to Yankee: New England, 1630—1730
The Great Alliance: Britain, Russia and the United States, 1941—1945
Cold War America: The United States from Truman to Kennedy
English:
American Literature, 1620—1865
American Literature, 1865—1940
American Literature, 1940—1980
Politics:
The Politics of Race
United States Government: The Politics of the Presidency
The American Policy Process
United States Foreign Policy since 1945

Assessment: see under appropriate subjects.

YOU WILL NEED

| Courses | A-level | O-level/GCSE |

Amer St   **BBC/BCC normally incl. English**   **A pass in a foreign language**

or other qualifications (IB, EB, Scottish Highers) at a comparable standard.
AS-levels: will be accepted.
Interview policy: special cases only.
Open days: candidates who are offered places will be invited.

Another significant development I alluded to in mentioning our greater 'knowingness' is increased *reflexivity* (Giddens 1991) in respect of discursive practices: there is a greater awareness and self-awareness about discursive practices, reflected for instance in the extent of media analysis of the campaigning styles of politicians in the recent (1992) British General Election. This greater reflexivity is manifest in what I have called the *technologization of discourse* (Fairclough 1992): the involvement of social scientists and other experts in researching, redesigning and providing training in public discursive practices on the basis of calculations of their instrumental effectivity – for instance, the effectiveness of advertisements in selling, or of interviews in selecting personnel.

What I am suggesting, in summary, is that commodification is not only leading to significant changes affecting particular types of discourse. It is also leading to a more pervasive and diffuse set of changes affecting public orders of discourse at a deeper and more general level, consequent upon the generalization of promotion as a communicative function. As I hope I have indicated, I view these developments with a certain amount of concern.

CONVERSATIONALIZATION OF PUBLIC DISCOURSE

Leech (1966) notes the 'public-colloquial' style of advertising – a public language with features of private, colloquial, conversational language. For instance, the following extract consists of the linguistic element (as opposed to the visual element) of a recent advertisement for Bird's Eye Fish Fingers (*Radio Times* 7–13 March 1992):

> More cod for the same price? There has to be a big catch. Don't worry, there's nothing fishy going on. It's going in. From now on our Cod Fish Fingers will be even bigger.

Conversational features include some of the vocabulary (*catch, fishy, going on*), simulated dialogue (hence the question *More cod for the same price?* and the imperative *Don't worry*), and the elliptical form of the question. Leech also notes the simulation of a personal relationship between advertiser and audience, which is evident in this example. This would include the simulated individuality of personalization ('synthetic personalization') already referred to above, including direct address. Personalization had previously been remarked on by Hoggart, Barthes and Marcuse. Hoggart (1957) writes of 'fake intimacy' and a 'phoney sense of belonging'. All this is subsumed under what I now want to call *conversationalization* of public discourse.

Conversationalization involves a restructuring of the boundary between public and private orders of discourse – a highly unstable boundary in contemporary society characterized by ongoing tension and change. Conversationalization is also consequently partly to do with shifting boundaries between written and spoken discourse practices, and a rising prestige and status for spoken language which partly reverses the main direction of evolution of modern orders of discourse – a development seen in optimistic terms by Williams (1989) because of its democratic potential (I return to this below). Conversationalization includes colloquial vocabulary; phonic, prosodic and paralinguistic features of colloquial language including questions of accent; modes of grammatical complexity characteristic of colloquial spoken language (what Halliday (1989) calls the grammatical 'intricacy' of spoken language); colloquial modes of topical development (as described by conversation analysts); colloquial genres, such as conversational narrative. At a more delicate level of analysis one might wish to distinguish various forms of conversationalization, depending for instance upon which of such features are most salient.

Conversationalization in commodity advertising is quite old: Leech claims that it was established by the 1920s, first in the USA. Cmiel (1990) shows that conversationalization of public discourse was a significant process in nineteenth-century America. However, the cultural and social matrices of the process, and therefore in an important sense the process itself, were markedly different from their contemporary form. The leading edge of nineteenth-century conversationalization was religious and political oratory, now it is, I believe, the mass media; conversationalization now affects a much wider range of institutions and domains (for example the professions – see the examples below); it is in a distinctively modern relationship as I argue later to 'expert systems' (Giddens 1991); and it appears to be tied in with contemporary cultural developments including contemporary forms of individualism (Bellah 1985) and conceptions of the self (Giddens 1991).

Conversationalization is a widespread and rather general concomitant of the commodification of public discourse, of which the colonizing spread of advertising genre is as I have argued an important dimension. There is for example conversational language in the Barclaycard text – for instance *the goods are yours* in (4), *that's all there is to it* in (5), *You'll find your Barclaycard can make life a whole lot easier* in (15) – though in this respect as in others it is hybrid. However, conversationalization appears to be a much broader tendency in contemporary public discourse. For instance, the private lives of public figures are treated as news in the popular press, and this shift in the content of news goes along with a shift in style towards private, conversational, language. This extract, a newspaper headline, is a brief illustration:

DI'S BUTLER BOWS OUT... IN SNEAKERS! (*Daily Mirror* 17 May 1984)

Note the colloquial term *sneakers* and the colloquial 'phrasal verb' *bows out* (here meaning 'gives up his job'), and the abbreviation *Di* for Princess Diana. The conversationalization of broadcast talk is discussed by Scannell (1989); and Tolson (1990) has discussed television interviews in terms of the emergence of 'chat' as an institutionalized form of conversation which is a key genre in contemporary media culture. Conversationalization is also a pervasive feature of politics in its contemporary mediatized forms. Jamieson (1988) for example has shown the evolution of the political discourse of US Presidents towards the highly conversational discourse of Ronald Reagan – effectively simulating intimate face-to-face interaction on the television screen, full of stories and anecdotes, personal and self-revelatory, with the actor's capacity to simulate conversational spontaneity and authenticity while reading ghostwriters' scripts.

Nor is conversationalization just a mass media phenomenon – it is also affecting public services and professions. The process is significantly different here, in that it is not mass communication but face-to-face communication, one-to-one (as in doctor/patient consultations) or small group (as in classroom discourse). *Counselling* for example is another institutionalized form of conversation, in therapy and various other domains to which it is applied, drawing upon and systematizing for instance the conversational figure of the 'good listener'. The following extract shows the conversationalization of medical discourse, presumably via the influence of counselling:

(a) (Prudence has said she's angry, frustrated and feeling suffocated, and going to work has not alleviated these feelings as she'd hoped they would. Katherine, the nurse practitioner, probes:)

K: What do you do with these feelings?

P: Keep them inside, yeah [laughs], that's probably//

> K://and fall asleep at eight o'clock.

P: And fall asleep at eight o'clock [laughs].

K: You know, most people, you must be very angry beyond your ability to manage it.

P: I am [laughs], I am.

(b) K: Tell me about your job and tell me, fill me in a little bit about what your life is like now.

P: (describes her 'normal day', on the go from 5.30 a.m. till 8 p.m.)

> K: And then you fall face forward on the floor.

(c) P: But he gets mad at me, like at night, sometimes I want to sit there and read a book or something and he gets mad. . . .

K: What's his anger?

P: He thinks his sex life is crazy, He thinks 'why do you want to read books', when you know it . . . (her voice trails off)

> K: When you could be having sex.

These are short samples of interaction between a patient and a 'nurse practitioner' from Fisher (1991). A nurse practitioner is a new category of health professional in the USA with responsibility for education and prevention as well as treatment, who combines 'caring and curing' according to Fisher, drawing upon the model of counselling discourse. The samples illustrate a conversational strategy used by the nurse practitioner to show empathy and be supportive – a strategy of *turn completion* where the nurse practitioner (K above) completes the turn, and the narrative, of the patient (P) in a conversational style which harmonizes with the patient's. Instances of the strategy are marked with an angle bracket on the left.

Let me just mention two further cases. First, conversationalization is I think inherent in 'learner-centred' styles of teaching, advocated for instance by the distinguished pychotherapist Carl Rogers (Rogers 1983). Second, contemporary management specialists stress 'conversational skills' as an important management resource, implying a significant degree of conversationalization in workplaces – see Margerison (1987), but also

Bellah (1985: 123ff.) on 'expressive individualism' and self-revelatory 'therapeutic' interactional style in work.

Conversationalization, then, is a pervasive feature of contemporary public discourse. It overlaps with the commodification of public discourse, but is a more general trend. It can perhaps be regarded as a part of a process of cultural democratization affecting contemporary societies, and it would seem to be associated with a widely noted breakdown of the divide between 'high' and 'popular' culture, and valorization of 'popular' values and practices (being 'nice' and 'ordinary' is, after all, the highest praise in the popular press these days for public figures such as royalty). One way of seeing the relationship between conversationalization and commodification would be as an appropriation of the former by the latter (see further below).

CONVERSATIONALIZATION AND AUTHORITY

Seeing conversationalization as part of a democratization of culture suggests that it is linked with a shift in authority relations in favour of the mass of the population, 'the public', and at the expense of politicians, bureaucrats, various categories of professionals, the media, and so forth. Conversationalization on this reading would constitute a linguistic/discursive form of recognition of the increased cultural authority of the mass of the population through an accommodation to and valorization of their private discursive practices in the public domain, which also democratizes access to the public domain. The 'sovereign consumer' thesis might be regarded as identifying those aspects of this general shift which have to do with changes in the economy and the market. According to Abercrombie (1991: 192):

> the shift from producer to consumer means that the capacity to determine the form, nature and quality of goods and services has moved from the former to the latter. This represents a profound change in social relationships. . . . This is not to say that the producer/consumer relationship is more fundamental than any other, but . . . change in patterns of authority between producers and consumers . . . affects social relations as a whole.

Actually, this formulation suggests that the shift in market relations and authority might spark off the more general shift in authority relations I am suggesting, through a more diffuse infection of other social relations in the public sphere by the democratized producer–consumer relation. And certainly the processes of commodification and consumerization of new domains of (professional, artistic, etc.) life would entail the extension of something analogous to the 'authority of the consumer' to areas which have not traditionally been conceived in terms of market relations between consumers and producers.

But there are difficulties with this democratic account of conversationalization. First, conversationalized discursive practices are more typically generated and imposed in a 'top-down' manner than in a 'bottom-up' manner. In other words, it is precisely those who according to the democratic account are losing authority that are generally the source of conversationalized practices. Members of 'the public' generally have little say, and it is difficult to see the process as a democratization if those who are supposed to gain have no choice, and no authority, with respect to it. Second, conversationalized practices may become imperative for members of publics, in their contacts with professionals or officials; and learning to be appropriately informal may become just, or largely, another hoop to jump through. Third, conversationalized discursive practices might be regarded not as eradicating the power of producers, professionals, bureaucrats, and so forth, but as backgrounding and disguising it, and making it more difficult to challenge.

There is another objection of perhaps an even more fundamental sort: the concept of conversationalization itself may be rather less coherent and rather more problematic than it appears to be at first sight. I have already suggested that it might be helpful to distinguish various forms of conversationalization according to which conversation-like features are most salient. But it is also necessary to consider *whose* conversational language is being drawn upon as a model; although conversation as a genre can be characterized in general terms, there are significant differences in conversational language and style across different social classes, strata and groups. It may be that, while particular discursive practices can reasonably be called 'conversationalized' in the sense that they do draw upon features of some forms of conversational language, they in no sense represent a real shift towards the discursive practices of the publics involved. It is also important to emphasize that what is at issue is the *simulation* of conversation; it may be that conversationalized practices are not particularly close to anybody's real conversational language.

Furthermore, it is important in assessing whether conversationalized practices are democratic to take account of the structures they are embedded within. Conversationalization in contemporary societies is closely tied in with the operation of 'expert systems'. Thus a major aspect of the technologization of discourse is the simulation of conversation in public institutional contexts: the calculated use of 'conversational skills', as Margerison (1987) and many others call them, to achieve institutional objectives – selling goods, keeping customers happy, keeping employees under control, and so forth. Promotional discourse is widely characterized by calculated construction of the consumer, the producer, and the consumer--producer relationship (as well as the product) which often involves strategic, instrumental use of simulated conversational language, and which seems to have more to do with shifting goods than conceding authority. And one finds a similar strategically motivated use of conversational language in, for example, various types of interviews used in a range of professional contexts (job interviews, doctor–patient interviews, disciplinary interviews in schools and workplaces, and so forth). One also finds quite explicit recommendation of such strategic use of conversational style on the part of the technologists of discourse, amongst whom one might include management specialists such as Margerison (1987), and social psychologists with an interest in 'social skills training' such as Argyle (1978).

Rather than opting for a democratic account or an 'engineered' account which sees conversationalization primarily in terms of technologization of discourse, I want to suggest that conversationalization is a profoundly ambivalent feature of contemporary orders of discourse. It may be substantively democratic, perhaps especially but not only in face-to-face interactions; it may be engineered, perhaps especially but again not only in mass-communication and promotional contexts. But it is a matter of real ambivalence, not just ambiguity, that is, not just a matter of deciding whether any particular instance is democratic or engineered. For even manifestly synthetic and engineered conversationalization puts democratization, and new forms of social relation and social identity in public, on the social agenda. It does so by making implicit validity claims (in the terms of Habermas 1984) – using language as if democratic relations obtained – which may in certain circumstances be openly questioned, evaluated and 'redeemed'. And even the most authentically democratic conversationalization in intention may be suspect in a society where strategically and instrumentally motivated action is so pervasive. This deep ambivalence is reflected in the reception of and response to conversationalization. People oscillate between trusting and cynical responses to conversationalization, and find it difficult to decide *which* interpretative posture to adopt in many cases. And people have various strategies for coping with conversationalization either as members of publics who are targets of it or as institutional employees who are trained to do it – I suspect that irony is a widely used strategy, which again suggests an unease and uncertainty about conversationalization.

A clearer understanding of the ambivalence and contradictions of conversationalization will no doubt come from detailed investigation of specific cases. For example, time-consuming conversationalized, patient-oriented methods of health care come into conflict with rigid economically imposed institutional structures (such as the regulation five- or ten-minute doctor–patient consultation period), and carefully engineered 'conversationalized' routines (taught to doctors in increasingly fashionable 'communication skills' courses) might be seen as a compromise – a way of reconciling contradictory imperatives, prized cultural values on the one hand, economic imperatives on the other (see Bell 1979). This suggests a dynamic relationship between authentically democratic and engineered forms of conversationalization.

Conversationalization constitutes, I believe, interesting evidence for debates over the 'authority of the consumer' and over shifting authority relations more generally, but it is by no means conclusive evidence. What it suggests is that one should treat claims of a real shift in authority in favour of consumers, or more generally publics, with a certain amount of caution. The ambivalence of conversationalization suggests a more uncertain and contradictory evolution of authority relations. Conversationalization cannot convincingly be simply dismissed as engineering, strategically motivated simulation, or simply embraced as democratic. There is a real democratic potential, but it is emergent in and constrained by the structures and relations of contemporary capitalism. It is noteworthy that conversationalization, and indeed the construction of people as consumers and the apparent attribution to them of 'the authority of the consumer', so widely take place in promotional contexts or other contexts where strategic objectives are paramount. The cultural value and significance of conversationalization is not predetermined: it is itself a focus of struggles to substantively democratize society and on the other hand to maintain existing hegemonic relations through a semblance of democratization, and its ambivalence is a symptom of the complexity and unresolved and contradictory nature of the current social settlement.

Finally, conversationalization, as an aspect of the commodification/consumerization of discourse and more generally, gives rise to moral issues. The technologization of discourse, the strategic and engineered discursive practices of which so many of us are not only the targets but also the producers, in advertising and promotional discourse but also more broadly, help to naturalize the manipulation of people for institutional purposes as a commonsense feature of our world. Democracy is, despite its real potential in conversationalized practices, often a mere façade. Moreover, there is the question of what effects such engineered conversation might have upon the 'real thing': can 'conversational skills' be widely taught and 'used' strategically without in some sense diminishing conversation? Can the practice of private, everyday life be institutionally appropriated on the contemporary scale without impoverishing the private domain? And if not, how can such practices of appropriation be morally justified?

NOTES

1 I would like to thank Nick Abercrombie, Russell Keat, Sarah Kiaer, Paula McNeany and Stef Slembrouck for comments on an earlier draft of this chapter.

2 I use the 'private' v. 'public' distinction to contrast the informal domains of 'ordinary', everyday life with more or less institutionalized domains of social life, including both 'private' sphere and 'public' sphere institutions (in the other common form of the 'private' v. 'public' distinction).

3 The contrast between 'consumers' and 'producers' in formulations of this claim can actually be misleading. What is meant is presumably a contrast between consumers and those who own or control production, not workers (those whose labour is deployed in production). The mass of the population are of course both producers in this second sense and consumers, and the claim suggests a shift in authority towards them (though not 'as producers').

4 Halliday (1985) distinguishes 'interpersonal' and 'ideational' macrofunctions of language which are simultaneously at issue in any text, the former appertaining to the identities of and relationships between discourse participants, the latter appertaining to the representation and signification of 'the world'.

REFERENCES

Abercrombie, N. (1991) 'The privilege of the producer', in R. Keat and N. Abercrombie (eds) *Enterprise Culture*, London: Routledge.

Argyle, M. (1978) *The Psychology of Interpersonal Behaviour*, Harmondsworth: Penguin.

Bell, D. (1979) *The Cultural Contradictions of Capitalism*, London: Heinemann.

Bellah, R. (1985) *Habits of the Heart: Individualism and Commitment in American Life*, New York: Harper & Row.

Cmiel, K. (1990) *Democratic Eloquence: the Fight over Popular Speech in Nineteenth-Century America*, New York: Morrow.

Fairclough, N. (1988) 'Register, power and sociosemantic change', in D. Birch and M. O'Toole, *Functions of Style*, London: Pinter Publishers.

—— (1989) *Language and Power*, London: Longman.

—— (1992) *Discourse and Social Change*, Cambridge: Polity Press.

Fisher, S. (1991) 'A discourse of the social: medical talk/power talk/oppositional talk?' *Discourse and Society* 2 (2): 157–82.

Further Education Unit (1987) *Relevance, Flexibility and Competence*, London: HMSO.

Giddens, A. (1991) *Modernity and Self-Identity: Self and Society in the Late Modern Age*, Cambridge: Polity Press.

Habermas, J. (1984) *Theory of Communicative Action*, 1, London: Heinemann.

Halliday, M. (1985) *Introduction to Functional Grammar*, Sevenoaks: Edward Arnold.

—— (1989) *Spoken and Written Language*, Oxford: Oxford University Press.

Hochschild, A. R. (1983) *The Managed Heart: Commercialization of Human Feeling*, Berkeley: University of California Press.

Hoggart, R. (1957) *The Uses of Literacy*, Harmondsworth: Penguin.

Jamieson, K. H. (1988) *Eloquence in an Electronic Age: the Transformation of Political Speechmaking*, Oxford: Oxford University Press.

Leech, G. N. (1966) *English in Advertising*, London: Longman.

Margerison, C. (1987) *Conversational Control Skills for Managers*, London: Mercury Books.

Rogers, C. (1983) *Freedom to Learn for the 80s*, New York: Merrill-Macmillan.

Scannell, P. (1989) 'Public service broadcasting and modern social life', *Media, Culture and Society* 11: 135–66.

Tolson, A. (1990) *Speaking from Experience: Interview Discourse and Forms of Subjectivity*, Ph.D thesis, University of Birmingham.
Wernick, A. (1991) *Promotional Culture*, London: Sage.
Williams, R. (1989) 'Writing, speech and the "classical", in *What I Came to Say*, London: Hutchinson-Radius.

Name index

Subject index

Abstract Expression 124–5
acceptance, advertising and 97
access: elitism of 25; to theatre 173–5
account planning 94–5, 96–8
accountability 200–1, 203
acute health services 211–12
Adelphi Theatre, London 177, 178
advertising 52, 91–101; and anxiety 72;
    art and 121–2, 123; as aspiration 93;
    awards 92–3; Bauman 63; codes of
    practice 92; commodification of
    discourse 255–6; communication as
    logical process 93–4; consumer
    research and approval 94, 95–7;
    conversationalization 261–2; cultural
    status 91–2; future 99–100;
    incorporation of consumer into 94–5,
    132; innovation 97–8; likeable 94–5,
    96–7; New Age religion 112; 'public-
    colloquial' style 261; quality and the
    award system 92–3; shift to
    irrationalism 85; status quo 95; values
    not products 98
advocacy movement 218–19
aesthetic realm 123–6
aestheticization of life 52–3, 130
altruism 202–3
architecture, theatre 177–8
art: advertising and 121–2, 123; aesthetic
    realm 123–6; as critical discourse
    126–9; de-aestheticization of 52–3; life
    and 124–5; potential for social change
    126; religion and 125–6; role displaced
    by commercial culture 122–3; style
    guides and 134; see also high culture
'Art et Pub' 158–9
arts centres 145
Arts Council of Great Britain (ACGB) 9,

10, 140, 152, 170; cultural policy and
    171–2; regionalism 152; theatre 169
Athena posters 155–6
audience: collective empowerment 182–3;
    cultural policy and concepts of 10–11,
    138–42, 144, 149–52; development
    173–5; heterogeneity 174; theatre 12,
    170–1, 174, 182–3; well-being and
    scepticism 35–7
Audit Commission 200, 216
authority: consumer see consumer
    sovereignty; of consumer preferences
    27–30; conversationalization and
    264–7; elitism, modernity and 24–7;
    erosion of 11, 43–4; internalization of
    102, 103–5, 110–11, 111–12; and
    legitimacy 45–6, 48; performance,
    theatre and commodity 183–5;
    producer see producer authority;
    professional 17, 228–30; resistance to
    see resistance to authority; transfer
    from producers to consumers 52–3
authority contexts 46–9;
    consumer–producer relation 49–51;
    interconnected 49
autonomy 36, 38

Barclaycard 254–5, 256–7, 261
Bauman, Z. see Name index
belief 45–6
belonging 58–9, 67–71, 71–2
Bisto gravy 99
Black Revolution 128
Bloomingdale's 121
boycotts, consumer 86, 87
British Film Institute 140
British Gas 242
British Standards Institution 86